Alan Harding
17·2·1985

THE RECORD SOCIETY OF LANCASHIRE AND CHESHIRE

FOUNDED TO TRANSCRIBE AND PUBLISH
ORIGINAL DOCUMENTS RELATING TO THE TWO COUNTIES

VOLUME CXXIV

The Society wishes to acknowledge with gratitude
the assistance given towards the cost of publication by
Greater Manchester County Council
Cheshire County Council
Lancashire County Council

© Record Society of Lancashire and Cheshire,
C.B. Phillips and J.H. Smith

ISBN 0 902593 14 5

Produced by Alan Sutton Publishing Limited, Gloucester
Printed in Great Britain

STOCKPORT PROBATE RECORDS
1578–1619

Edited by
C.B. Phillips and J.H. Smith

PRINTED FOR THE SOCIETY
1985

COUNCIL AND OFFICERS FOR THE YEAR 1985

President

Professor A. Harding, B.Litt., M.A., F.S.A., F.R.Hist.S.

Hon. Secretary

A.P. Jenkins, M.A., c/o Lancashire Record Office,
Bow Lane, Preston, PR1 8ND

Hon. Treasurer

B.W. Quintrell, M.A., Ph.D., F.R.Hist.S., c/o School of History, Liverpool University, 8 Abercromby Square, Liverpool 7

Hon. General Editor

P. McNiven, M.A., Ph.D., c/o John Rylands University Library of Manchester, Oxford Road, Manchester, M13 9PP

Other Members of Council

J.J. Bagley, M.A., F.R.Hist.S.	Mrs J.I. Kermode, B.A.
Professor W.H. Chaloner, M.A., Ph.D.	B.H.G. Malet, M.A., Ph.D.
Miss E.A. Danbury, B.A.	P.J. Morgan, B.A., Ph.D.
R.N. Dore, M.A., F.R.Hist.S.	M.A. Mullett, B.A., M.Litt., Ph.D.
K. Hall, B.A., D.A.A.	C.B. Phillips, B.A., Ph.D.
B.E. Harris, M.A., Ph.D.	Professor J.S. Roskell, M.A., D.Phil.

J.R. Studd, B.A., Ph.D., F.R.Hist.S.

CONTENTS

Preface	vii
Acknowledgements	viii
Introduction	xi
Provenance of the documents	xv
Selection of the documents printed	xvii
Editorial conventions	xxi
General	xxi
Wills	xxii
Inventories	xxii
Specimen transcripts	xxiii
Index of decedents	xxiv
Stockport Probate Records, 1578–1619	1
Index of persons and places	143

To death we must stoupe, be we high, be we lowe,
but how and how Sodenly, few be that knowe:
What carie we then, but a sheete to the grave,
to cover this carkas, of all that we have?

(Tho. Tusser, *Five hundred pointes of good husbandrie*, ed. W. Payne and S.J. Herrtage (English Dialect Society, VIII, 1878), p. 66).

PREFACE

The origins of this volume lie in a short course mounted by the Extra-Mural Department of the University of Manchester in Spring 1975 when 50 people came together to discuss the possibility of serious research into the history of Stockport. Out of that preliminary skirmish there emerged a group of 29 people who formed, with their tutors, Dr. C.B. Phillips and Dr. J.H. Smith, the Historic Stockport Research Group. Each year since then the group has met during the winter months at Pendlebury Hall in Stockport under the auspices of the Extra-Mural Department to transcribe and analyse probate records for the Stockport area. Photocopies of the records from the Cheshire Record Office were kindly loaned by Stockport Public Library with the support of Stockport Borough's Historic Stockport Research Committee.

Over the ten years that the group has been in being, there have been a number of changes of personnel and two sad deaths but the members as a whole have displayed great stamina and fortitude in identifying, transcribing and analysing the documents. They have also developed great skill in palaeography and in the interpretation of archaic and dialect words and expressions as well as becoming expert in many facets of 16th, 17th and 18th century life. The membership of the group is as follows:

Mrs. A.M. Ashworth	Mrs. S. Levenberg
Mrs. E.E. Barnett	Mrs. S. McKenna
Mrs. D. Bates	Mrs. C. Nunn
Mrs. S. Cobbing	Mr. T.F. Oldham
Mrs. H. Coutie	Mrs. D.M. Oldham
Mr. R. Fox	Mr. J. Oldham
Mrs. R. Fox	Mr. D. Richbell
Mrs. L. Gaunt (deceased)	Mrs. M. Riding
Mr. R. Gee	Mrs. J. Robinson
Mrs. S. Gelletly	Mrs. K. Smith
Miss M.K. Gilligan	Mr Sutton
Mrs. V. Grey	Mrs. D.J. Wadsworth
Mrs. G. Haigh	Mrs. M. Walker
Mrs. L. Hamilton	Mrs. M. Washington
Mr. S.J. Hart	Mr. G.C. Warren (deceased)
Mrs. A. Kell	Mrs. C. Wilkes
Mrs. A. Lee	Mrs. Worthington

The present volume comprises all the known probate records for Stockport township to 1620 held at Cheshire Record Office, but it represents only a part of the group's work. The records after 1620 have also been transcribed and it is hoped that they will form a companion volume to this one. The group has also transcribed several hundred records for other townships in Stockport parish and these will be deposited in Stockport Public Library. Additionally, the group is now completing an exhaustive analysis of the probate records for Stockport township.

C.B. Phillips
J.H. Smith

Manchester
May, 1984.

ACKNOWLEDGEMENTS

A project of this size and nature depends on the help, support and goodwill of a great many people and the editors wish to record their thanks to Professor Owen Ashmore who offered early and continued support and guidance, and Professor T.S. Willan for his helpful observations. Mr. Brian Redwood and his staff at the Cheshire Record Office and Mr. David Reid at Stockport Public Library have given invaluable help to the group. Miss Eileen Simpson, senior assistant archivist at the Cheshire Record Office, made invaluable comments on the draft of our introduction. Thanks are also due to the Teachers' Centre at Pendlebury Hall for the fine accommodation they provided. The Rector of Stockport, the Rev. A.M. Fairhurst, kindly gave us free access to the parish registers and the John Rylands University Library was helpful to us in many ways and on many occasions. Mrs. Hazel Gordon of the Department of Extra-Mural Studies and all the Secretaries in the Department of History have given great secretarial support in the preparation of the text and we also thank Mrs. Jenny Kermode and Dr. Peter McNiven for their editorial advice and guidance. Finally, it only remains to acknowledge the work of the members of the group and, on their behalf as well as our own, to thank Mrs. Shirley McKenna whose vigour and devotion as secretary to the group have contributed so much to its continued health and resilience.

INTRODUCTION

Stockport in the late sixteenth and early seventeenth centuries was one of some 650 or so market towns in England and Wales and one of thirteen in Cheshire.[1] The free borough of Stockport, created a few decades before the Black Prince made the town a market in 1260, remained a seigneurial borough until incorporation in the nineteenth century.[2] It is not until the early eighteenth century that there is evidence of significant industrial development but by the 1760s Stockport had become one of the earliest factory towns and, somewhat unusually at that time, an urban rather than a rural centre of industry. The description in the 1769 edition of Daniel Defoe's *Tour* highlights the impact which such new manufactories had on contemporary observers:

> A large and handsome town. . . . It is inhabited by a great number of gentry and well filled with warehousemen who carry on the check, mohair, button and hat manufactures. Here the raw silk is chiefly thrown and prepared for the Spitalfields silk weavers by six engines the buildings of which are of prodigious bulk, one of them containing above 45,000 movements which fill the spacious room up to the fifth storey and are all put in motion by one wheel that goes by water. . . . At this place poverty is not much felt except by those who are idle.[3]

This is very different from the Stockport which is the subject of this volume, for the factories were a consequence of the recent introduction of the silk industry itself from Derby.

In the late sixteenth and early seventeenth centuries William Camden and William Smith noted Stockport as a modest market town and the site of a locally important bridge; neither of them offered any estimate of the market's importance which can be used to compare it with the other markets in Cheshire.[4] In his *Britannia* of 1673 however, Richard Blome estimated the importance of each market, rating Stockport's as 'very considerable'.[5] While this was a more impressive rating than, for example, the 'inconsiderable' market at Tarvin, it would seem inferior to the 'well served' market at Macclesfield, where Blome found 'very large and fair buildings' while Stockport's buildings produced no comment at all. The fact that Camden and Smith offered no opinion of Stockport whereas Blome found the market considerable might suggest that the late seventeenth century market had grown in importance compared with that of 1600, but such a conclusion might strain the evidence too far. These sixteenth and seventeenth century writers all noted the salt industry in Cheshire, and Blome commented on the button industry at Macclesfield and on the light leather industry at Congleton, but none mention any manufacturing at Stockport. Yet in the early seventeenth century Stockport cloth was a recognised commodity at London.[6] The nature and extent of this and other industries have yet to be established for the period covered by this volume. Table I, which lists

x   Introduction

the given status or occupation of the 64 deceased included in this volume, represents a starting point.

Table I

Status and Occupations Declared in Probate Records

	Males	
Not given	14	
alderman	1	
baker	1	
butcher	1	
carpenter	1	
clergyman	3	
cooper	1	
cutler	1	
haberdasher	1	
husbandman	3	
linen-draper	2	
mason	1	
mercer	2	
shearman	1	
shoemaker	1	
tailor	2	
tanner	1	
webster	1	
webster: linen	2	
webster: wool	1	
wheelright	1	
yeoman	8	50

	Females	
Not given	2	
spinster	2	
widow	10	14
		64

The expansion of industry in eighteenth-century Stockport was associated with an increase in population from about 3,000 in 1750 to 5,000 in 1780 and to 15,000 in 1801.[7] No reliable sources exist for the population of Stockport in the period covered by this volume. The 1563 enumeration of households by diocesan bishops is confused for Stockport. In the 1664 hearth tax the township of Stockport comprised about 1333 people in 289 households.[8] Whatever the precise size of the population in the late sixteenth and early seventeenth centuries our general expectation would be that it followed the national trend and increased in the years from the 1540s to the 1650s.

The eighteenth-century increase in population no doubt meant that most Stockport residents then depended on the market for their daily necessities. We would expect this dependence to be greater than that of their mid-seventeenth century predecessors who would themselves be more directly involved in agricultural production, some of it for their own consumption.[9] Alongside these agricultural pursuits existed the manufacture of Stockport and other cloth and, no doubt, a range of craft manufactures and services common to most rural centres: tanners and shoemakers, blacksmiths and wrights and masons were ubiquitous and, together with alehouse keepers and innkeepers, their presence in Stockport would not be surprising. What is of interest to the historian of our period is, on the one hand, the numbers following these crafts and services and their wealth or poverty, and on the other hand, the presence of any men involved in distributing Stockport cloth, of wholesalers and retailers distributing goods not made in Stockport, perhaps through 'shops', and the presence of more specialised or sophisticated service or manufacturing occupations. Stockport's place as the ecclesiastical centre of a large parish may also have meant a more marked clerical presence in the town than its own population required. However, it would be surprising to find a wide range of specialist occupations at so early a date as 1578–1619 in a small town in a pastoral region where agriculture and other occupations were normally closely integrated. This volume and its companion will make it possible to test Stockport's place in the national economy and that of Cheshire. The 1660 poll tax for some mid-Cheshire market towns gives occupations which could be compared with those revealed by probate records in Stockport.[10] The development of Stockport can be set against the background of two competing models of small towns in the national economy. One argument is that there were too many Stockports and that in the sixteenth century they entered a period of gradual but permanent decline as the urban hierarchy which was to characterise nineteenth-century England gradually evolved in the late seventeenth and eighteenth centuries. The other, more optimistic, interpretation sees the level of services in such towns developing in the seventeenth century and their numbers increasing to an extent that allowed the replacement of those that decayed by new ones arising. In this view it was not until the later eighteenth and nineteenth centuries that such towns were pushed down by the rise of other larger urban centres and by developments in communications.[11]

All these are questions to which the Historic Stockport Research Group is turning its attention. However, because the free borough of Stockport remained unincorporated, we are deprived of many of the categories of archives which prove so helpful for incorporated towns. The gild records, freemen's rolls and apprenticeship registers, corporation minute books and records of town courts, which historians of mighty Chester, or of little Liverpool, have put to such good use for this period,[12] are absent because Stockport had no machinery to create them. In the manorial court any civil actions brought should have related to

xii   *Introduction*

values of less than £2 so that much litigation went to higher courts. The manor court rolls which do survive offer evidence of land transactions and land management, of licensing and business in the market, although for all these purposes the rolls have to be used with care.[13] The court records also tell us about the lordship of the Warren family over the town, a jurisdiction which they maintained against their feudal superiors as well as against disgruntled Stopfordians.[14] A systematic study of the court rolls remains to be made, into which would also have to be fitted the various family and estate archives containing material on the town, and records such as inquisitions *post mortem*.[15] The Warren family's property included the advowson of the parish, and their influence on the town was also exercised through the church and the parish authorities.

Probate records have much to say about all these topics, and the absence of the classes of records used by historians of corporate towns enhances the importance of probate records for Stockport's historians. Nevertheless, just as court rolls or inquisitions do not necessarily mention all forms of tenancy, or all a deceased's lands, so too probate records present problems for their users.[16] Probate records comprise wills,[17] inventories, bonds to indemnify the Diocesan and/or his officials in case of actual or alleged non-performance of their duties by executors or administrators, probate accounts showing how the administrators or executors disposed of monies, process papers in litigation about a deceased's affairs, and the administrative records of the deaneries and the consistory court involved in probate. One of the first problems to be faced is whether or not the religious statements in wills are those of the deceased or those of the person who wrote the will. Real estate in wills poses difficulties: it does not need to be mentioned; if it is mentioned, not all of it may be mentioned. Historians are uncertain as to what the prisers, the people who drew up the list of the deceased's goods, and sometimes debts and/or credits, which comprises a probate inventory, were supposed to list; and how the prisers arrived at their valuations of the goods. The prisers themselves may have been less than honest or thorough, or they may have been deceived by intrigue close to the deceased. Probate accounts provide at least a total of the deceased's goods if the inventory is missing, and can amplify and even extend our knowledge from the contents of the inventory relating to debts or credits. There are no probate bonds in this volume, and the process papers, which can be mines of information on an unexpectedly wide range of issues, deal only with the deceased's state of mind at the time the will was made. Despite all the problems which may arise, probate records remain a valuable source for many aspects of historical enquiry and they have been printed by record societies for over 150 years. Some editions, both early and recent, have confined themselves to extracts of wills and/or inventories; others have omitted wills altogether and printed only inventories. Extracts always raise doubts in the mind of the reader as to what has been left out, and better sense of inventories can be made with the deceased's will to hand. In this edition we have excised only the common form from wills and inventories, and in any event, as described below, we have calendared that material. We have also printed all the known surviving probate records, according to the Cheshire Record Office, relating to the township of Stockport for this period. We intend that this *total* approach to the probate records of Stockport, none of which have been printed before in their entirety, will create in a conveniently usable form a body of evidence which will go a long way to answering the questions about Stockport's past, and about the wider perspective of similar towns elsewhere, which were raised above, as well as perhaps prompting scholars to raise other issues.

Provenance of the Documents

The probate records printed in this volume are all in the care of the Cheshire County Record Office, the Diocesan Record Office for Chester Diocese. This edition comprises a calendar and transcript of 112 probate documents relating to 64 people: table II categorises the documents.

Table II

Numbers and Types of Documents

No. of deceased		No. of documents
3	will only	3
16	inventory only	16
39	will and inventory	78
1	will and inventory plus memo	3
1	will and inventory plus renunciation	3
1	inventory and accounts	2
1	accounts	1
2	will and inventory plus litigation papers	6
64		112

Throughout the period of this volume and until 1858 the Church of England usually had initial responsibility for probate matters.[19] The documents in this volume were dealt with by the Diocese of Chester. From a sample survey, by class members, of the printed indexes to the records of the prerogative courts of Canterbury and York, it seems that no Stockport person used these jurisdictions in our period.

We do not intend to discuss fully probate procedures within the sixteenth- and seventeenth-century diocese, and we have made no reference to the probate act books of the period. Nevertheless, three procedural points need to be made. Firstly, the three classes of probate documents into which the Chester Diocesan material is now divided in the Cheshire Record Office are: *supra, infra* and

xiv   Introduction

consistory court. Documents are referred to by year of probate, prefixed by the letters WS., or WI., or WC.; thus Robert Ryle's documents (below, p. 1) are WS.1578. These classes were inherited by the Record Office and are the basis of the printed indexes used to identify the Stockport documents.[20] Most documents come from the *supra* or *infra* classes. *Supra* documents relate to personal estates valued at £40 or more, *infra* documents to those valued at less than £40. The third class of documents emerged at an uncertain date as a result of process in the consistory court which led to wills and inventories being filed with the court's papers. However, no process papers relating to many of these consistory court wills and/or inventories are known; process papers survive in the court records relating to wills and/or inventories now filed in the two main sequences of *supra* and *infra* documents (e.g. James Tellier, below, pp. 44–47); process papers are the only surviving documents for a few deceased (see the projected volume II of this edition for references to these cases) and, finally, some process papers are filed in the main sequences of documents and are not known in the court sequence (e.g. Alexander Torkinton, below, pp. 40–44). In our text we have indicated the class of each individual's documents (below, p. xxii) and noted it also in the alphabetical list of deceased (below, pp. xxiv–xxv). The second procedural point is that the grant of probate endorsed on each bundle of documents appears to mark the usual end of contact between executors/administrators and the diocesan or deanery officials. No probate bonds, a strand of evidence for probate procedure, are known for Stockport residents of this period. Only a few probate accounts of Stockport people survive as evidence of contact with church officials subsequent to the date of probate (e.g. Edward Doughtie, below, pp. 96–99). It may however be that such bonds and accounts were routinely produced but have survived less frequently. In some few cases litigation about the deceased's estate occurred, and in such cases the order of events was dislocated from the norm (see James Tellier, below, pp. 44–47 and comments in the will of John Robinson, below, pp. 103–104).

The third point is that J.P. Earwaker, whose pioneer work did so much to make these records available, stated that the wills produced for enquirers at the Chester Diocesan Registry, at the end of last century, were 'originals' and not copies.[21] If by 'original' he meant documents bearing the testator's mark or signature or prisers' marks or signatures, then, for this period the researcher anticipating evidence of literacy amongst Stockport testators and prisers will be disappointed. None of the documents in this edition bear a testator's mark or signature. Witnesses' signatures or marks are recorded and, in a small number of instances, so are the marks or signatures of prisers, as opposed to the listing of their names in the preamble to the inventory. A few of the wills and inventories are expressly stated to be copies (e.g. below, p. 121), but most appear in fact to be a version other than that authenticated by the testator or prisers. If Earwaker used 'original' to mean the will or inventory, signed by the testator, or by the prisers, then, so far as the Stockport documents of this period are concerned, we have found no evidence to support him, although there are some such documents later in the century. Perhaps Earwaker meant merely to distinguish

Introduction xv

the loose paper or parchment copies of the Chester Registry from the bound, parchment, registered copies usually consulted by readers at the prerogative courts.[21]

Selection of the Documents

The ancient parish of Stockport comprised, besides the township of Stockport itself, thirteen other townships: Bramhall, Bredbury, Brinnington, Disley, Dukinfield, Etchells, Hyde, Marple, Norbury, Offerton, Romiley, Torkington and Werneth. The boundaries of the manor, borough and township of Stockport have been established and mapped with some accuracy.[23] For three reasons it was decided to restrict documents in this volume to those of residents of Stockport township. Firstly, this gave the volume an identifiable nucleus and geographical coverage – the market town and its immediate environs. Secondly, by placing some emphasis on the market town of Stockport, which was not untypical of many other small unincorporated market towns, we draw attention to one of a class of towns which requires more study if its role in sixteenth- and seventeenth-century England is to be fully understood. Thirdly, for the purposes of funding, Stockport township fell within the present concern of the Recreation and Culture Division of Stockport Metropolitan Borough, who paid for the photocopying of the documents. For comparative purposes, they also funded photocopying for some of the townships outside Stockport but in the Metropolitan Borough's area. Thus the Research Group has not transcribed records for Heaton Norris which was not in the sixteenth century part of the Borough or township of Stockport, but which is now in the post-1974 Borough; neither has it worked on the records of Hyde, which was a township of the ancient parish but is not now in Stockport Borough. But the group has transcribed records for Brinnington and Offerton for example, townships of the ancient parish outside the free borough but in the present Borough. Some residents of Stockport township in our period were quite specific in their wills about where they lived, for example, Hugh Mottram of the township of Stockport (below, p. 74), but others, testators and their prisers alike, were content with 'Stockport', or 'parish of Stockport'. Documents with these vague attributions have been included in this collection if they satisfied any one of two conditions: residence in property in Stockport, e.g. George Daniel of the Hillgate (below, p. 14), or at named places in the township, e.g. Heaviley or Nangreave; or described in the parish register as of Stockport, for the register appears to identify people by township.[24] These criteria, inevitably, proved indecisive in a number of cases, and we shall print in the next volume documents for those deceased about whose residence we could reach no firm conclusion and who may, or may not, have been resident in the township of Stockport, a group we refer to as 'query Stockport township'. Readers can make their own judgement about their membership of the market town community. A glance at Heginbotham's list of the mayors of Stockport will show that these criteria will exclude some mayors of the town, especially gentry mayors who lived outside it.[25] Another person with a prominent role in Stockport whose will would not be printed here is the schoolmaster, William

Nicolson (d. 1598), who lived at Reddish. Some of these records will be included in volume II.

The mechanics of selection were as follows. Indexes to the probate records were compiled and printed by this society over a century ago. They were based on the finding aids then available in the Diocesan Registry. Although amplified and checked by the Cheshire Record Office, these printed indexes remain the essential finding tool today.[26] Class members used the indexes to compile a list of all deceased described as of Stockport (in any form), Brinnington, Bramhall, Etchells, Offerton and Torkington, and named places in these townships. A separate group of class members then went through the indexes again and drew up a check list. Photocopies of the will, inventory, accounts, bonds, litigation papers and any other papers relating to the deceased were then made, including the contemporary office endorsement written on the outside of the folded bundle of documents sometime before it was stored in the Diocesan Registry. From these copies any 'Stockport' residents who clearly did not live within our area of interest were excluded, and the rest grouped into townships or into a group designated as 'query Stockport township'.

One factor which influenced the selection of documents was, of course, their survival. The survival of usable documents for a given year is irregular, and we have made no attempt to relate this to the number of registered burials, nor to the probate procedures of the period, nor to the vagaries of subsequent archive storage. Table III summaries the survival of documents. Some documents which appear in the indexes have been lost or are no longer fit for use.[27]

Table III
Dates* of Documents Printed

1578	1	1600†–1604	10
1588	2	1605–1609	7
1591	4	1610–1614	20
1592	1	1615–1619	16
1596	1		
1599	2		
			64

* i.e. Probate date, year beginning 1st January, for each deceased.
† no documents for 1601.

Introduction xvii

Notes to the introduction

1. Calculations by Dr. A.D. Dyer in 'The Market Towns of Southern England, 1500–1700,' *Southern History*, I, 1979, pp. 125–126, based on William Smith, *Particular Description of England* (London, 1588) and John Speed, *Theatre of the Empire of Great Britain* (London, 1611). Dr. Dyer's figures modify those of Prof. Everitt in *The Agrarian History of England and Wales, IV, 1500–1640*, ed. Joan Thirsk (Cambridge, 1968), pp. 467, 589 sqq., by isolating markets listed at particular dates, whereas Prof. Everitt counted those listed at some point between 1500 and 1690. Speed counted thirteen market towns in Cheshire, and this agrees with the version of the 'Vale Royal of England' as printed in G. Ormerod, *History of Cheshire* (3 vols; London, 1819), I, pp. 109–111.
2. The borough charter of 1206 X 1239 and the market charter of 1260 are printed in H. Heginbotham, *Stockport Ancient and Modern* (2 vols; London, 1882, 1892), II, pp. 291–293, 297.
3. See J.H. Hodson, *Cheshire 1660–1780* (Chester, 1978), pp. 150–151, where Defoe is quoted.
4. Wm. Camden, *Britain* trans. Philémon Holland (London, 1610), p. 610 says rather confusingly that the river Mersey '. . . after it hath among other small townes of meaner note watered Stockport. . . ', Ormerod, *Cheshire*, I, pp. 109–111.
5. Richard Blome, *Britannia* (London, 1673), pp. 56–57.
6. A.P. Wadsworth and J. de L. Mann, *The Cotton Trade and Industrial Lancashire* (Manchester, 1931), p. 14.
7. S.I. Mitchell, 'Food Shortages and Public Order in Cheshire 1757–1812', *Trans. Lancs. and Cheshire Antiq. Soc.*, LXXXI, 1982, p. 43.
8. British Library, London, Harleian Ms. 594, f.100; Public Record Office, London, Exchequer, Lay Subsidy Returns, E.179/86/145 (on microfilm in the Cheshire Record Office).
9. For this paragraph see P. Clark and P. Slack, *English Towns in Transition* (Oxford, 1976); Thirsk, *Agrarian History of England and Wales, IV;* pp. 80–81, 83; L.A. Clarkson, *The Pre-Industrial Economy in England 1500–1750* (London, 1971), Ch. IV.
10. *Northwich Hundred: Poll Tax 1660 and Hearth Tax 1664*, ed. G.O. Lawton (Record Society of Lancs. & Cheshire, CXIX, 1979).
11. Clark & Slack, *English Towns in Transition*, esp. pp. 7–8, 110. For the opposite view, and a general discussion see *Urban History Year Book 1979;* and Dyer, *Southern History*, I, pp. 123–134. See also P.J. Corfield, *The Impact of English Towns in the Eighteenth Century* (London, 1982); and *The Transformation of English Provincial Towns*, ed. P. Clark (London, 1984), p. 21.
12. For example, see *Liverpool Town Books 1550–1603*, ed. J.A. Twemlow (2 vols; Liverpool, 1918, 1935), and *The Rolls of the Freemen of Chester* ed. J.H.E. Bennett (Record Soc. of Lancs. and Cheshire, LI, 1906), or *A Calendar of Chester City Council Minutes 1603–1642*, ed. M. Groombridge (ibid., CVI, 1956).
13. W.M.P. Taylor, *A History of the Stockport Court Leet* (Stockport, 1971); Eric Kerridge, *Agrarian Problems in the Sixteenth Century and after* (London, 1969), p. 24. For agriculture, see above note 9. For licensing in Lancashire at this time see W.J. King, 'Regulation of Alehouses in Stuart Lancashire', *Trans. Hist. Soc. Lancs. and Cheshire*, CXXIX, 1980; see also P. Clark, *The English Alehouse: a Social History 1200–1830* (London, 1983).
14. Heginbotham, *Stockport*, I, pp. 123–124; II, pp. 264–265; B. Coward, *The Stanleys Lords Stanley and Earls of Derby 1385–1672* (Chetham Soc., 3rd series, XXX, 1983), p. 115.
15. *Cheshire Inquisitions Post-Mortem* ed. R. Stewart Brown (Record Soc. Lancs. and Cheshire, LXXXIV, LXXXVI, XIC, 1934, 1935, 1938). The Cheshire Record Office and the John Rylands University Library of Manchester hold relevant family archives.
16. A convenient guide to the literature of probate inventories is M. Overton, *A Bibliography of British Probate Inventories* (Newcastle-upon-Tyne, 1983). For wills see many works listed therein, and especially R. Sharpe France, 'Short Guides to Records: Wills', *History*, L, 1965; G.G. Alexander, 'The Custom of the Province of York', *Miscellanea* (Thoresby Society, XXVIII, 1928); Henry Swinburne, *A Brief Treatise of Testaments and Last Wills* (London, 1590).

xviii   *Introduction*

17. Strictly speaking, what we here refer to as a will was properly called a will and testament. In the will the deceased disposed of real estate, and the testament dealt with personal estate. By our period the two functions were usually combined in one document, referred to as a will in this introduction.
18. So far as we know. Inevitably the editors may have missed some printed editions, and we should be grateful to be told of any; we exclude from this short extracts such as that from Alexander Torkinton's will (below, pp. 40–42) printed in J.P. Earwaker, *East Cheshire* (2 vols; London, 1877, 1880), II, p. 106.
19. Except in the period of the Interregnum. See C. Kitching, 'Probate during the Civil War and Interregnum', *Journal of the Society of Archivists*, V, 1976.
20. See below, note 26.
21. *Wills at Chester 1621–1650*, ed. J.P. Earwaker (Record Soc. Lancs. and Cheshire, IV, 1881), p. xii.
22. The problem of the exact origin and status of these documents is complicated by, for example, the two hands used in James Tellier's documents (below, p. 44–45); or the two differing versions of Ellen Taylior's inventory (below, pp. 77–79), each in a different hand.
23. E.g. in *The Report upon the Proposed Municipal Boundary and Division into Wards of the Borough of Stockport* (1837); see also Taylor, *Stockport Court Leet. The Place Names of Cheshire, Part I*, ed. J. McN. Dodgson (English Place Name Society, XLIV, 1970), p. 257 *et seq.*, describes the townships and their modern mutations.
24. E.g. Christopher Piggot 'of Stockport' in his will, was buried as 'of Stockport' according to the parish register, 5 June 1614. Raphe Winnington 'of Stockport' in his inventory, noted as of Offerton, parish of Stockport in the index to wills, was buried as 'of Offerton' in the parish register, 11 March 1613/14. We have classified Piggot as a resident of Stockport township, and excluded Winnington.
25. Heginbotham, *Stockport*, II, pp. 266–69.
26. The indexes for this period are: *An Index to the Wills . . . at Chester, 1545–1620* ed. J.P. Earwaker (Record Society of Lancs. and Cheshire, II, 1879); *A Collection of Lancashire and Cheshire Wills not now to be found in any Probate Registry* ed. W.F. Irvine (ibid., XXX, 1896), which does not contain any Stockport names of this period; 'An index to the wills . . . in testamentary suits . . . at Chester, 1437–1620', ed. W.F. Irvine, *Miscellanies relating to Lancashire and Cheshire*, III, (ibid., XXXIII, 1896) and 'An index to the wills . . . at Chester commonly called infra wills . . . 1590–1665', ed. W.F. Irvine, *Miscellanies relating to Lancashire and Cheshire*, V, (ibid., LII, 1906).
27. E.g. Lawrence Chetham's documents of 1591 are missing. Chetham's Library, Manchester, Piccope MSS, vol. 10, p. 36 is the abstract of the now lost will of Edward Warren of Stockport, 1611, printed in *Lancashire and Cheshire Wills and Inventories at Chester*, ed. J.P. Earwaker (Chetham Soc., n.s., III, 1884), p. 231. We have not consulted the manuscript of the abstract.

EDITORIAL CONVENTIONS

All the documents for each individual are printed in the order in which they were originally made: will, inventory, then any other. The arrangement of the volume follows the date of the grant of probate for each deceased's estate. There is an alphabetical list of decedents, with summary of documents and probate date on pp. xxiv–xxv. Documents are printed according to the following conventions.

GENERAL

1. Documents have been numbered by the present editors for use in the format of this volume only.
2. Burial entries are from *The Parish Register of St. Mary, Stockport 1584–1620*, ed. E.W. Bulkeley (Stockport, 1889).
3. Office endorsements, where these survive, may record the person to whom probate was granted. The name of this person is recorded at the end of the decedents' entry.
4. Documents are in English unless otherwise stated.
5. Where there are multiple copies of a document this is noted and variations, other than spelling, are indicated in a footnote.
6. Where documents are originals, it is indicated whether signatories sign or mark. On other documents it is noted where a mark is indicated.
7. Dates between 1 January and 24 March are rendered e.g. 24 March 1635/36. Where a date is in regnal years without an A.D. date the latter is given in [ ].
8. Place names in calendar are modernised if known, otherwise left in original spelling (EPNS Cheshire followed). Personal names are given in the original spelling.
9. Standard extensions are silent.
10. All roman numerals have been rendered in arabic.
11. In lists of debts in wills, and in valuations and lists of debts in inventories, all values have been placed in columns for £ s d; other indications of £ or s or d have been omitted. Valuations have been left in the original denomination, e.g. 14d has not been altered to 1s 2d nor has 33s 0d been altered to £1 13 0d. For valuations in whole numbers of shillings an O has been entered in the pence column.
12. In the texts of wills and inventories, sums of money expressed in words have been transcribed as such but such sums rendered in figures have been given as follows, retaining denominations:
13s 0d, 13s 4d, £1 but £1 0s 10d, 14d, 33s 4d.
13. All contemporary indications of totals, e.g. *summa totalis* have been rendered as Sum. Where necessary, corrected totals have been suggested [*recte* £3 3 3d and where no total was given in the MS one has been supplied in [ ].

xx *Editorial Conventions*

14. Erasures which are legible are indicated by ⟨ ⟩
    Other erasures are indicated by [erasure]
    Gaps are indicated by [ ]
    Doubtful readings by [?]
    Interlineations by [*interlined*]
    Blanks in MS – [blank]
    Gaps caused by damage – [damaged]
    Unable to read [illegible]
15. NS – nothing stated.
16. There is a separate sequence of footnotes for each document and the notes are placed in an indented position at the end of each document.

WILLS

1. In all wills the preamble, comprising date, identity, place, status, age and health, has been summarised; within this summary exceptional statements are given in their original form. The standard forms are variations on 'sick in body but of sound mind' or 'aged in body but of perfect remembrance' and only significant departures from these forms are given.
2. Will and testament, or will, is indicated by the letters W.T., or W., before the date of the will.
3. In all wills the statements appointing executors and overseers or supervisors have been summarised.
4. Revocations of former wills and testaments have been omitted.
5. The records of witnesses have been summarised but include name, status and residence as and when given.
6. At the head of the preamble, on the right of the page of this text, the letters S., I., or C. are used to indicate to which class the documents belong. One of these letters prefixes the letters Pr. which are followed by the probate date. Thus for Robert Ryle (below, p. 1) S. Pr. 25 August 1578 means that his documents are in the *supra* class and probate was dated 25 August 1578.
7. Where the testator states that he or she has set hand and seal, mark, or mark and seal, this is indicated at the appropriate point in the transcript by H. and S., Mk., or Mk. and S.

INVENTORIES

1. The preamble has been summarised, the summary giving the name, status and residence of the deceased, the date on which the inventory was taken and the place, where such information is given. The descriptive phrase, e.g. goods, cattells and chattells, is given in full. The name, status and place of residence of prisers are noted, where such information is given.
2. *Imprimis* and item are omitted throughout.
3. Where there is no will the class in which the documents are to be found, and the probate date, are given at the right hand side of the preamble, using the formulae indicated for wills at 6. above.

Editorial Conventions xxi

The will and inventory of John Robothom, No. 28, is given below in full, with the calendared sections of text rendered in *Italic*. These full transcripts can be compared with the edited versions on pages 60–61 of the volume.

In the name of god Amen the tenthe Daie of Aprill in the yeare of our lord god 1609 I John Robothom of Stockport within the Countye of Chester husbandman, beinge sicke in bodye yet whole in mynd and in perfect memorye, laude and praise be given to god the Almightye Doe make this my present Testament Contayninge my last will in manner and forme followinge First I comend my soule unto allmightie god my maker and Redeemer and my bodie to the earthe from whence itt came: and to bee buried in the Church or Churchyard of Stockporte where it shall please my verie good Landlord George Elcocke to thinke good: Item I give and bequeathe to my Landlord his Daughter Alice Elcocke one litle Coffer the fyer Iron and the table in the house all which shee shall have after the Deceasse of Katherin my wyffe: Item, the residue of all my goods unbequeathed I doe wholie give them to Katherin my wyffe my funerall beinge Discharged *Item I Doe make the said Katherin my wyffe my full executor. Item I doe make my Landlord George Elcocke of Stockport yeomann the supervysor of this my last will that it bee performed in wittnes whereof I have caused this my last will to bee made these beinge Witneses whose names are under written*
Elizabeth Seddonn
John Lowe

      Debts which I doe owe

Imprimus to Willm Dickinsonn Aldermann	2s	6d
Item to Wil'm Dickinson in the padacar		16d

A true Inventorie of all the goods of John Robothom Deceased as it was prised by John Lowe, John Cottrell Christopher Pigott and Edward Warren Aprill the 19th 1609

Imprimis 2 brasse potts and 2 leads	5s	
Item in pann mettell	2s	6d
Item in pewter	5s	
Item in Iron ware	3s	
Item in trene ware	6s	8d
Item 4 litle bords and one forme	4s	
Item in chaires and stooles		12d
Item in woorke loomes	4s	
Item in chests and bords	12s	
Item in flaxe	7s	
Item in beddinge and bedstocks	16s	
Item in Bacon	8s	
Item 2 wheeles		6d
Item in qushens		8d
Item 1 litle sheepe	2s	
Item in his Apparell	14s	
some £4	11s	4d

INDEX OF DECEDENTS

47 Allen, Mary, I, Court, 15 July 1614.
 3 Andrew, Thomas, W, Court, 20 April 1588.
61 Arderne, Mary, widow, W Memo I, *Supra*, 1619.
44 Ashton, Ralph, mason, I, *Supra*, indexed as Richard, 13 July 1614.
31 Benesson, John, I, *Infra*, 6 July 1610.
59 Bennison, Edward, tailor, I, *Supra*, indexed as Bennetson, 29 October 1617.
42 Bibbye, Edward, linen webster, WI, Court, 13 May 1614.
16 Burdsell, Thomas, I, *Supra*, indexed as Buerdsall, 10 June 1603.
 4 Burges, John, I, *Supra*, 22 January 1590/1.
24 Chorlton, James, linen draper, WI, *Supra*, 13 December 1606.
55 Crossley, Ellis, woollen webster, WI, *Infra*, 13 December 1616.
 6 Daniel, Alexander, WI, Court, 17 September 1591.
 8 Daniel, George, yeoman, WI, Court, 8 December 1592.
34 Daniel, James, webster, WI, *Infra*, 4 January 1610/11.
62 Dickinson, William, alderman, WI, *Supra*, 20 May 1619.
 7 Diconson, Thomas, linen draper, WI, *Supra*, 18 October 1591.
53 Doughtye, Edward, rector, IA, *Supra*, 14 January 1616/17.
40 Elcock, Dorothy, widow, WI, *Supra*, 28 September 1613.
32 Fallowes, Robert, WI, *Infra*, 14 September 1610.
41 Gardner, Robert, cowper, WI, *Supra*, 1 April 1614.
45 Gerard, Richard, parson, W, *Supra*, 1614.
51 Hall, Edward, I, Court, 29 March 1616.
18 Haryson, Wm., lynen webster, WI, *Infra*, 27 April 1604.
54 Hibeart, Issabell, widow, WI, *Infra*, 25 October 1616.
30 Houlme, Henry, mercer, I, *Supra*, indexed as Hulme, 25 June 1610.
56 Huitte, Siciley, widow, WI, *Infra*, indexed as Cicely Smith, 17 January 1616/17.
64 Hulme, Wm., WI, *Supra*, 16 November 1619.
11 Hunt, Raphe, yeoman, WI, *Supra*, 7 September 1599.
39 Hurst, Margaret, spinster, I, *Infra*, 22 April 1613.
 5 Jackson, John, I, *Supra*, 1591.
15 Kelsall, John, butcher, WI, *Infra*, 11 February 1602/3.
49 Kenyon, Richard, rector, A, Court, 15 November 1615.
20 Latham, John, I, *Infra*, 15 October 1604.
27 Lowe, Alexander, mercer, W, *Supra*, 31 March 1608.
33 Marsland, Margaret, widow, I, *Infra*, 23 November 1610.
17 Mores, Ellen, I, *Supra*, 1603.
37 Mottram, Hugh, wheelwright, WI, *Supra*, 13 May 1612.
 2 Nabbs, Richard, I, Court, 27 February 1587/8.
50 Norton, William, I, Court, 8 March 1615/16.
25 Pickering, Margaret, widow, WI, *Supra*, 22 January 1606/7.
43 Piggot, Christopher, haberdasher, WI, Court, 1 July 1614.

Index of Decedents xxiii

14 Ridgewaye, Hugh, WI, *Infra* 21 May 1602.
57 Rigbie, Lawrence, WI, *Infra*, 14 February 1616/17.
60 Robinson, Jane, widow, WI Ren, *Supra*, 26 October 1618.
58 Robinson, John, yeoman, WI, *Supra*, 30 April 1617.
63 Robinson, John, yeoman, WI, *Supra*, 6 October 1619.
28 Robotham, John, husbandman, WI, *Infra*, 12 April 1609.
 1 Ryle, Robt., yeoman, WI, *Supra*, 25 August 1578.
46 Sclater, Henrie, husbandman, WI, *Supra*, indexed as Slater, 14 July 1614.
12 Seele, Henry, yeoman, WI, *Infra*, indexed as Steel, 20 June 1600.
10 Shawe, Robert, carpenter, WI, *Supra*, 8 June 1599.
    Smith, Cicely, *see* Huitte, Siciley.
 9 Smyth, John, baker, WI, *Supra*, 25 February 1595/6.
35 Swyndells, William, husbandman, WI, *Supra*, 19 February 1610/11.
38 Taylior, Ellen, widow, WI, *Supra*, 26 May 1612.
23 Tellier, James, cutler, WI, *Supra*; Lit, C; indexed as Taylor, 6 November 1606.
52 Thomston, Blannch, widow, WI, *Infra*, 19 July 1616.
22 Torkinton, Alexander, tanner, WI Dep., *Supra*, 1605.
29 Torkynton, Issabell (or Elizabeth), widow, WI, *Supra*, 27 March 1610.
19 Walmeslie, Anne or Agnes, spinster, I, *Infra*, 8 June 1604.
48 Warren, Jerome, taylior, WI, Court, 19 August 1614.
36 Whitachers, John, shoemaker, WI, *Supra*, 23 April 1612.
26 Williamson, James, yeoman alderman, WI, *Supra*, 24 June 1607.
13 Wood, Roger, yeoman, WI, Court, 26 February 1601/2.
21 Wynn, Nicholas, shearman, WI, *Infra*, 26 October 1604.

1. ROBERT RYLE OF THE BOTHAMS, STOCKPORT, YEOMAN.

S.Pr. 25 August 1578.
Will [no statement about health and age.]   W.T. 26 July 1578.

First I comend my soule to the proteccon of Almyghtie god by the blood sheedinge of whose onelie sonne even Christ Jhesus I hope assuredlie to be saved and my body I bequeath to the earth to be entered and buried underneath my forme belonginge to my house of Bothamms within the parishe church of Stopport. Item I give grannt and bequeath all my landes and tenements which nowe I enjoy or of right ought to enjoy within the Realme of England to Edward Ryle my sonne and to the heires of his body lawfullie nowe begotten and to be begotten for ever accordinglie as by my sundrie deeds and grannts by me before this tyme made sealed and delivered doth appeare and for default of such issue to Ales and Elizabeth Ryle my daughters and to the heires of theire bodies lawfullie begotten and for defalt of such issue then to the right heires of me the said Robert for ever. Item my mynd and will is that all my debts shalbe paid of my whole goods and the rest by my executors and overseers shalbe devided into three equall parts whereof one parte I geve to Ellen my wyffe for and in the name of her third part the second parte I geve to Ales and Elizabeth Ryle my said daughters for and in the name of their childs parte and the third parte I will and appoint to discharge my funeralls and buriall. And one cowe calfe I geve to Dorothie Ryle my goddaughter and one blewe coate I geve to John Ryle my brother and one tawenye coate I geve to Edward Ryle my sonne And what of this last parte remayneth I whollie geve to Ellen my wyffe Item my will and my mynd is that my armour shalbe and Remaine in the hands of Edward Ryle my sonne to serve his prince withall when occasion needeth the parcells be knowen.

Executor: John Torkenton, gent.
Overseers: Robert Bridge and Henrie Booth.

These be due to me
Imprimis in the hands of Robert Ryle of Tharston which was of the goods of Sir John Leighe of Northenden the Parson which 16s I geve to Anne Leighe my servant 16s
Item in the hands of Thomo Johnson of Bredburie one halfe yeares rent which he withholdeth from me wrongefullie .   .   8s
whereof 4s I geve to the said Anne Leighe and the other 4s I geve to my godchildren .   .   .   .
Item I have in keeping of Mr William Tatton of Northenden one bedd of joyned worke with one tester over the same which bedd I did lend to the said William and he promised to deliver the same when I required it.

Witnesses: Willm Swindles, Edmund Shelmerdyne, Hughe Ridgway, Edward Ryle senior, and John Ryle and the executors and overseers, with others.

2   Stockport Probate Records

Inventory: Robert Ryle of the Bothams, Stockport, yeoman. Taken: 8 August 1578.
Of: goods. Preamble of inventory in Latin, rest in English.
Prisers: Thomas Massie, Thomas Buerdsell John Browne and William Swindells.

	£	s	d
1 mare and 1 horse price		53	4
2 oxen price	4	8	10
2 kyne	3	0	0
1 cow stirke		15	0
1 calfe		7	0
1 hogge		10	0
2 ewes and 2 lambes		10	0
1 cowe		20	0
husbandrie ware		21	0
1 websters lome and the furniture		8	8
1 iron cader		2	8
1 trivit			16
1 brasse pan		10	8
More brasse } in Pewter		24	4
2 drinkynge potts			12
al Tryne ware		6	0
Iron ware in the house		3	4
bords tresses and shelves		3	0
3 cheres and stoles			18
bedstockes		5	0
2 Cofers and 1 old arke		6	0
2 fetherbeds and 2 bolsters		20	0
1 mattres 1 bolster 2 pillowes		6	8
4 coverlets 4 blankets 1 coverynge		16	0
al lynens		16	0
harneis		10	0
hey		15	0
corne	5	0	0
fuell		5	0
his apparell		30	0
Sum	28	17	4

Office endorsement: probate to executor John Torkenton, gent.

2. [RICHARD] NABBS OF STOCKPORT, [buried 11 January 1587/8[1]].
C.Pr. 27 February 1587/8.
Inventory of: goods [damaged] debts.   Taken: [damaged] 1587.

Stockport Probate Records 3

Prisers: John Hillane and Gorge [sic] Woode plus two other names illegible.

	£	s	d
two kyne and 1 Calf	4	0	0
his Apparell		40	0
one phether bedd a matteris, a chaffe bedd 4 bolsters one pillowe 4 Coverletes 4 blanketes 3 paire of Sheetes	3	13	4
towe sheetes		7	0
7 pewter dishes 3 pottingers eight sawcers 1 salt 1 candle sticke		8	8
1 pott 1 pann 1 litle kettle 2 Skelletes a fryne pan, a spit, agryd Iron a chining knife and a Iron gratte		2	8
one litle forme 1 table standinge one frame, one stand bedd and a trundle bedd		10	0
5 Coffers		13	4
3 stounds a flashkeett a barell A knedinge trought 3 wodden dublers 2 piggens a brandreth of Iron, 3 nogens, 2 pookes and a lanterne with all other implementes about the house		10	0
2 blanketes		5	0
one bolster			12
one coverlet		4	0
Sum	13	18	0
[*recte*	12	15	0]

Debtes inwarde

	£	s	d
Sir Richard Buckley	4	0	0
Edward Walley of Whitcroft		30	0
George Wood		47	0
John Hall haith a cowe of myne hyred within 3 years, 1 yeare cometh up at May daye next, and so consequently for 3 years 5s yearlie, or els for no payment to fatch her whom		15	0
Robert Marshowe for the hayre of a cowe		5	0
the same Robert		4	0
Also the same Robert Marshowe five nobles and ten grootes for A horse		16	4
Robert Milnes dwelling lying at Norburye more payd		20	0
Jane Lowe			13½
Hughe Wishall		4	4
[damaged] for Piggatt		3	4

[Uncertain length of document missing]

[New sheet]

	£	s	d
[damaged] nely			14
[damaged] Marsland		20	0
the presaid Robert Dawars		5	0

debtes outward
in Charges the yere of his lyinge and funerals 27 0
the mortuarye the probation and wrytinge up the will and Inventories . . . . [blank]

> 1. We identify this badly damaged inventory as that of Richard Nabbs from the only burial entry of a Nabbs in Stockport parish register. Probate was granted to Matilda Nabbs, widow, of Stockport.

3. THOMAS ANDREWE OF STOCKPORT [buried 21 Feb. 1587/8].

C.Pr. 20 April 1588.
Will, sick. W.T. 12 February 1587/8.

Fyrst I bequeath my soule into the hands of Almightie god haveinge my full truste and confidence in the meritts and passion of my onelie lord and Saviour Jesus Christ with a most assured hope therein onelie to bee saved And for the order and dystribucon of my goods: Fyrst my Will is that my debtts and funerall expences shalbee taken of my holle goods before anie Division thereof bee made: then my Will is that alice my Wife shall have the full thyrd parte of my holle goods remayninge, and the other 2 parts to bee equallie Devyded amonge my Children: Item my Will is that Alice my wife keepinge her sole and unmaried shall have the bringinge upp of my children and governemente of theire porcycons untill they come to Lawfull age And that shee may bee the better able to bringe theime upp: my will is that shee shall have the lease which I have of Olyver dodge as alsoe the yeares yett unexpired which I have in a certen peece of grounde called Knott Crofte And also the bargin which I have of William Wakefield in A peece of grounde for Certen yeares yet to come: Item my will is that if my saide wife bee nott able to bringe upp my Children and to paye theime there porcons and that the same doe so apeeare unto Mr Frannces Elcocke: That them my saide Children shall allowe forthe of theyre porcons suche resonable parte towards thire maintenans as the saide Mr Elcocke shall thincke conveniente: Item my will is that my saide wife shall have the rent of my 2 howses under the banke towards the bringinge upp of my children untill my sonne Thomas come to the age of 21 yeares if shee doe keep her seelf sole and unmaried And then I doe geve the saide 2 houses unto my sonne Thomas and to the heires male of his bodye Lawfullye to be begott And for want thereof then to the heires male of my sonne John Lawfullie to bee begotton, And for defaulte there of then to the heares male of my sonne Nicholas Lawfullye To bee gotton, And for default thereof then to the right heires of mee the saide Thomas and theire heires for ever Provyded always that my sonne Thomas shall geve of his porcion to everye one of my younger Children in money 13/4d where uppon hee to have the Cubbord in the Chamber and the Longe table in the howse: Item I geve to Elizabeth Hall my servannt A peticote Clothe of Redd.

Executors: Mr. Frances Elcocke, testator's wife Alice and son Thomas.
Witnesses: Nicholas Elcocke and George Daniell, with others.
Office endorsement: probate to executors.

Stockport Probate Records 5

4. JOHN BURGES OF STOCKPORT [buried 7 January 1590/1].

S.Pr. 22 January 1590/1.
Inventory of: goods and cattle. [No date taken].
Prisers: Otiwell Dodge, Thurstan Matlaye, Homfray Bridge.

	£	s	d
one cowe		40	0
one Swyne		4	0
in pulline		4	0
in corne		6	0
in straye and haye		4	0
in peuter and brasse		6	8
in treene ware		6	0
in bedding		20	0
[Sum	4	10	8]

Office endorsement: probate to testator's wife Jane Burgess and son-in-law Robert Shaw.

5. JOHN JACKSON, [OF STOCKPORT, buried 21 July 1591].

S.Pr. [day and month illegible] 1591.
Inventory: [whole of preamble too damaged to read, except for deceased's name; one priser was Alexander Torkenton.]

	£	s	d
Two kyne at	4	0	0
one heffer at		30	0
one Mare at		10	0
the halfe of three yonge beastes to be divided at Martynmas nexte		20	0
three Swyne at		18	0
fowre hennes at			16
in pewtar at		20	0
in Brasse at		26	8
one grate of Iron and in other Iron ware at		16	0
in bordes formes Tables Sylinge Stoles Cheares bedstyddes Rackes Manger and suche lycke at	10	0	0
in Stowndes [damaged] Earthen pottes and such lycke at		20	0
one fournes and one [damaged]		30	0
in Coffers and arckes at		24	0
three sylver Spoones at		12	0
in fewell as Woodde and Coles at		30	0
in Haye at		30	0
in Corne and Maulte at	4	10	0

6   *Stockport Probate Records*

one Tacke of grownde taken of William Nicholson of the wood halle	4	6	8
Calfe Skynnes and Sheepe skynnes undressed at . . .	14	10	0
Dressed Lethars at		13	4
beddinge Sheetes pyllowe beeres pyllowes Quyssions naperye [?] ware and suche lycke at	8	0	0
in apparrell [illegible]	[?3]	0	0
one Sworde in the [damaged]		5	0
Sum	63	13	0

6. ALEXANDER DANIELL OF HILLGATE, STOCKPORT, WEAVER.
C.Pr. 17 September 1591.
Will, [left hand margin torn away]. Health: visited by god's [damaged].
26 August 1591.

First I commend [damaged] bodie to the earth etc in the church yard of Stockport nere unto my deceased wifes and for [damaged] of my worldlie goods It is my mynde and will that my debtes which I owe to Anie personne or persons and my bequest and funeralls shalbe paid and discharged of my whole goods I give my sonn [damaged] lowme that he weave in I give my son Allexander A lome he worketh in and for [damaged] it is my mynde that James weave it and give Alexander and Richard eyther of them [damaged] of hose and the rest take himself, I give Robert my sone A linien lowme and a wollen [damaged] sonne Richard A wollen lowme he worketh in I give my sonne James 5 lb. of whyte woll [damaged] my reeds rathes helds ware stocke and whatsoever belonginge to weavinge I give my sonne [damaged] and James Equallie Amongst them And all the rest of my goods, I will shalbe [damaged] my five sonnes by equall porcions I give James my sonne a coat cloth [damaged] ground I assigne to Alexr. my sone and his Assignes It is my mynd that James my [damaged] chamber at my sonne Richard howse late in the [damaged] assignes and a doale in the Longshut head duringe the terme of the lease the [damaged] chamber.

Executors: testator's sons Alexr. and James.
Witnesses: Robert [damaged] and George Reddiche.

Debtes which I owe	£	s	d
To James my son		12	5
To Robert my sone	[illegible]		6
To Richard my son		6	0
To Alexr. my son		3	6

Inventory: Alexander Daniell.   Taken: 6 September 1591.
Of: goods, chattells and debts.
Prisers: Homfrie Bridge, George Daniell, Robert Hudson and George Reddiche.

	£	s	d
2 kyn	3	6	8
6 sheepe		20	0
in brasse and pewter		22	0
in Iron ware		4	0
in corn and haye	4	10	0
in fewell		3	0
5 lowmes withall thinges to them belonginge		33	4
wooll and wollen yearne		7	0
one pece of bacon and in butter		8	0
in beddinge		30	0
his Apparell		23	0
in bordes and treene		3	4
‹in› one pack saddle and a harrow		3	0

[Sum 15 13 4]

Debts outward as Appeareth by the will   27 [?]5

Office endorsement: probate to executors.

7. THOMAS DICONSON OF STOCKPORT, LINEN DRAPER.

S.Pr. 18 October 1591.
Will, partelie vysyted with Sickenes.   W.T. 12 September 1591.

Knoweinge death to be certeyn to every creature and the houre thereof unknowen, meanynge that Amytie and frendshippe shall and maye be had and contynued Amongest my children and frends after my deceasse do make and declare this present Testament herein contayninge my last will in manner and forme Followinge, that is to weete: First and pryncipallye I do commend my soule into the hands of Almightie god my creator redeemer and onlye Saviour by the merytes of whose sonnes precious bloodsheedinge I trust unfaynedlye to be Saved and to Inherytt his Eternall Kyngdom, And my bodie and boones I do commytt to the earth from whence yt came to be buryed in the parish churche of Stockport in such manner and place as my executors thinke meete and convenyent. And whereas I have purchassed A certayne burgage in Stockport afforsaid now in my occupacon, I do geve grant bequeath and will the same burgage and all buyldings gardens and appurtenances to the same belonging unto William Diconson my Eldest sonne to have and to hold the said burgage with thappurtenances unto the said William my sonne and to the yssue of his bodie lawfullie begotten or to be begotten And for want thereof I do geve bequeath and will the same burgage unto Rauffe Diconson my sonne and to the yssue of his bodie lawfully begotten or to be begotten, And for want of such yssue I will bequeath and geve the said burgage with thappurtenances unto Joane Diconson my Daughter and to the yssue of her bodie Laufullye begotte or

8   *Stockport Probate Records*

to be begotten, yf she the same Joane do take the advyse and councell of my father and Twoe bretherne my executors and be ruled and governed by theym and att theire appoynetement, And yf the said Joane have no yssue upon her bodye Lawfullie begotten, or that she refuse the governance of my said father and bretherne my executours, Then yt is my mynd and will that the same burgage with thappurtenunces shall remayne unto the right heires of me the said Thomas Diconson theire heyres and assignes forever, To hold of the capitall Lord or lords of the fee thereof by the rent and Service affore due and Accustomed, And for the order and dystribucon of my wordlye gooddes Chattells and Debtes, yt is my mynd and will that all such debtes as I owe of Right or conscyence to anie person or persons shall be payd and Discharged of my wholle goodes, my funerall expences deducted of the wholle, and this my last will performed of the wholle, Item I geve of my said wholle goodes to the poore within Stockport 20s to be delyvered and bestowed att the Discrecons of my executors Item yt is my wyll that all waynescotte or Sylinge and all glasse in or about my howse shall remayne unto William my sonne and his assignes, The rest revercon and Remaynder of all my said gooddes Chattells and Debtes whatsoever I will shalbe Devyded into three equall and just partes, The fyrstparte whereof I geve and bequeath unto the said William Dicenson my sonne, the second parte I will and bequeath unto the said Rauffe my Sonne and the thryd and last parte I geve unto the said Jone my Daughter, Of which said parte due to the same Joane my Daughter yt is my will that the some of Fourtie pounds shall remayne in the hands of my executors hereafter named untyll such tyme as they have had Suffycient Tryall whether the same Joane wilbe advysed by my said father and bretherne my executors and be ruled governed and bestowe herselffe at and to theyre appoynctement or nott, If she be Then yt is my will that the same Jone shall have the said fourtie pounds And yf she will nott, nor will be governed by them Then yt is my mynd and will, That the said William and Rauffe my sonnes shall have the said fourtie pounds, That is to weete eyther of theym such parte thereof as my said father and bretherne my executors thinke good and appoynt att theire Discrecons. Item I geve of my whole goods to my Servant Anne Woodd the some of 20 shillings Also yt is my mynd and will that my said three children and eny of them and all and eny theire childs parte and porcons of gooddes and all things to them belonginge Shall be att the governance and Rule of my executors and be under the Tuycon custodye and use of the same my executors untyll my said Children shall Severally accomplesshe the age of 21 years.

Executors: my trustie brethern William Diconson and Fauffe Diconson.
Supervisor and overseer: my father John Diconson.
Witnesses: John Diconson and George Reddich.

[The Debts owed and owed to are written in two columns: l.h. col.]

Dettes which I the said Thomas Diconson do owe	£	s	d
Unto my father John Diconson	3	0	0

Unto my brother Rauffe Diconson 6 0 0
Unto Alex Holme 10 0
                 Sum 9 10 0

Dettes owinge to me the same Thomas Diconson
Of Thomas Grenes 2 hoopes seede barlie 6 0
Of the same Thomas left unpayd for seede oats 3 0
Of Hughe Cenyan lent money 30 0
Of Hughe Cenyan wyffe lent money 14 6
Of Rauffe Nicholson 13 8
Of Richard Robinson 12 0
Of George Elcocke 5 0
Of Allex Elcocke 12
Of Nicholas Persyvall 3 4
Of John Hough of an ould Reckonynge 3 0
Of William Chedle lent money 40 0
Of Robert Brucke 6 0
Of Thomas Ridgewaye 18
Of Mr Robert Bridge 14
Of Katheryne Bradburye 4 10
Of the same Katheryne for as much fyne Yarne as oved 4 yards
and A quarter of clothe . . . .
Of Rauffe Holme for 4 hoopes of otes 6 6
Of William Norres 4 17 6
Of Peter Heyes of lent money 4 0 0
Of Alex Mosse 4 0
Of Robert Lees for 3 thrave of Straye 12
Of John Chowcliffe lent money 10
Of Alex Knott 9
Of John Gibson 9
Of Alex Knott 2 0
Of John Chorlton 3 0 6
Of Mr William Dokenfyld 10 0
Of Robert Knowles 53 4
Of Mr Wynnyngton of Offerton for Mr Bowdon . . . 29 0
Of the same Mr Wynnyngton 48 0
Of William Hudson 15 0
Of Ambrose Chetam 6
Of William Norres 2 4
Of William Hudson 6 0 0
Of Alex Andrew 8 0

[r.h. col.]
Dettes also owynge to the same Thomas Diconson
Of Laurence Moores 20 0

Of my brother Robert for the dett he receaved of the said
Laurence Moores		43 4
Of Thomas Greenes		8 0
Of young Mr Arderne		5 6
Of George Hampson of Heaton	3	0 0
Of John Chorlton[1]		49 4

Dettes owing to me the same Thomas in the countrie as appeare by my Dette booke.

Of William Tollie		8	11 11
Of Richard James			57 0
Of John Spragg			15 2
Of Phillippe Andrew			57 6
Of Phillippe Gardner			55 0
Of Walter Amsden		22	4 2
Of Edward Wall		15	6 9
Of Mr John Townesend		13	12 0
Of George Bardell		17	0 0
Of Franncis Smyth Junior		5	0 0
Of Franncis Smyth the elder		3	10 8
Of William Smyth		10	0 0
Of Henrye Rowe			40 0
Of Mr Quynye		26	0 0
Of Charles Benton		20	0 0
	Sum[2]	193	10 6

1. Total thus far £43 11s 2d.
2. Recte £196 1s 4d. Totals 1 and 2 do not include yarn for 4¼ yards of cloth. Total debts in the country £152 10s 2d.

Inventory: Thomas Diconson of Stockport, linen draper.

Taken: 23 September 1591.

Of: goods chatells and debts.

Prisers: Rauffe Nicholson, Peter Hey Alexander Torkenton and Thomas Shelmerdyne.

	£	s	d
twoe kye	4	10	0
one mare		53	4
one Swyne		14	0
one frying pan and one dryping pan		2	6
3 hacking knyves			8
one Spitt			4
2 payre pott hookes			10
2 gawberts and one yron showing horne			14
for 1 fyre yron			18

one Rakentree 6
one payre tonges and A fyre shovell 6
one brendrett and one breade yron 2 0
one Lanterne 8
the best brasse pott 20lb weight 10 0
another brasse pott 13lb. weight 5 0
another brasse pott 13lb weight 4 4
another brasse pott 8lb weight 3 0
one ould lyttle brasse pott 8lb weight 2 6
one yron pott 23lb weight 4 0
one pan beinge the best of 15lbs weight 10 0
one other pan of 13lbs weight 6 0
one Leade of 30lb weight 3 0
one other Leade of 13lb weight 13
one Skellett and one ladle of brasse 12
6 ould pewter dishes and one sasar weyinge 11lb and an halffe 4 0
7 pewter dishes and 5 sasars weying 18lb 9 0
2 bottells one kair one possett cuppe and one salte of pewter of
    4lb weight 2 4
6 trenketts and one Sasar 3lb weight 2 0
3 brass candlestycks of 4lb weight 3 4
2 lyttle candlestyckes A Scummer and A fyre Dysh of brasse 4lb
    weight 3 0
one Dosen case trenchers and 2 Dosen of trenchers . . . 12
A Drynckyng cup and 2 glasses 6
one bread grater 2
one hetchell 10
one halffe hooppe 12
2 Syffes 3
A Salting tubbe with A kyver 14
one lyttle esshen 6
one breweing kayre 16
4 stounds 16
4 piggens 4
3 chesfatts 6
2 wodden platters 4
one churne and A churne staffe 8
one lyttle Chist in the Kytchyn 12
2 thicke short bordes in the kytchin 8
2 lyttle trestes in the kytchin 6
A trest behynd the kytchin dore and A Swyne Tubbe . . . 6
one hacking bord 2
one Kneyding Tubbe 20
10 earthen pottes 10
3 gallons of butter 6 0

3 Sawen bords in the milkhowse   15
one Chist in the milkhowse 5 0
one cubbebord in the milkhouse 6 0
the cubbord in the buttrye and the bords there . . .   6 8
one bord in the stable   8
A throw for A brewing kayre and A Spynnyng wheele . .   12
3 Sawen bordes in the stable   12
19 peeces of Tymber in the heyhowse and Turffe Howse . .   8
8 bordes lying under the hey 2 8
in woodd and Turves to the fyre 13 4
in coales 6 0
one Loade of fyrre woode   12
one Sadle and 2 brydells 3 4
one pytch forke and one padle   12
one Sadle cloath   6
A weight beame and Scales and one dogg chayne . . .   20
in thaye in the barne 3 10 0
in Swynes gresse 4lb   12
8 bords and 2 basses lying in the Streete and other 4 peeces of
   tymber 12 0
2 sackes and one poak   12
A fetherbed A mattresse A bolster A blankett and A cadowe
   upon the highe bed in the parlour 34 0
upon the Truckell bed in the same parlour A matterasse, A
   bolster A pillow A coverlett and A blanckett . . .   16 0
in the cloth house A matterasse with A bolster and three
   blankettes 6 0
upon Another bed over the kytchin three blankettes A coverlett
   and A bolster 11 0
upon the bedd in the high chamber over the howse A fether bed
   A bolster 2 pillowes A matterasse three blanckettes . .   45 10
a cadow for the same bed 20 0
the hangings and frynge for the same bed 14 0
fyve graye blankettes 5 0
A Remnant of Round canvas 2 4
one halfe dosen of sett Quysshens 11 0
5 quysshens made of listes 3 1
4 other quysshens 2 0
7 slippinges of lynnen yarne 3 0
in Asses   12
in unnyans and garlycke 30 rysses 3 0
A wheele and A cradle   20
one malte arke 4 0
one bord in the high parlour 13 4
one bord in the high chamber 6 8

Stockport Probate Records   13

the Sylings in the 2 high chambers	5	0	0
the table in the howse and one forme there and one forme in the highe chamber		4	0
the lyttle round table with one foote			16
the Sylinge in the howse		20	0
10 buffett Stooles		10	0
one closse Stoole			18
the Standinge beds in the highe chamber over the kytchin		12	0
the best bed in the other highe chamber		53	4
the Standinge bed in the chamber belowe and one trucle bed		18	0
one chist in the Same chamber		10	0
one other chist		3	4
one other chist		2	6
in malte 9 hoopes 16d the hoope		12	0
one Silver cuppe		40	0
one dosen Silver spoones	3	0	0
A Silver pyn and ould Silver		3	4
A capon A hen and A cheeken			16
A axe and a Shovell			8
oates in A Sacke			12
wheat in the highest chamber		2	8
one lyttle bord			2
all his apparell	4	0	0
apparell that belonged to his wyffe			
A peticote		13	4
A wolsted kyrtle		6	8
A gowne		30	0
in lynnyns in one boxe 25 peeces		13	4
4 shurts		9	0
4 smockes		6	0
19 table napkyns		10	0
one Syffe clothe		3	4
2 fyne bord napkyns		2	0
4 other table napkyns course ones			16
3 pillowe beeres		4	0
one Towell			16
one other Towell			16
one payre flaxe shets		7	0
one payre sheetes of teaw of hempe		6	0
one payre canvas sheetes ould ones		4	0
5 sheetes of canvas		8	0
one fyne sheete		10	0
3 other flaxen sheetes		13	4
one table cloth			20
one other table cloth		2	0

14   Stockport Probate Records

one Remnant of holland cloth		2	6
one other Remnant of holland			9
14 yards lynnen cloth		23	4
hey in Offerton		6	8
whete there unthreshed		33	4
in otes there unthreshed	7	0	0
one leasse of A tenement in Offerton valued to	60	0	0
one other leasse of certain other ground in Offerton valued to	40	0	0
his parte of Another leasse of ground in Bramall valued to	15	0	0
his part of another leasse of ground in Heaton norres	12	13	4
one book for certeain ground called Longe rakes valued to	5	0	0
all the glasse about the howse	[	?[1]	]
one Chist in manchester		10	0
cloth unsold in the countrie	3	16	8
cloth unsold in manchester	5	9	0
in gold and Silver	45	12	0
Sum	258	11	11

    1 This could be either £10 or 40s. No *recte* figure can be given.

Detts outward as appear by the will of the Deceassed admount in the whole to the some of £9 10 0d.

Detts inward as appeare by the same will admount in the whole to the some of £193 18 6d.

Office endorsement: probate, and tuition of Wm., Radi and Joanne Diconson, to executors.

8. GEORGE DANIELL OF HILLGATE IN THE TOWNSHIP OF STOCK-PORT, YEOMAN.   C.Pr. 8 December 1592.
Will, sickness in my body.   W.T. 29 November 1592.

Knowinge deathe to bee certeyne to Everie creature and the hower thereof unknowne meaninge that Quyetnes, love and Frendshippe shall and maie be had and conteyned amongest my wyfe and freends after my decease, doe make and ordaine this present Testament herein conteyninge my last will in manner and forme Followinge: That is to witt First and principallie I doe commend my soule into the hands of Almightie god my Creator Redeemer and onlie Saviour by the merites of whose Sonnes precious bloodsheedinge I trust unfennedly to bee saved and to Inheritt his Eternall Kingdome And my bodie and boones I doe committ to the Earthe from whence itt came to bee buried in the parishe Churche or Churchyarde of Stopporthe afforesaide at the will and discretion of my freends and executors hereafter named And for my burgages lands and heredytamentes whatsoever in Stopporthe afforsaide nowe in myne owne occupacion and all barnes buildinges and premisses within the lytell yate at my howuse it is my will and I geeve and bequeathe the same unto Ellen Daniell my wyfe for and duringe all hir naturall lyffe keepinge hir in my name soole and unmaried, And all my other lands burgages and heredytamentes whatsoever in Stopporthe, together with all my said lands After the Deceasse of my said wyfe or Immediatlie from or after shee eyther marriethe or miscariethe and all revertions thereof, I wholilye geeve the same unto Francis Daniell my nephewe and to the yssue of his bodie Lawfullie begotten or to bee begotten And for wante of suche yssue I geeve and bequeathe the same to Alexander Daniell his brother and to the yssue of his bodie Lawfullie begotten or to bee begotten And for wante of suche yssue I geeve and bequeathe the same unto William Daniell sonn of William Daniell my nephew and to the yssue of his bodie Lawfullie begotten or to be begotten. And for want of suche yssue to the Right heires of me the said George Daniell theire heyres and Assignes for Ever, To hould of the capytall or cheefe lord or lords of thee fee thireof by the Rents and Services affore due customed And for the order and distribution of my goods, cattells, chattells, and debtes I geeve and bequeathe the same as followethe First I geve to Alexander Daniell my saide nephewe the some of 40s. in monie to bee taken of my said whole goods ⟨Item I geeve my nephewe Francis Daniell my greate brass brass pott⟩ before anie devision be made therof to be paide to him at the feast Daie of the purification of our Ladie 1593. Item I geeve litell William Daniell sonne to William Daniell my nephewe one Cowe which his father hathe in his keepinge To be taken of my said whole goods. Item I geve my said nephewe Frances Daniell my greate brasse pott which was his father's. Item I geeve to Ellen my wyfe my cloake and all the rest of my apparell I geve to the saide Frances my nephewe and I Charge the same Frances of his porcion of my goods to geeve to Joane his Sister Tenn Shillinges in monye, Item I geeve Twentie Shillinges To bee peaide at the first daie of maie next to the hands of Robernet Dodge maior of Stockporthe Towarde the makinge the makinge [sic] of A peymente in the Hilgate begininge Anendest my cosen William Stable Dore and soe towards Mr. Elcocke front [?]as farr as the monie will reeche And the peymente to bee of the breathe of tow yards and one halfe yarde and a Chanell in the midest. Item I geve Raphe Daniell wyfe 3s. Also it is my will that all my weyne scott or Silinge and all bords formes bedstockes woodden wear yorne ware and husbandrie ware shale remeaine at my house duringe my wyffe lyfe if shee keepe in my name and Soole and unmaried and shee to have the use and occupacion thereof And after her decease or Immediately after shee marie or miscarie, I geeve the same to whomsoever enterethe uppon my burgages and Landes by force of this my last will and Testamente The rest revercon and Remender of all my goods cattells and chattells, and Debtes whatsoever I will shalbe equallie devyded betweene the same Ellen my wyffe and the said Fraunces my nephewe, by even portions And yt is my will that my bringinge forthe and funerall Expences shalbee paide of 45s. which I leave in my howse.

Executors: Ellen my wyfe and the said Fraunces my nephewe. And it is my will that my neyboure Godfrey Heron [?] shall have the use and occupacion of all

16 *Stockport Probate Records*

suche monie as is due to my nephew Frances Daniell by fource of this my last will for and unto the use of him the same for the tyme and space of Sixe yeares next ensuinge the date hereof by which tyme I trust the same Fraunces will bee [damaged] the same his selfe.

Witnesses: Hughe Buredsell, William Daniell, George Reddishe.

Debts owinge to mee the saide George Daniell.	£	s	d
Of Robeart Seele of brammall		40	0
Of Rondulfe [?] holme of Offerton		27	4
Of henerie Fogge of Offerton		38	0
Of ould good wyffe Dodge of the hill toppe		10	0
Of Raphe Seele and his wyffe		8	0
Of Thurston Rowson Alias matley		15	0
Of widowe Newton of Impshaweyate and Alexander hir sonne		2	6
Of blanche henyson widowe		2	6
Of litell John henshaw		7	0
Of Ales bekerstaffe		3	8
Sum	7	14	0

Inventory: George Daniell of hillgate in the township of Stockport, yeoman.
Taken: 6 December 1592.
Of: goods, cattells, chattells and debts.
Prisers: Homfrie Bridge, Otiwell Heyginbothom, Thurston Rowsen alias Matley, and Robert Jynnie [?]

	£	s	d
in Cattell	5	6	8
in horse fleshe		40	0
in Sheepe		35	0
in heye		20	0
in Corne		35	0
in fewell		6	8
in husbandrie ware and Iron ware		20	0
in bords formes Sylinge and bedstockes		16	8
in Chistes		10	0
in pewter brasse and leads		20	0
in Treene ware and wooden loomes		3	4
in Cheares, stooles and Quishens			16
in beddinge		40	0
in A bord clothe and towells			16
in bookes		10	0
in Beasse and Chattels	9	10	0

his Apparell	20	0
in Readie moniey	45	0
Sum	31 1	0

his Inward debtes as Appeare by his last will and Testament admount in the whole to the Summe of £7 14s.

Office endorsement: probate to executors.

9. JOHN SMYTH OF STOCKPORT, BAKER. S.Pr. [25 February?] 1595/6. **Will**, [faded in places]. Health: troubled with infirmities in my body.
W.T. 22 October 1595.

I commend my soule into the handes of Almightie god my creator Savior and redeemer, by the merytes of whose blessed sonnes bloodsheding I [damaged] unfainedly to be saved, And my bodie I comytt to the earthe from whence yt came to be buryed in the parishe churche of Stockport afforesaid Item I gyve and bequeathe unto Margerie Smythe my welbeloved wiffe my burgage messuage tenement and howse with thappurtennances in Stockport afforesaid wherein I nowe dwell with all landes and all others commodyties and proffettes to [damaged] belonginge duringe the terme of her naturall lyffe yf she fortune to Survyve me the said John [damaged] my deceasse [damaged] name soole and unmaryed Item I gyve and bequeathe unto the said Margerie my wiffe the full [damaged] one third parte of [damaged] goods cattells chattells [damaged] moveable, Except a foulden bord A presse, one Cubbord and three pairs of bedstiddes which I will and my mynd is that they shall contynew and remayne in my howse where they now be, and contynewe revert discend or come to hym or them to whom I shall hereafter in or by this my testament and last will gyve and bequeathe the same, my burgage unto, After the deceasse of my said wiffe, provyded allwayes that it is my will that Margerie my wiffe shall have the use and occupacion of the said foulden bord, presse Cubbord and three bedstiddes duringe her naturall lyffe yf she kepe her in my name soole and unmaried, Item from and after the naturall deceasse of me the said John Smythe and the said Margerie my wiffe or from and Imedyatlie After she eyther marye or myscarie After my deceasse I gyve and bequeath my Sayd burgage, messuage tenement howse landes groundes and appertenances within Stockport afforsaid and all comodyties thereunto belonging unto John Smythe sonne of my brother Robert Smythe Clerke, and to the heires of his bodie lawfullie begotten or to be begotten, And for want of suche Issue I give and bequeathe the same to Edmonnde Smythe one other sonne of the said Robert Smythe my brother and to the heires of his bodie lawfullie begotten or to be begotten, And for want of suche Issue I gyve and bequeathe the same to the Issue of Rondulphe Smythe my brother [damaged] begotten or to be begotten and theire heyers, And for

18 *Stockport Probate Records*

want of such Issue I gyve and bequeathe the same unto my Servant and nephew John Burgesse, and to the Issue of his bodie lawfullie begotten or to be begotten And for want of such Issue I gyve and bequeathe the same unto the Right heires of me the said John Smythe theire heires and assignes forever Provyded alwaies and yett neverthelesse yt is my mynd and will that the estate of the sayd John Smythe my said brother Robert his sonne and the Issue of his bodie lawfullie begotten or to be begotten, of in and unto the said burgage and premysses, And for want of suche Issue, That the right and estate of the said Edmonde and the Issue of his bodie lawfully begotten or to be begotten (of in or unto the same burgage) And for want of suche Issue that the Right and estate of the Issue of my said brother [damaged] Smythe lawfully begotten or to be begotten and theire heyres, Shall Stand and be uppon these condicons hereafter expressed That is to weete that [damaged] of them be mynded to Alyenate or sell his right estate and Interest unto anye man person or persons whatsoever of all or any parte of the said burgage [damaged] premisses which cometh in truste or distended to him theym or anie of theym by this my present last will and testament, That then he or they [damaged] shall alyenate and sell that unto the said John Burgesse or his Issue, (yf he or they be myndfull to have the same), And shall Abate to the said John [damaged] Issue, the somme of fyve poundes of [damaged] England, that others would gyve for the said burgage or of the pryce the same burgage [damaged] soev[er] refuseth so to do to have no benefyt of the said Burgage nor Anie parcell thereof by this my last will and Testament but his and their interest in [damaged] and unto the same burgage to Surceasse, and the same burgage and premisses to discend to the next heire in the Intayle afforsaid after hym or them Succeedinge.

[The will is too damaged to print after this point. John Burgess, James Fell, Thomas Rysinge and his sons William and John, Edward Smythe and the testator's brothers Robert and Randolph all receive bequests. The testator left a bequest to the mayor of Stockport; and 20s to each servant in his employment at his death.]

Dettes owyng to the said John Smythe	£	s	d
of Rauffe Reddich of baguley as appeareth by one Indenture	40	0	0
of the same Rauffe behynd of oxen pryce		30	0
lent hym by younge Sympson		40	0
lent hym 2 yeres synche to buy A horse		13	4
Sum	44	3	4

Receaved hereof			
at the last Reckenyng I was behynd		5	0
for cheese		5	0
A field at Tervyns 2 yeres		40	0
for one mare		46	8
in otes		24	0

in otes an other tyme		24	0
in otes an other tyme		20	0
one cowe		40	0
one other cowe		48	8
one fatt swyne		20	0
gresse for my oxen		10	0
the exchange of one cowe		3	4
one browne heffer		43	4
[in margin] sum received	16	10	0

dettes also owing to the said John Smythe

of Rauff Reddiche for one mare and A cowe	5	6	8
for ground		26	8
for the exchange of A cowe		20	0
in money		20	0
behynd of Oxen and A cowe		14	0
half gresse of A cowe		5	0
due to me	9	7	8

due to my wiff of the same Rauffe one peece of gold about £3 the peece and 2 other peeces of 10s the peece

Sum	24	0	0

Dettes also owying[1]

of [damaged] as appeareth by A byll [damaged] .
of John Warren as appeareth by A bill
of Richard Ogden as appeareth by [damaged] his handes 8s whereof I [damaged] hym the one
of Alexander Elcocke as appeareth by a bill
of George Elcocke son of the same Alexander
of James Low as appearethe by a bill

more of the same James		3	0

of John Lowe
of Robert Smythe of bradburie
of Randulphe
of Alexander Mosse
of Thomas burdsell
of Joane Crosley widow
of William [?] for 5th [sic] hopes barlie 4s the hoope lent money 10s for the hyre of one cow 6s 8d and for [worke] with my draught 13s 4d .

off Thomas Garnett		13	0
of the same Thomas for leadinge his bryde wayne			
of [?] Adshed of Adlington		21	6
of Rauffe Clayton of merple		7	[?]
of the said [?] Adshed of Adlington		7	4

20 Stockport Probate Records

of younge Thomas Bordman	2	8
of Thomas Nicholson of Addeswoodd		20
of Robert Torkenton of handford	6	3
of William Richardson Thomas Combes and Worthington	38	0
of Rauffe Downes	14	6
of Rauffe Woolfondym	7	6

Sum 33 [?] [?]

[More debts owing to the deceased[2]]

Thomas [?] of Riddiche	7	4
of Thomas Garnett more for 2 daies worke with my draught	3	4
of Thomas Adshed of Adlington for Asshes	12	0
of Roger Woodd	3	[?]
owe hym for thresshing 2 dayes and An halff		
of Olyver Heginbotham	3	4
of Mr. Warren of Poynton 18s receevon whereof for baking 6s 8d resteth	11	4
of Mr Lowe for kyddes		17
of the same Mr Lowe for one hoope asse		
baking and leading hey and cowes		
of Myles Sharshall		
of James Fell		
of Reynold Makyn	18	0

Sum 5 15 [?]

dettes which the same John did owe

To William [illegible] for 2 hoopes salt	[blank]	
To Mr Lowe for a boke	3	4
To Mr Low for a mucke wayne	6	0

Sum 9 4

Sum of the whole [illegible] dettes   90 16 10

1 This section of the debt list is extensively damaged, and many amounts are lost. We have left these blank.
2 This heading illegible except for the word owing. From the net total of the debts we deduce that it refers to more debts owed to the deceased.

Inventory: John Smyth of Stockport, baker.   Taken: 21 February 1595/6.
Of: goods cattells chattells rightes credyttes and debtes. Original document, authenticated by the prisers at the foot of the sheet.
Prisers: Raphe Nicholson, Sampson Huntte, Raphe Seele and Raphe Johnson the elder.

	£	s	d
one grey geldinge	3	13	3
one white geldinge	3	0	0
one blacke geldinge		40	0
one Readd cowe	3	0	0
one blacke cowe		40	0
one other blacke cowe		30	0
in hey by estymacion two wayne loads		26	8
one carte with Iron bound wheels		33	4
one mucke wayne one mucke carte leaves		11	0
one paire wheeles		3	4
one corne wayne		7	0
fyrewoodd at the bakehowse		4	0
tenne loads of gorses		13	4
one loade of kyddes			20
certen gorses yett growing in bentley hey in Heaton Norres		33	4
Piles and coale rakes in the bakehouse and 2 bordes			12
oates by estymacion 20 hoopes		35	0
5 peckes barlie malte		6	0
3 hoopes oate malte		5	0
4 wisketts one Syffe and one Ryddle		2	0
candle rysshes			2
certen course barlie malte			20
3 Seckes		3	0
2 trestes in the highe chamber			4
one wyndowe sheete one coffer one forme in the highe chamber and one cheese crate		3	4
one ould paire of bootes			20
one flock bedd one bolster 2 blanckettes one ould coverlett and certen fethers in the highe chamber		7	0
in the parlor 4 coverlettes		18	0
one blankett			20
one ould fether bedd one pillow 1 bolster and 1 mattrasse		24	0
7 paire hempe sheetes		21	0
4 table napkyns, 3 fyne pillow beeres 4 other pillowbeeres 3 hand [damaged]		7	6
one lyttle peece valure and one lyttle peece velvett			8
2 fyne towells		3	0
certen ould silver by estymacion one ounce		4	6
3 round bord clothes		2	0
2 yds, quart, lynnen clothe			16
other lynnen clothe, 9 yardes and an halffe at 6½d the yard		5	1½
2 coffers		8	0

In the parlour beneathe

| A fetherbedd a bolster 2 pillowes | | 30 | 0 |

2 pillowe cases and one paire fyne flaxen sheetes	10	0
2 ould coverlettes one blanckett	3	0
3 bedstydds which are to remeyne at the howse	4	6
one presse also to remeyne	13	4
one cubbord in the house and one foulden bord also to remeyne att the howse	32	0

In the lower chamber and in the highe chamber beneath

one Turnell	4	0
one lyttle trestle		4
one head yoake 1 payre clyvis 2 oxe bowes one other oxe yoke	2	8
2 yokes unbound		12
one Iron teame		16
2 mattockes	2	8
one hammer one payre pynsers and 3 iron wedges	2	6
2 siccles		3
1 hand saw		4
1 paire hynd most horse geeres with an iron tordwith		12
1 pigg foot		4
one ould harrowe with pynnes		20
one axeltree		6
one long bast and one lyttle bord		14
in turves by estymacion 6 carte loads	7	0
one hackney saddle and 2 packe saddles and some furnyture	4	0
one Sword	2	0
one other sword pawned	3	0
a carte sadle 3 paire horse geeres 3 hombarghes 3 horse collers 1 payre thille homes	8	6
one henne crate		4
one paire bedstocks		12
5 oxe bowes		4
one weighe beame		3
2 axes, one bill 3 ould ogers one gorge, A Spoakeshave, 3 horselocks and one lyttle cheyne of Iron	4	8
2 forks 2 muckhookes one spade 2 pitchforks A staffe A poole axe	[amount illegible]	
one sawe		16
one nasse one wymble and one paire ploughe irons A ploughe staffe	3	0
one payre gowberts, one ould grydle and other ould iron	3	0
one carte rope		6
one plowe beame foure axeltrees 2 plowes	3	10
certen fellies for wheeles	2	8
6 netherhedds		8
balkes under the hey and other fyre woodd	6	0

9 Sawen bords	3	0
1 turffe wayne chest	2	6
in mucke	10	0
one fyre Iron one fyre shovell one paire tonngs one Rakentree and pott hookes	5	0
2 Spytts and one byrd spytt	2	0
22 pewter dysshes and 8 sasars weighing 44 pounds with 5 pottingers	22	0
one pewter quart and one pynt two pewter salts and 4 spoones		16
5 brasse candlestyckes	3	4
one brasse chafyndysshe	2	6
foure brasse potts 2 possenytts 57lb weight	20	0
one cawltherne of brasse weight 16 lb	5	4
2 brasse pannes one skellett one kettle 15 lb weight	10	0
a frying pane		14
A lead		9
one chuffen weight 12 lb et dd	4	0
2 hackynge knyves		4
one morter and one pestell	2	0
one Round bord		20
foure cheeres	2	6
2 lyttle cheeres and 2 buffett stooles and other stooles		20
7 treyne dyshes one dosen trenchers		6
one growle stound	4	0
one chorne and staffe		8
2 barrells, 2 Ryndletts	4	0
other tryne ware	5	0
one breweinge kayre	4	0
in earthen potts and muggs		20
bords in the buttrie	2	0
one reame pott		4
one tennet		3
[Line illegible]	2	0
2 esshens A pigenne and the bords under them		21
one Lanthorne		4
one chamber pott		2
4 quarters salte beefe	26	8
one fornace	6	8
2 drynckynge potts		4
one uewe bowe	2	0
4 quysshens		16
all his apparell	46	8
fyre woodd in the streete and certen coales		14
one Jacke	5	0
60 Asshes standinge and 11 lyinge uppon the ground fallen	6 0	0

24 *Stockport Probate Records*

ground taken of Mr. Low.	10	0	0
certen ground called Walle butts		13	4
ground taken of Willm Norres		42	0
ground in Ettchulles or money certen yeres . . .	17	2	0
in Redie money	24	18	0
10 Silver Spoones weighing 8 ounces		32	0
one psalter			6
Sum	111	17	9½

his Inward detts as appeare by his last will and testament admount in the whole to the some of £90. 16s. 10d.

his outward detts as appeare by the same his last will and testament admount in the whole to the some of 9s. 4d.

The praysers names
[Signed] Raphe Nyklesson
          Sampson Huntte
          Raphe Seylle
          X the marke of
          Rauphe Johnson.

Office endorsement: probate to Robt Smith.

10. ROBERT SHAWE, OF STOCKPORT [OF THE MOORE SYDE WITHIN THE BOUNDS OF STOCKPORT¹], CARPENTER.

S.Pr. 8 June 1599.
Will, trobled with Sicknes.   W.T. 31 December 1598.

Firste and prinsepally, I Comende my Soule unto god allmightie And my bodie to the Earthe from whence it came to be buryed in the Churche yarde of Stockporte. Allso I do will and my mynde is. And I do geve and bequeath unto Roberte Shawe my base begotten sonne 1 th[sic] leade a lossett my Coate and a peare of hose. Allso I do geve unto John Benesone Junior one wether hogge. he the said John Benessonne, gevinge, unto either of his sisters 6 th[sic]d Item I do geve unto William Benessonne sonne of John Benessone one Cuttinge Axx. And all the reste of that little portion of goods that god hathe blessedme wyth all. I do device geve and bequeathe unto my two daughters Ellinne Shawe and Eme Shawe equally betwine them. They the saide Elline and Emme payinge doinge and dischardgine my debtes Legaseyes and funerall Expenses.

Executors: Ellinne Shawe, testator's daughter, and Rawffe Tayler testator's neighbour.
Witnesses: Rawffe Tayler and James Smithe.

Inventory: Roberte Shawe of Stockport, carpenter. Taken: 3 June 41 Eliz. [1599].
Of: goodes.
Prisers: James Smith, Hughe Mottrom, Rawffe Tayler and John Heigham.

	£	s	d
In pewter and brasse .		13	4
one little Arke one Cowfer and one peare of bedstocks		6	0
one little borde and Trine ware .		3	4
Rackes and tonnges .			12
in bedclothes Linnen and wollen		11	0
his Apparrell .		10	0
[Sum	2	4	8]

Office endorsement: probate to Ellina Shawe.

   1 Buried 2 June 1599.

11. RAPHE HUNT OF STOCKPORT, YEOMAN.   S.Pr. 7 September 1599.
Will, [damage to top and bottom]. Health: sick in body.   W.T. 25 July 1599.

Knowinge death to bee certayne to everie creature and the howre thereof uncertayne doe make and ordayne this my present testament contayninge heerein my last will in maner and forme followinge first and principallye I doe commend my soule into the handes of almightee god my maker and redeemer by whom I trust to bee one of the number of those that shalbee saved; and my bodie to the earth from whence it was taken to bee buried in the churchyard of Stopford neere unto the place wheer my father lyeth buried. Item for the order and distribution of my goodes as followeth my mynd and will is, that my debtes and funerall exspences shalbee payd and discharged of the whole goodes. Item wheeras the house and groundes wheeruppon I now dwell are in the disposition and orderinge of my master, my mynd and will is, and I doe most humbly beseeche his woorship that it would please him to accepte of my sister Elizabeth as tenante to the same both for the kyndnes I have found with her at all tymes and especiallye for the great paynes shee hath taken with mee in this my extreame sicknes. Item I geeve and bequeath unto my said sister Elizabeth all my goodes moveable and unmoveable and whatsoever I have heertofore made profitt, or commoditee of in and upon the same house or groundes I doe freely geeve unto her, my debtes and funerall exspences as aforesaid beeinge payd and discharged of the whole. Item I geeve unto my said sister Elizabeth my best band; Item I geeve unto Richard Gloover alias Johnson my best sute of apparell and my best hatt my orrenge colored stockinges my girdle and spotted band and my shooes. Item I geeve and bequeath unto my sister Margerie the wyffe of

Raphe Allen two hoopes of barley and two bandes. Item I geeve and bequeath unto my sister Jane the wyffe of John Dickenson of heweston one hoope of barley. Item I geeve unto my brotherinlawe Raphe Allen one payre of strawe colored knit stockinges: Item I geeve unto James Buerdsell my blacke dublet, and Jerkyn my hose that are made for beneth the knee, my second hatt, and a paire of Carsee stockinges Item I geeve unto Ellyn Hunt my sisterinlawe my byble: Item I geeve to Raphe Pycrofte and Robte Hardman my two best handkerchers: Item I geeve to Francis Smith my purse with twoo ringes and 5 or 6 litle bend peeces of silver Item I geeve to Robte Withinton my woork daie hose, and to Alex Rode my litle cambrige band: Item to Raphe hollinshed my bowe and arrowes and a paire of bowles: Item to Francis Withington a woork daie dublet and a black paire of breeches and [illegible] coate. Item I geeve to Ann ‹Raphe› Allyn daughter of my Brotherinlawe Raphe Allyn all the rest of my bookes.

Executors: my sister Elizabeth Hunt and my neighbour Thomas Buerdsell.
Overseers: Edward [damaged].
Witnesses: Elizabeth Hunt, Tho. Buerdsell, Ed. Rodes, Tho. [damaged].

Inventory: Raphe Hunt of Stockport.　　　　　　　　　No date given.
Of: goods and catells.
Prisers: Raphe Seele, Tho. Buerdsell, Edward Rodes, Robte Woodd.

	£	s	d
a fetherbed and a boulster .		24	0
2 Coverletes and 2 blanketes		13	4
one mattris		5	0
3 sheetes		6	0
one standinge bedd		10	0
one ould brasse panne		10	0
one ould brasse chandler			18
three pewter dishes		2	6
3 coffers		10	0
a litle truckell bed		2	0
a litle Iron grate			20
a brasse morter and a pestill		2	0
an ould chaufer and a posnet		4	0
an ould swoord and a dagger		3	0
3 ould axes, and a hand sawe			18
nagers chisells and other Iron stuffe		2	0
an Iron hacke, a forke with a mucke hooke and a dubbing bill			16
an ould payre of ballances with a leade pound			4
an ould bruinge leade		10	0
an ould square table		2	4
another litle round table			16
a litle keare and a stoond eshin and kimnell		2	6
earthen pottes			8

bookes	6	8
his apparell	33	4
in barlie	46	8
in hey	10	0
more in hey which is sould	22	0
in wood and turves	3	4

[Sum 11 19 0]

Office endorsement: probate to executors.

12. HENRIE SEELE OF STOCKPORT, YEOMAN. I.Pr. 20 June 1600.
Will: sick. W.T. 12 June 1600.

First and principallye I commend my soule into the hands of Almightie god my maker, trustinge faithfullye to bee saved by the precious deathe and passion of our Lord and Saviour Jesus Chryste, And my bodie to the earthe from whence it came, hopinge to have a Joyfull resurrection Item I geeve and bequeathe to my Brother Raphe Seele all my goods and househoulde stuffe remayninge at my house in Brinnyngton And I bequeathe to my daughter Ellyn buckley alias Taylier my cloake The reste of all my goods and Cattayles bothe moveable and unmoveable (I beinge honestly broughte home and my Funerall expences discharged) I whollye geeve and bequeathe to Frances Taylier daughter of Edward Taylier deceased.

Executrix: the said Ellyn Taylier.
Witnesses: James Williamson Alderman, John Wynne, Thomas Crosley, John Reddiche, Richard Glover and George Reddiche.

Inventory: Henry Seele of Stockport, yeoman. Taken: 13 June 1600.
Of: goods and cattayles.
Prisers: James Williamson alderman, John Wynne, Robte Bexweeke and Willm hudsonne.

	£	s	d
his goods in Brinnington one ould nagge		13	4
one greate arke		13	4
one Turnell			16
twoe other arks			20
one payre of bedstocks			15
one disheboard			12
one meate boarde and one forme			20
in the highe chamber, one board, one forme, twoe breads, 10 arrowes, 2 brydles, 2 ould paynted cloathes one ladder, one ould bottle one ould sythe		2	0

28 Stockport Probate Records

one Vargis barrell			1
in the chamber belowe, 2 axes, one noger, one spade, one bill, one sicle, one wymble, one hande sawe, one mattocke, one hammer, one payer mittens, one wollcombe . . .		4	0
one boarde one ould forme and one stoole			12
one harrowe		2	0
seven ould boards one cliste of wood belowe in the shoppe . .		2	4
one water boarde and twoe breads in the house			9
one oulde sadle, and one ould forke			8
corne sowen uppon the grounde his parte		[blank]	
	[Sum	2	6	6]

his goods in Stopporth

one brasse pott		7	0
one fryinge pann and one grid Irone		2	0
one Fether bedd		10	0
one duble coverlett		6	8
one pillowe and one boulster		6	0
one whyte blankitt		3	4
one blankett			20
2 ould peere of blanketts			6
one payre of Sheetes		5	0
2 sherts and fouere sherte bands		5	0
one table napkyn and one andkerchaffe			12
one cloake		11	0
one gowne of fryce		5	0
one ould blewe coate		3	4
2 payre upper ends of hoase		2	0
2 dublets		3	4
2 payre of netherstocks		2	0
one payre of garters			2
one ould payre of shoes			4
2 ould hatts			8
one girdle one bagge one dagger one knyfe and one payre of glooves		2	0
2 bowes one broken bowe all of Uewe 11 arrowes and one quyver		6	8
2 bowe castes			6
one chaire and one quishon			12
one coffer		8	0
one arke			6
one payre of tayler sheares			4
	[Sum	4	6	0]
	[Sum	6	12	6]

13. ROGER WOODD OF STOCKPORT, YEOMAN. C.Pr. 26 February 1601/2.
Will: damaged throughout. Health: sick in body. W.T. 4 February 1601/2.

I comend my soule into the hands off the allmightie god my creator Redeemer and onelie Saviour and my bodie to be buried in the parish church of Stockport [near *or* next] to my Mother [illegible] my worldlye goods my will as followeth Item yt is my mynd and will that my wyffe shall have all my goodes chatells and dettes whatsoever or wheresoever they be and that After her decease [hereafter text and interlineations illegible].

Executors: jointly, testator's wife and brother Robert Wood.
Overseer: Robert Raddick.

Debts owe more [sic] to mye Roger Woodd	£	s	d
Off Elen Smyth off Levensholme		16	0
More off Elen Smyth for one fyre yron		4	0
More off Elen Smythe for one ketle pan		3	4
More off Elen Smyth for towe hens			16
More off Elen Smyth for a Rakentree and one peare of kynves [sic]		2	0
More off Elen Smyth for one [damaged]		2	0
Off Huge Smyth for two stones		2	0
More off Huge Smyth for one pick forck			12
Off Thomas Mosse off the church yarde [damaged]		3	0

[The remaining nine lines too damaged to read; for total see inventory.]

Inventory: Rodger Woodd. [No date given.]
Of: goodes or cattelles.
Prisers: James Fell, William Rydgeye, Edward Rodes and John Cartwryght.

	£	s	d
in bedinge		12	0
in his bodily Reparrell		4	6
in arkes and cofferes		5	0
one paire of bedstokes			12
in bordes and [illegible]		2	0
in tryen ware		2	0
in yearthen potes			6
in Iorene ware		3	8
in puter and brasse		8	0
one ladder and [illegible]			6

⟨Sum 38s 6 8d[sic]⟩
[*recte* 39s 2d]

30   *Stockport Probate Records*

Sume goodes and deptes as appereth in the will is £6   14   2d.

Office endorsement: probate to executors.

14. HEW RIDGWAYE, WITHIN THE TOWNSHIP OF STOCKPORT.
I.Pr. 21 May 1602.
Will: damaged throughout. Health: sick in body.   W.T. [damaged] 1602.

[Damaged portion mentions testator's daughter Jone, and proceeds:]
I do also give Roberte all my work loomes in the smithey morover [damaged] is the Rest of all my goodes shall be equaly deveyded [damaged] my Sonne John my Sone Roberte and my doughter Jone my Funerall Expences beinge firste tacken up of the whole morover my will and mynd is with the consente of my maister that my wyffe shall occupoy that little ground I have deuringe her lyfe and that after her desseace then my Sone Roberte to injoye it peinge unto his Brother John at Such tyme or tymes as they shall agreye upon the full and Just Some of feyffe ponds hopinge to foynd my good maister tractuble unto it morover I do give unto my doughter Jone one wheyt Ewe and a wheyte lamb I do allsso consitute ordene and macke my Trusty and well beloved frends John Sydbothom and my Brother in lawe Alexander Knote my lawfull executors and Olyver Dodge to be oversyer of this my will in manner and forme aforsed my will and mynd is my doughter Jone shall have the halfe of the chamber over the Feyld Syd.
[Rest of will too damaged to print.]

Inventory: Hewes Ridgwaye.   Taken: 1 May [1602].
Of: damaged; prisers' names at foot damaged: include Myles Herod.

	£	s	d
threi Coye one sterke towe barren coy one incalffe	7	[?]	[?]
one coupel and towe ewe hoges for the sheipe		13	4
one yonge Swyne		6	0
in Geisse henes and ducks		5	0
in Brasse		19	0
in Beuter [sic]		2	0
in Bedinge		50	0
in sheites and other linins		24	0
in arkes and Coffers		20	0
in Bedstockes		4	0
in Hempen yerne		13	0
in Corne and malte		19	0
in Backin		6	8

in Bordes and formes	6	6
one dishebord	2	6
one turnell	2	6
in treine ware	7	0
yorthen potes		20
one ould leade		12
fee for a closse for one yeare	22	0
in quishons	2	0
one ould cheire and stooles		6
in Eyrone ware within the housse	5	4
more in eyron ware within the housse	3	0
towe lades		12
towe more lades		4
toules for the Smitheye	44	8
for his owne aparrell to his backe	24	0
for one heyffer	3	4
for one parcel of timber	3	0

[2 lines damaged]

Office endorsement: probate to executors.

15. JOHN KELSALL OF STOCKPORT, BUTCHER. I.Pr. 11 February 1602/3.
Will: faded. Health: Sicknes and infyrmyties in my bodye.
W.T. 16 November 1602.

Dreadinge the uncerteyn tyme of my departure out of this transytorye worlde [illegible] be certen to every creature and the houre thereof unknowen, meanynge that Amytie [illegible] the contynuance thereof shall and mey be had and contynued Amongest my wyffe and children [illegible] deceasse, and for the discharge of my conscyence, do make and declare this present testament [illegible] herein my last will in manner and forme followinge that is to saye. First and pryncypallye I do comend [illegible] into the handes of Almyghtie god my creator redeemer and onelye savyor, by the meryts of whose [illegible] bloodesheedinge I trust to be saved and to Inherytt his everlastinge kyngdome, And my bodye and bones [illegible] to christiene buryall in the Parishe church yard of Stockport above mentyoned in such place as my frendes and executors thinke meete and convenyent And for the order and distribucon of my worldlye goodes chattels cattells and debts. It is my mynd and will as hereafter followeth. First yt is my will that any [illegible] as I owe of Right or conscyence to anye person or persons my funerall expences the probacon of this my last will [illegible] legacies hereafter mentyoned shalbe paid done and performed of my whole goodes before anye divysione be made [illegible] which legacies hereafter followe I gyve and bequeath to Willm kelsall my sonne the somme of foure marks which Raphe [illegible] oweth mee in full discharge and satisffaction of his childes parte or porcon of my goodes to be due to him [illegible] reason of my naturall deceasse consyderinge how good I have bene to him alreadye, Item I gyve to Edward kelsall Richard kellsall Robert kelsall my sonnes and to Jane my daughter every one of theme 12d a peece in full recomp [illegible] satisfaction and discharge of there and every of there childes parte and portion, due or to be due or belong to theme or anye of them, or after or by reasone of my naturall deceasse consyderinge how good I have bene [illegible] alreadye. The rest of my goods cattells and debts I will shalbe devyded into three equall porcons The first parte whereof I give Frances kelsall my wyffe, the second parte to Alles my doughter and the third and parte to John kelsall sonne of my sonne Edward. Item yt is my mynd and will that all such assignements as I have heretofore made of my howse shall stand and bee good and effectuall according to the tenor and true meanynge thereof.

Executors: William Nicholson of Stockport and Thomas Didisburye of Withington Yf god call for mee I give my sonne Edward the rent of the shoppe in baguleye [?'s] ocupacon.
Witnesses: Thomas Elcocke, George Reddich.

	£	s	d
Debts that John Kelsall oweth			
to Thomas Elcocke		24	0
for a dublet clothe and buttons and sylke		6	0
more lent		14	0
Rec of this 6s in tallowes.			
more			9
to Thomas Andrewe		5	0
to Edward mottershed		5	6
The debts owinge to John kelsall			
of James Willyamsone the younger		3	11
of Henrye Ryle of holt either 2 hoopes of Barlye or to be paid one saynt Andrewes daye next		7	6
of John Collyer of Streete house lane		6	0
of Thomas Hulme malte man		3	3
of William Norres		3	8
of Raphe Ryle	fore	markes	
of Thomas Walker the younger		3	0
of Richd bagaley		3	4
of the wyffe of John Cheet		5	8
of Henrye pownall of Hathorne for beeffe			18
of George bowdon gent lent money		2	0
of John pott of the edge for beeffe			16

Inventory: John Kelsall of Stockport, butcher.   Taken: 9 February 1602/3.
Of: goodes chattells credytts and detts.

Prisers: Alexander Wood, John Robynson, alderman, Otywell Dodge and Nicholas Blomeyley.

	£	s	d
two ‹Syyne› Swyne		36	0
in pullene		2	8
three flitches of bacon		25	0
in pewter		15	0
in brasse mettell		42	0
A brasse mortere A pestill and a brasse candlestick		2	0

In the highe chamber over the parlor and butterye
of [sic] fetherbedd one bolster one chaffe bedd Two matteresses 2 coverlettes two blankettes and three payre bedstockes and 3 formes 40 0
one Table 5 0

In the parlor above in the house
a fetherbedd a bolster a pillowe one coverlett one blankett and one payre bedstockes 28 0
 ‹13 4›
fore payre of rownd sheetes 13 4
one bord 2 formes 6 0
three ould coffers 5 0

In the lyttle parlor belowe
one ould fetherbedd, one bolster one coverlett one blankett, A bord and three Settells and bedstockes 15 0

In the lytle buttrye in the kytchin
A coverlett A blankett 10 0
A greate stound two barells for beare one lyttle stound, An eshon A tinne dishe A kymnell A lossett twentye kannes and cuppes 15 0

In the kytchyne
A brewinge keyre A greate stound a litle stound two eshens, A turnell A kymnell 10 0

In the highe chamber over the kytchin
in turves three wysketts and one Spinnynge wheele . . . 4 0

In the fyre howse
two bordclothes 4 napkins 4 0
four cheares 16
one longe bord 2 formes one littlye bord and Settles one other thicke bord 13 4

34   *Stockport Probate Records*

In the highe chamber over the house

a coverlett A blanckett one ould spinnynge wheele and other thinges there .	5	4
one peece of bacone .		16

In the buttrye above in the howse

A cubbord 2 shelffes two beere barrells one Ale pott kannes poottes and glasses	11	0
in Iron ware	11	0
one salt coffer .		6
3 quyshens and stoules		6
one womans sadle and a brydle .	6	8
2 dosen trenchers		4
in coales .		8

In the stable and back sayde

in hey rackes and mangers and wood .	10	0
all the glasse aboute the housinge		12
Ale and Barlye malte	17	4
all his bodielye apparell	16	0

Sum [blank]
[Sum 18 14 4]

his Inward dettes as appeare by his last will
admont in the whole to [blank]
his outward debtes as appeare by the same
will in the whole [blank]

Office endorsement: probate to testator's wife Frances Kelsall.

16. THOMAS BURDSELL [OF STOCKPORT, buried 30 May 1603.¹].

S.Pr. 10 June 1603.

Inventory of: goods.   [No date given.]

Prisers [names at foot of document]: Henerie Holland, Robert Wood, John Whiticors and Thomas Newton.

	£	s	d
fower kye	9	0	0
one swyne		9	0
in bacon .		10	0
in Beddinge	4	0	0
in Linines .		30	0
in graye yorne .		10	0
in bodiley apparell		26	8
fowre bedstedes		26	8

in coffers and arkes		16	0
one table one rounde bord one benche with one Forme		20	0
one small coborde with one disheborde		6	8
in cheares and stoules with one [?senles]		3	4
fowre quishines		2	0
in Brasse and pewter	3	8	0
one Leade			20
in trine ware		10	0
towe seckes and one littelle bage		2	0
in yron wardes		15	0
one lanteronn and one [?bruche]			6
one oulde wiskete and towe siffes			6
one ould book			18
in Ladels			15
in barleye		10	0
in mallt		5	0
Sum	26	15	10
[*recte*	26	15	9]

1. Buried as 'Old Thomas of the Churchgate in Stockport'.

17. ELLINE MORES [OF STOCKPORT, buried 18 June 1603].

S.Pr. [year only] 1603.
Inventory of: goods. [No date given.]
Prisers: John Wharmbey and William Ridga [damaged].

	s	d
1 ould arke		[damaged]
3 muge potts		2
1 littell bowck		2
1 ould stownd		1
2 canes		3
3 woden platters		2
Ould bredes		1
Dishes		1
1 nogin		1
2 littell Kettells		6
1 creset		4
pothoacks & tongs		4
1 fyre Iron		8
3 sheets		16
the rest of her bedclothes		16
1 skert of a pettecotte	2	0

36 Stockport Probate Records

1 ould pettecotte & wastcote		8
1 yard of red cloth		22
all her smale linnen clothes	4	0
1 silke hatt		8
1 paire of ould showes		4
1 pewter charger		4

18. WILLIAM HARYSON OF THE HILLGATE IN STOCKPORT, LYNNEN WEBSTER. I.Pr. 27 April 1604.
Will, sickness and infyrmities in my bodie. W.T. 7 January 1600/01.

Knowinge Death to be certeyne to every creature and the houre thereof unknowen – meanyng that Amytie love and frendshippe and the contyuance thereof shall and maye be had and contynued Amongest my wiffe and children after my Deceasse, do make and ordeyne this present testamet [sic] conteyninge herein my last will in manner and forme followinge: That is to saye first and pryncipally I do comend my Soule into the hands of Almightie god my creator Redeemer and onelye Saviour, by the meryts of whose sonnes precyous bloode sheddinge I trust Unfenynedlye to be saved and to Inherytt his eternall Kyngdome And my bodye and boones I do comytt to the earth from whence yt came to be buryed Under or neere to the two highest formes above the Font and next to the font above the same, And for the ordering and distrybucon of my worldlye goodes cattells and detts: It is my mynd and will that the Same shalbe Gyven and devyded in maner and forme followinge: Fyrst my detts to be payd of the whole and that done, First and gyve of my whole goods to Ales my wyffe all such goods as are att my howse and brought to me by her when I did marye her, And to John Haryson my sonne fyve shillings in money which 5s yt is my mynd and will he have in full Recompence of his chylds porcon of my goods consyderinge he had att one tyme foure pounds in money of me heretofore and other goods and things And to my Daughter Jane I gyve in full Recompence of her porcone, with that she hath alreadye the Lowme she hath bene Accustomed to worke in and three Reedes at the dyscrecon of my executors to be delyvered: The rest of my said goods It is my mynd and will shalbe devyded Into three equall and Just parts: The first parte whereof I gyve and bequeath to Ales Haryson now my wyffe accordinge to the custome of the cuntrie, the Second parte I gyve and bequeath to Ellen Haryson my Daughter, And the thryd and last parte I do reserve to myselffe to dystcharge and paye my funerall expences and legacies, And after the same done and performed I will the revercon of my parte shalbe equallie devided betwixt the said Ales my wyffe and Ellen my daughter by even porcones.

Executrices: testator's wife Ales and daughter Ellen.
Witnesses: James Dyckson, Edmond Shelmerdyne, Thomas Broocke and George Reddich.

Inventory of: William Harrysons goods who was buryed the 16 of Aprill.[1]
Prisers: [at foot] Reynold Haryson, Alex Boardman, Laurence Darbye and Rauff Jackson. [no date given.]

	£	s	d
one lowme which is gyven		12	0
one lowme		8	0
one lowme		13	4
one Lath			16
in Reeds		20	0
in laches			16
in temples and shuttles			12
one pynne wheele			4
in brasses and prynes			2
one Warstocke, and Ryngs			18
one payre ballance			4
two ould arks			12
one yarne beame			4
two Wisketts			2
one ould baskett			1
in turves			4
in bedstocks		3	0
five od boxes		2	8
one table		6	8
in his wearinge clothes		6	8
in beddinge		13	4
in tryeene ware			16
in pewter and brasse		6	0
one fryinge pane one broach and toungs		3	0
2 old cheeres and stooles			6
4 ould coffers		6	8
one barryne cowe		26	8
	[Sum 6	17	9]

1. Parish register agrees.

19. ANNE[1] WALMESLIE [OF STOCKPORT, buried 13 April 1604].
I.Pr. 8 June 1604.
Inventory of: goodes and cattels. [No date given].
Prisers: [names at foot of document] Thomas Bordman, Richard Hankesson, John Sutte and John Ouldam.

38   *Stockport Probate Records*

		s	d
one wosted curtell		5	0
2 red petticotes		5	0
one ould apperan			6
in linines			18
one ould payre of house and showes			6
	Sum	12	6

Office endorsement: probate to William Carrington.

    1. Office endorsement has 'Agneta', status: spinster.

20. JOHN LATHAM [OF STOCKPORT, buried 20 June 1604].
                                            I.Pr. 15 October 1604.
Inventory of: goods.   [No date given].
Prisers: George Wood, Richard Walker, John Ouldam and Thomas Bruckshall.

		s	d
for apparrell for his bodye		2	0
one blanket one coverlet and 2 oulde shetes		2	0
one cofer and a peare of bed stockes		2	0
in yren ware			13
in tryne ware and wodden ware			12
	Sum	8	1

Office endorsement: probate to Ellinae Lathome, relict of deceased.

21. NICHOLAS WYNN OF STOCKPORT, SHEARMAN.
                                            I.Pr [26?] October 1604.
Will: [first part damaged and indecipherable, proceeds:] W.T. [damaged] 1604.

Item I give and bequeath unto my sonne Nicholas Wynn my qwarte brasse pott one chaffing dish and towe of my best pewter dishes Item I geve and bequeath unto dorithie Tomlynson my doughter these parcels hereafter named which she fetched away from my howse I not knowing of most of thym viz The best Coverlett, one whyte blanket, a partie [?] colourd Irish blanket one spitt, one breadyron, one backspittle foure pewter dyshes, dyvers litle stoles one salting bowk Towe brass Candlesticks and eight shillings which I lent her moreover I geve unto my said doughter dorithy the biggest brass pann saving one, the biggest brasse pott but one and the biggest kettle pann and three of the worst pewter dishes. Also I give and bequeath unto my said doughter dorithy towe rough kettle panns and one old skellett. Item I geeve and bequeath unto my said sonn

John my best skellett, one frying pann, one fyre Iron with rackentrees, one payre of tonngs and one spitt and my worst brasse pann and the beast brasse pott. Item I give and bequeath unto my Sonn John his children fyve old pewter dishes and three socers to be devyded amonge thym. Item I give and bequeath unto my soninlawe James Chorlton my worst sheres. Item my mynde and will is that everie chyld I am granndfather unto shall have everie one of thym 12 pence a pece. And my mynd and will is that my sonn John shall have the rest of my goods not bequeathed towards the paying of my debts and the discharging of my funerall expence.

Executor: testator's son John.
Witnesses: James Chorlton, Edmond Shelmerdyne, James Fearne and Tho. Symkyn.

Inventory: Nicholas Wynn of Stockport, shearman. Taken: 16 October 1604.
Of: goods and chattells.
Prisers: Thomas Garnett, Edmond Shelmerden [sic], Robert Gardner and James Fearne.

	£	s	d
Pannes and kettles viz Three pannes, three kettles, and twoe skelletts		10	7
foure brasse pottes		16	0
one Chafinge dish			10
Twelve ould pewter dishes and three sawcers		6	0
one oulde table, trestle, benche and forme and other ould bordes		3	0
one litle brotch one ould fryinge pann, one payre of pott hookes one payre of tonges, one Rakentree one oulde fyre Iron			20
Twoe payre of Shermans sheeres		2	8
workinge bordes and handle stockes			8
one Twyneter		4	0
Three stooles and a Chayre			4
one flocke bed, one Coverlett, foure blanketts, three boulsters, one pillowe		20	0
Two payre of sheetes three shirtes foure bands and one handkercher		7	0
his apparrell		20	0
one ould Arke			4
one sheerebord			6
paynted Clothes			8
in monie[1]		30	0
in Debt owing 13s 4d. to hym by his son John	‹Somme is 4	14	3›
	Sum [erasure] 6	17	7

40   *Stockport Probate Records*

[The signatures of the prisers have been copied at the foot of the document and Tho. Simkin signs the copy as 'wytnes hereof'.]

1. This and the following item have been added in another hand; as a consequence the total was altered in the same hand.

Office endorsement: probate to executor.

22.   ALEXANDER TORKINTON OF STOCKPORT, TANNER.
                           S.Pr. [date and month illegible] 1605.
Will, visited with weakness and infirmitie of bodie.   W.T. 19 September 1605.

I commende my soule into the hanndes of Almightie God my maker and preserver, And my bodie to be buryed in the Churche of Stockport on the Southe syde thereof, hopinge in the merites of Jesus Christe my Savioure and redeemer to be one of that small number that shalbe saved. Item I give and bequeth unto Izabell Torkinton my wyfe Threescore and Tenne poundes of lawfull money of Englande in recompence of her parte and portion of my goodes: And all the Brasse, Pewter, beddinge, lynnens, houshould stuffe and Implements whatsoever. Item I give and bequeth unto Izabell Bradley the daughter of Charles Bradley late of Rediche in the Countye of Lancaster husbandman deceased Thirteene pounde six shillinges Eighte pence of lyke lawfull money. Item I give and bequeth unto John Birche of Levensham shoomaker Thirteene poundes six shillinges eighte pence, towardes the bringing up of Alexander Birche my godsonne, and the reste of his children. Item I give and bequeth unto William Nicholson of Stockport other Thirteene poundes six shillinges eightepence lykewyse for and towardes the bringinge up of his Children. Item I give and bequeth unto Ellen Nicholson the daughter of Raffe Nicholson of the Townes ende, fyve poundes. Item I give and bequeth unto Alice Nicholson the daughter of William Nicholson late of the Woodhall in Rediche afforesayd deceassed, Tenne poundes to be putt forthe for her beste proffett and advantage, and the same to be delivered unto her when shee shall accomplishe the full age of Sixeteene: And if she departe this lyfe before she shall accomplish the sayde age: Then my mynde and will ys that Dorothye Nicholson another daughter of the same William Nicholson late of the Woodhall afforesayde deceassed, shall have the foresayd summe of Tenne poundes delivered unto her shortelye after the deceasse of the sayde Alice: And if the sayde Dorothye doe deceasse lykewyse before the sayd summe of Tenne poundes shalbe in suche sorte due and payable unto her as afforesayd: Then my mynde and will, ys, that Frannces Nicholson the Yongest sonne of the sayde William Nicholson late of the Woodhall afforesayd deceassed shall have the sayd summe of Tenne poundes to his owne proper use and behoofe for ever. Item my mynde and wyll ys further, That the pore artificers and tradesmen of the towne of Stockporte, shall for and towardes theire better helpe and furtherance in theire trades and occupations have the use and occupation of the Summe of Thirteene poundes sixe shillinges Eightpence of my goodes, for the space of Three Yeares, and soe from three Yeares to Three Yeares for ever, withoute anye interest payinge for the same, to be soe Imployed and bestowed att the oversighte of the Maior and Twoe of the moste Aunciente Aldermen dwellinge in the sayd Towne of Stockport for the tyme beinge, provyded Alwayes, That if the sayd Maior and Aldermen for the tyme being, that shall have the disposinge of the sayd money, shall eyther by negligence or other wyse, lett oute the same to unthriftye persons soe that the stocke or any parte thereof be wasted: that then the sayd Maior and Aldermen theire executours and administratours shall of theire owne propper goodes make upp the sayd stocke agayne to be lett oute as afforesayd to the use of pore artificers and tradesmen for ever. Item I give and beequethe unto Margerye Ogden my landeladye Sixe poundes, hopinge she will use my wyfe kyndelye after my deceasse. Item I give and bequeth unto Alexander Mosse of Stockport Butcher Tenne poundes. Item I give and bequeth unto William Torkinton of Stockporte my cosen, Twentye shillinges: And unto John Torkinton his servante fyve poundes. Item I give and bequeth unto Ellen Smithe the wyfe of Thomas Smithe late of Stockport deceassed Fouretye shillinges. Item I give and bequeth unto Mr. Arthur Storer Twentye shillinges. Item I give and bequeth unto Thomas Symkin Clarke of Stockport Twentye shillinges. Item I give and bequeth unto John Robynson Tanner fourtye shillinges and one sute of my apparrell. Item I will give and bequeth for and towardes the fyndinge and maynetayninge of an Usher for the publicke schoole of Stockport Tenne poundes for ever. And the same to be soe bestowed accordinge to my intente and true meaninge and not otherwyse, att the oversighte of Mr Gerard Parson of Stockport, and William Dickinson nowe Maior of the same towne, and twoe of the moste Aunciente Aldermen thereof: And att the oversighte of the Parson, Maior and twoe of the moste Aunciente Aldermen of the sayd Towne forever. Item I give and bequeth unto everie one of my Godchildren Twoe shillinges. Item I give and bequeth unto Ellen Lynney of Stockport Twentie shillinges. Item I bequeth will and leave unto my executors heereafter named towardes the bringinge of my bodye to the earthe, and for and towardes the discharge of my funerall expences costes and charges thereunto belonginge, the summe of Tenne poundes of currante money of Englande. And if the same be founde to be too litle: Then my mynde and will ys, That my sayde executors shall take parte of the Residue of my goodes not bequethed for the defrayinge of the sayd charge att theire discretion accordinge to the truste I have reposed in them. Item my mynde and will ys and I doe hartelye desyre, that the Clerk, John Ouldham and some boyes that can singe, doe fetche my bodye from my house, and accompanye the same unto the churche in singinge of psalmes to the prayse of God. And for theire laboure I give and bequeth everie one of them sixepence. The residue of all my goodes chattalls and debtes after my funerall expences performed and theise my legacies conteyned in this my presente Testamente fulfilled I wholye give and bequeth unto Peter Hey John Bolande and William Nicholson equallye to be devyded amongst them.

Executors: Izabell Torkington my wife, Peter Hey and John Boland. Hey and Boland are to have £3 each for their work as executors. Mk. and S.
Witnesses: Ri. Gerard, William Dickinson and Tho. Simkin.

Inventory: Alexander Torkington of Stockport, tanner.
Taken: 26 October 1605.
Of: goods and chattells. Original inventory authenticated at foot by three prisers.
Prisers: Alexander Boswell [signs Bossevylle], Raphe Dickinson [signs Raffe Diconson], Godffrey Hearon and Edmonde Shelmerden [Mk.]

	£	s	d
in ready money	4	10	0
his apparrell		40	0
in the house one standingebed with a Tester and Trucklebed		26	8
one fetherbed, mattresse 2 blankettes and a caddow		33	4
2 bolsters, 2 pillowes, one payre of sheets, and twoe pillowe beares		20	0
3 chestes in the house		12	0
one cupbord and one table in the house		16	0
Brasse		16	8
Pewter		20	0
in an highe chamber, one standingebed, and beddinge there remayninge	3	0	0
newe lynnen cloth		18	0
6 shirtes		9	0
other lynnens	3	0	0
corne and malte		12	4
one malte arke, one salting turnell, 3 chestes and 3 arkes		27	0
Bacon and grease		3	0
one halfe hoope and pecke with other implementes			16
one Barrell of Beefe		5	0
Treene ware		8	6
bordes and earthen pottes		2	0
woodd, turfe and coale		30	0
Barke	5	0	0
one oulde bedstead with bordes		2	6
one ould paire of scales one swinglefoote, hettchell and a spynningewheele			16
Lyme		3	0
worke loomes, ladders, baskettes and other implementes belonginge to his occupation		7	8
flax		2	3
one fyre yron, shovell tonges, brundrett, dreepingpan fryingpan, 2 spittes, golbertes, and other yron ware		9	0

twoe silver spoones		10	0
Butter and cheese		8	0
chayres, stooles, cushins bellowes and other implementes . .		6	0
Sum	33	0	7

Debtes owinge to the Testator

by James Worthington and George Bradley		44	0
by George Chorleton the father and George Chorleton his sonne	11	0	0
by Robert Dodge	11	0	0
by Thomas Simkin		40	0
by Thomas Houlte and John Henshall	11	0	0
by Edward Ryle, Robert Woodd and William Torkinton . .	7	14	0
by Roger Chewe and Reginalde Hollingworth	5	10	0
by William Bate and Hughe Bate	7	14	0
by Edward Thorniley Raphe Collier and George Brookshall .	11	0	0
by Peter Hey	56	0	0
by William Nicholson	5	0	0
by John Boland	57	19	8
by George Rawlinson alias Harrison		55	0
by Mr. Gerard	6	0	0
by Raphe Nicholson		30	0
Sum	198	6	8
Sum 231 7 3			

Depositions relating to will of Alexander Torkington of Stockport, tanner. With original signatures. Transcript:

Depositions of wittnesses taken att Stockport the 29th daie of October: 1605. for the probation of the Last will and Testament of Alexander Torkinton late of Stockport in the Countie of Chester Tanner Deceased, before Richard Gerard Bachelor in Divinitie and Parson of the parishe Churche of Stockport afforesayd by vertue of a Commission from the Right Worshipfull David Yale Doctor of the Lawes bearinge Date the 24th daie of October. 1605. as followeth.

William Dickinson of Stockport in the Countie and Dioces of Chester Lynnen Draper of the age and [sic] 62 yeares or thereaboute sworne and examined deposeth and sayth: That the will shewed unto him with the preamble thereof ys the same that he did as a witnes signe att the desyre of the sayd Alexander Torkinton deceased: And that he was presente and did heare the same read before the said decedent signe seale and deliver the sayd will as his dede: And that the sayd decedent was of good and perfect memorie, when he did soe signe, seale and deliver the sayd will. And further he saythe not.
[Signatures]   William Dickenson, Ri: Gerard.

44   Stockport Probate Records

Thomas Simkin of Stockport afforesayd yoman of the age of Fortie three yeares or thereaboute sworne and examined deposeth and sayth in all thinges as the above named William Dickinson hathe deposed and sayd.
[signatures] Tho. Simkin. Ri. Gerard.

Office endorsement: probate to executors.

23.   JAMES TELLIER OF STOCKPORT, CUTLER.   S.Pr. 6 November 1606.
Will: Probably a copy, not signed by testator, but witnesses signed it.
Health:[1] sick in body.   W.T. 1 June 1606.

I give and bequeath my soule into the hands of almightie god hoping assuredly and not dowting but by the meritts, Death and passion of Jesus Christ to be saved at the great and generall daie. And my bodie to be buried in the Churchyard of Stockport or els where it shall please the almightie to appoint. Also I give to James Williamson of Stockport Tellier 10s 0d: which he oweth mee. and to Francis Robinson 6s 8d which he (likewise) oweth me. Also I give unto Margery Robinson and Jane Robinson 5s 0d a peece and to John Grantham of Stockport showmaker my best suite of aparell. All the rest of my goods Cattls and Chattlls my funerall expencs, legacies, and detts discharged I give unto margery Tellier my wife and James Tellier my son equally to be devided betweene them and if it Chance the said Margery and James to die that then all my goods Cattls and Chattls moveable and unmoveable to be devided amongst the Children of my brother in lawe John Robinson equally except £10 which then shalbe given to Robart Vaudraie. And to see this my last will and testament performed and done in maner and forme abovemenconed I make and Apoint my welbeloved brother in lawe John Robinson of Stockport my sole executor not only to see this my last will executed but also do earnestly intreat the said John Robinson to take the tuition of James Tellier my son and to take both the boie and his portion and to see him orderly brought up and the said portion of goods belonging to my son to be put to his most proffitt and advantage. ‹witnesse whereof›.
                       ‹25 old sheepe and 8 lambs› [sic]

Detts owing to mee James Tellier	£	s	d
John Smyth of Heaton		20	0
Thurston Rawson		5	0
Sir William Damport knight	5	0	0
Ambrosse Robinson		20	0
Roger Orme		4	0
Thomas Sadler			16
Raphe Broocke		5	0
Thomas Williamson		3	0
James Walmersley	3	12	0

Stockport Probate Records 45

John Matly	4	0
John Cartwright	10	0
Thomas Anndrewe	10	0
The naile man	15	0
[Sum 13	9	4]

Detts owing by mee James Tellier

Unto my brother in lawe John Robinson	26	8
Unto George Gemings	5	0
Unto George Adshedd	6	0
[Sum 1	17	8]

Witnesses: Otywell Dodge and Wm Nicholson, who both sign.

Codicil: new sheet, different hand from those on will.

The Sixt Daie of June 1606 James Taylor beinge moved by John Granthame of Stockport Showmaker his brotherinlawe to have in remembrannce three silver Spoones and one Brasse Pott whitch the said John Granthame hadd formerlie pawned for the some of 22s 0d to the said James Taylor The Foresaid James Taylor beinge in perfect remembrance answeared as followeth in presence of divers Credible and Honest persons vizt There is one of the foresaid Spoones already made away And for the other two with the pott My mynd and will is that John Granthame my brotherinlawe shall have them.

1. Buried 9 June 1606. 'dyed of the plague'. Noted as no. 36 so to do.

Inventory: James Taylor of Stockport, cutler.   Taken: 25 November 1606.
Of: goods Cattlls and Chattls.
Prisers: Sampson Hunte, John Cartwright, Otywell Dodge, Thurston Rawson [all sign].

	£	s	d
In Silver and gold	14	18	4½
7 peeces of pewter 2 Candlesticks and a salt		3	6
one brasse pott		10	0
2 kettle pans 1 little possnett a ladle and a skellet		4	0
a Frying pan a payre of tongs a spitt a bread Iron a Fyre Iron and a payre of potthookes		2	4
bedding vizt a Feather bedd 2 bowlsters one pillowe 2 blanketts and a Coverlett		16	0
Linens vizt 3 pillowe beeres 1 flaxen sheete and 5 rownd sheetes		13	4
one Beddsteede		3	4

46 *Stockport Probate Records*

3 great Chists 2 litle Chists and an arke	13	4
2 Chayres and a stoole		6
4 piggens with Dishes and trenchers		12
6 wheele and a Bill	2	0
his Bodyly aparrell	50	0
4 lbs of Colloured Wooll	3	4
2 kyne 3	6	8
25 sheepe vizt 7 lambs 12d a peece 11 weathers 2s – 6d a peece 7 owes 12d a peece		
all the sheepe	41	6
in wooll 3 stonne	30	0
4 silver spoones	10	0
9 newe daggers which came from Manchester	13	0
6 daggers	7	4
2 swords and a skeane	15	0
7 sword hilts at 6^d a peece	3	6
4 dagger hilts att		16
2 damaske hilts with pomells		12
17 fisken handls		10
a dozen of wyre handls		14
a Dozen of Dagger Chapes a dozen of sword Chapes and five lockers		16
7 bunches of scales and an halfe	2	4
6 score pownd of Iron in hilts and pomells	5	0
10 pownd of old dager blades		10
21 Chapes		10
a vice a dressing beame and his towles	3	8
old sword blades rapier blades and dagger blads but we remaine uncertaine whether they wilbe claimed or no	6	0
old scabards		2
a grindle stonne	2	0
a long powle		2
4 daggers in Manchester not veiwed nor valewed		
more by William Nicholson for the part of a Closse called the bent and a tupp	20	0
Robert Hardman 5s which was received by him in Manchester		

[Sum 32 19 8½]

Detts due to the Testator

John Smith of Heaton Norris		20	0
Thurston Rawson		5	0
Sir William Damport knight	5	0	0
Ambrosse Robinson		20	0
Rodger Orme		4	0

Thomas Sadler		16	
Raphe Broocke	5	0	
Thomas Williamson	3	0	
John Matley	4	0	
John Cartwright	10	0	
Thomas Andrewe	10	0	
The nayle man	15	0	
John Robinson elder	10	0	
William Nicholson for Cloath	10	4	
[Sum	10	17	8]

In Tacks of ground

One Cloasse lett to John Warren for Five yeares . . .	16	13	4
one parcell of ground let to George Elcocke for Foure yeares .	6	8	0
another parcell of ground to the said George Elcocke for one yeare		46	0
one parcell of ground to James Williamson for Five yeares att .	8	13	6

More due by bound bill or otherwise as Followeth

A bownd due by William Hartley and Robert Barlowe of . .	21	0	0
Peter Damport	7	0	0
Nicholas Williamson	2	0	0
Ellis Odcroft		20	0
William Nicholson	4	0	0
Sampson Hunt	2	0	0
Ottiwell Dodge	3	0	0
James Hunt		30	0
uxor James Tellior nowe wyffe of Robert Hardman . . .		22	0
James Wallmsley	3	12	0

Out of which Foresaid detts and goods is to be deducted the some of 37s 8d which the said Testator did owe as is apparant by his will.
sum totall is £122 2s 8½d besyde the deduction of 37s 8d.
[*recte*: 122 4 6½]

Litigation paper, C. n.d., damaged. Margery, wife of Robt Haldman [sic] and relict of James Tailor of Stockport, versus John Robinson, executor of the last will and testament of James Tailor.

Office endorsement: probate to executor.

24. JAMES CHORLTON OF STOCKPORT, LINENDRAPER.

S.Pr. 13 December 1606.
Will: sick in body.   W.T. 5 August 1606.

First I bequeath my Soule into the hands of Almightie god my maker and into the hands of his Sonne Jesus Christ my savior and redeemer by whose meryts death and passion I hope to be saved and by no other waye nor avenue whatsoever Item my will and mynd is that after my death my goods be devided into three partes, the first parte to my Selffe, the Second parte I gyve and bequeathe unto Agnes my wyffe, And the thrid parte unto Elizabethe Chorlton Margrett Chorlton and Ales Chorlton my Three daughters and to the most proffett and advantage of the forsaid Elizabethe Margrett and Ales: And yf it shall please god that anye of my daughters shall dye before they come to yeares of discretion or maryage That the Survyvor or Survyvors of the said daughters shall have the said thrid parte with all proffytes that [illegible] Aryse of the said parte untill they shall comb to yeres of discrecon and be thought meete to governe the Same themselffs: Also the remaynder of my parte my funerall expences discharged my will is that yt Shalbe devided equallye betwene Agnes Chorlton my said wiffe, Elizabethe Chorlton Margrett Chorlton And Ales Chorlton my daughters.

Executors: Agnes Chorlton my wife and my well beloved brother in law John Wynne of Stockport. H. and S.

Dettes due and owinge unto me James Chorlton	£	s	d
John Willyamson of Stockport		6	8
James Walmersley of Stockport butcher		3	0
Ambrose Robinson off Stockport		9	0
John Cartwright of Stockport		16	10
[blank] Barnes of Staffordshire – 33s 4d due by A bill in the hands of the bayliffe of Stoone			
Thomas Broocke shoemaker at the daie of his maryage 5s. for a sword			
Robert Haryson alias Hughes		2	6
Thurston Rowson alias Matley		2	0
Richard Smythe de Nangreave			20
Alexander Aspynall		2	0
John Sidebothom	6	13	0
Sum	10	18	0

Witnesses: Willyum Dickenson, Wm Nicholson and Francis Hankinson.

Inventory: James Chorlton of Stockport, linendraper.

Date taken: 10 September 1606.
Of: goods cattells chatells and dettes.

Prisers: Henrye Holme, John Bowland, John Reddiche the elder, and James Ferne.

	£	s	d
In the stable			
two packe horses, two packe sadles and furnyture to the same belonginge	6	0	16
one old packe sadle and a hackney sadle		5	0
a frame for Inckle weavinge			20
27 sawen bordes, cratches and other impleyments		12	0
hey by estimacon 2 loades		16	0
2 siffes 3 wisketts			10
one swyne		13	4
3 ladders			16
certen Sclate			12
in fewell		2	0
In the parlor			
on the highe bedd one fetherbed a chaffebedd a coverlett 3 blanketts 2 bolstrs 2 pillowes		40	0
on an other bed under the wyndow 2 chaffe bedds a bolster a coverlett and a pillow		12	0
on the bed betwene the other two bedds a fetherbedd a bolster and a pillow a coverlett and six blanketts		52	0
a standinge bedstid and paynted clothe over itt		12	0
a truckle bed and one other bedstidd		8	0
4 chistes		13	4
one round table			6
6 paire sheets ould ones		16	0
5 flaxen Sheetes		16	0
two table clothes one towell napkyns and other napryeware		12	0
In the highe chamber over the parlor			
one bedstid		4	0
one arke one litle bord and other ympleyments		[damaged]	
in malte		[damaged]	
in Seckes and poakes		[damaged]	
one paire shermans sheares		[damaged]	
In the Buttrie			
in earthen ware and Tryene ware		[damaged]	
in bordes		2[1]	
pewter		4[1]	
in brasse Iron and leade		11	0

50   Stockport Probate Records

In the fyre howse

one brasse pann		13	4
more in brasse pottes, skelletts candlestickes and other brasse		25	0
in pewter		30	0
one Cubbord and cubbord clothes		14	0
in Stooles and cheeres		5	0
one bord in the house and A frame and other od thinges		10[1]	
A Lanterne			6
A hedginge bill 2 pytcheforkes A sword A dagger one other bill one broken poale axt		10	0
in Quyshens		4	0
one bible		10	0
a fyre Iron Spittes tonnges A fyre shovell and other Iron ware		10	0
in tryene ware		2	0
one Sawen bord			9
in beaffe and bacon		[illegible]	
in wheat	3	8	0
in lynen clothe and packe clothes and cordes	20	2	2½
one Shovell and A hatchett A hammer and 2 paire pynsars		2	0
in chattells	33	10	0
in Redie money	4	11	2
his bodylie apparell		30	0
Sum	89	3	7½

Dettes owing unto hym as appeare by his will in the whole . 10 18 0

1. Pence column damaged.

Office endorsement: probate to testator's relict Agnes.

25.   MARGARET PICKERING OF STOCKPORT, WIDOW.

S.Pr. 22 January 1606/7.
Will, sick in body.   W.T. 10 January 1605/6.

I give and bequeath my soule into the hands of almightie god my Creator savior and Redeemer assuredlye hopeing by the merritts of Christ his passion to be one of his elect and chosen ones and my bodie to be buryed in christiann buryall Item I give and bequeath to my brother Thomas Greene my best cowe here in Stockport Item I give to my brothers fiyve Children eche of them fyve shillings Item I give to my sister in lawe my best petticoat Item I bequeath to Richard Normansell Thomas Normansell and Urian Normansell each of them 3s 4d Item I give to Elizabeth Pott my saddle Item I give to Katheren Howley a coffer at her house which was my brother Edwards Item I bequeath to Margarett Jackson my best gowne Item I give to Margarett Wharmby one Waste and one Apron Item I give to George Knight my best hatt lyened with taffatie and my best safegard which was never worne Item I give to Katheren Swyndells my worke daie gowne my peticoat with redd fringe my best hoes and shoes and one stomacher Item I give to Elizabeth Wakfeld my worke daie petticoat and my ould hatt Item I give to Margerie Piggott one teare of hempe smock Item I give to Raphe Allen a little Cambrick patlett to be for a bannd all the rest of my goods whatsoever moveable and unmoveable after my debts paied and my legacies and funerall expences discharged I give and bequeath to my sister Elizabeth Greene.

Executor: testator's welbeloved sister Elizabeth Greene.

Further I give and bequeath unto Edward Jackson 3s 4d.

	£	s	d
Debts which I owe		[blank]	
Debts oweing unto me			
Thomas Pickering	8	0	0
Thomas Pickering for his table behinde	2	0	0
Item the same Thomas for two ladders[?] as they be praised		[blank]	
George Chowlerton of Didisburie Due at Candlemas next		9	0
[Sum	10	9	0]

Witnesses: Richard Normansell and George Knight.

Inventory: Margaret Pickering of Stockport, widow.

Taken:[damaged] February 1605/6.

Of: goods cattells and debts.

Prisers: Sampson Huntt, William Wharmbye, Thurston Role[s]ton, John Twyffoard and George Newton.

	£	s	d
one cowe paid for a hariott		53	4
4 Kyne and 3 heffers	14	0	0
2 swyne		13	4
in wheat unthreshed		21	0
in otes threshed and unthreshed		27	0
barelie threshed and unthreshed		29	0
in Rye		10	0
in haie	3	13	4
2 carttes and a paire of Iron bound wheeles		30	0
in mault		5	0
in silver spoones		18	0
in toawe		13	0

52 Stockport Probate Records

in yarne		17	0
in flax undressed		15	0
in linseed		2	0
in ladders		5	0
in harowes and ploughes		6	0
one colecart		5	0
in coffers and boxes		12	0
turnells Kimnells and onpouderinge tubb		10	0
Sackes window sheetes and poakes		13	4
2 bruinge caires		5	0
one Saffe		2	0
in maundes baskets wiskets and sives		4	0
in butter and cheese		26	0
in beeffe and Baccon poudered		40	0
in Beddsteedes and Bedding	6	0	0
in linines and naperie wares	4	6	8
in Otemeale and greates		8	0
Brasse and Peweter	4	10	0
in leades		5	0
Iron wares		20	0
in earthen pottes and glasses		3	4
in treen wares		16	0
in tables formes and stooles		6	0
one Spininge wheele and reeles		1	4
in Quishions		8	0
in husbandrie wares		2	6
in Pullen		6	0
in Apparell and her Sadle	5	15	0
in worthinge			10
Sum	60	18	0
[recte	61	4	0]

Office endorsement: probate to executor.

26. JAMES WILLYAMSON OF STOCKPORT, YEOMAN.

S.Pr. 24 June 1607.
Will: probably a copy, not signed by testator, witnesses' signatures.
W.T. 29 July 1606.

Consyderinge this dangerous tyme of Sicknes, the frayltie of flesshe and the mutabilitie of this transytorie and troblesome world, beinge of good and perfect Remembrance thankes be gyven to Almightie god, knoweinge death to be certen to every creature And the houre and tyme thereoff unknowen, do make and declare this present testament conteyninge herein my last will in maner and forme followinge, Fyrst and pryncipallye I do commend my Soule into the hands of Almightie god my creator redeemer and onely Saviour, By the meryts of whose Sonnes most precyous Bloud sheedinge I trust unfaynedlie to be saved, and to Inherytt his everlastinge kingedome, And my bodie and Boones I do commytt to Chrystyen buryall to be layd in the parishe Churcheyard of Stockport before mentyoned in suche manner and place as my frends and executors thincke meete and convenyent, And for my burgage and lands in Stockport with it appurtenances I gyve grant and bequeath the same burgage with all commodyties to it belonginge unto John Wyllyamson my sonne, And to the heires males of his bodie lawfullie begotten or to be begotten, And for want of such Issue I gyve and bequeathe the same to Thomas Wyllyamson my sonne and the heyres males of his bodie lawfullie begotten or to be begotten, And for want of such yssue to Rondulphe Wyllyamson my sonne and the heires males of his bodie lawfullie begotten or to be begotten, And for want thereof the same to Remeyne to the right heires of me the said James Willyamson forever, to·hold of the Cheeffe lord of the fee thereof by the rentt and Service affore due and accustomed, And yett it is my mynd and will that the same Thomas Willyamson and Rondulphe Wyllyamson my sonnes and either of them and theire assignes, from my naturall deceasse duringe theire naturall lyves and the longer lyver of theym Shall have and occupie the said Burgage as Tennantes: Payeinge to John Wyllyamson my eldest son yerlie, duringe the said tyme and terme the somme of Fyve shillings of lawfull money of England at the feast of the nativitie of St John baptist and St martin the buyshoppe in Wynter by even and equall porcones. And for the order and distribucon of my worldlie goods cattells and debts It is my mynd and will as followythe, First it is my will and mynd that all such detts as I owe of Right or conscyence to anye person or persons and my funerall expences shalbe paid and taken uppe of my whole goodes before anye division be made thereof, Item I gyve of my whole goodes to John Wyllyamson my sonne the longe bord and Cubbord in my howse nere the marketstid, Item I gyve to Thomas Wyllmson my son the mare which I paid for to James Walmsley. Item I gyve to margerye my daughter my brasse panne and greate brasse pott and one Coffer, all three remayninge in my shoppe, Item I gyve to every god child I have 12d to be taken as afforsaid of my whole goodes, The rest and resydue of my goodes cattells and detts It is my mynd and will Shalbe devyded Amongest all my children by even and equall porcones.

Executors: John Wyllyamson and Thomas Willyamson, testator's sons.
Supervisors: testator's nephew James Wyllyamson and testator's old servant James Fearne.
Witnesses: James Fearne, James Willmson the younger and George Rediche.

Detts which I the said James Wyllyamson do owe	£	s	d
First unto John Karre	3	8	0
Item to [blank] Lightbowne of bolton		14	0

54   Stockport Probate Records

Item to Anthonie Garlicke for a peece of white		25	0
At which tyme he left two peecs of clothe with me; the one of the price of 27s. the other of 17s, It is my mynd he have eyther his two peecs of clothe or ells money for them: they remayne with my other clothes.			
Item to Willm Goddard		3	9
Item to Francis hutchinson which I have Turned hym over to receave of Sir Edward Warren and John Kirke of henfabancke his Suertie.		26	8
Item I owe the same frances for dyinge three Reddes . . .		16	0
Item to george Whitaker		12	0
Item to george Newton		13	4
Item to John Lees malteman		9	9
Some is besides 26s. 8d. turned over	10	0	22
[*recte* £9 8s 6d excluding 26s 8d; including 26s 8d:	10	15	2]

Dettes owinge to me the said James Wyllyamson

Of Olyver Dodge by bill which bill remayneth in my shoppe .		58	0
Of lawrence bradley by bill also remayninge in my shoppe . .		55	4
Of humfrey Davenport by bill also remayninge in my shopp .		26	6
Of george Elcocke by bill also remeyninge in my shoppe . .		37	0
Of Mr. Willyam holme and his wiffe which was due before he maryed her Wytnesses hereof henrye bridge which last somme I gyve to my sonne Randolphe		46	8
Of the executor of my late brother Thomas Willyamson . .		24	5
Of the executors or admynistrators of Thomas Smyth of Crosse-Acres deceassed		33	0
Of Ric Walker of Chedle		5	9
Of Justynyan Cartwright			12
Of John Olyver		5	0
Of henrye Woodd of Chedle			20
Of Thomas Andrew			21
Of frances Elcocke		7	8
Of George Barrett of Wymeslowe		7	6
Of ould Mrs. Warren which I paid for her to francis Hutchinson for dyinge blewes and other colours		20	4
Of Lawrence Gibson left unpaid for fryces		14	0

Dettes also owinge to me the said James Wyllyamson

Of homfrey henshaw for A mare		20	0
Of henrye heywarthe of Derbyshire		5	0
Of Nicholas Boothe		4	8
Of Ellice Tym, and John burgesse dwelling near Hope or Castleton	6	10	0
Of Robert bancroft of marple		7	0

Of William Rocroft	27	
	and od money	
Of John halle of priestfields	5	4
Of Sir Edward Warren for 2 yards 3 quarters broade clothe at 4s. 8d the yard and nyne yards red at 2s the yard and 4s 8d. Suertie for hugh Jamyeson And for 4 yards and An halfe of broade clothe at 3s. 8d. the yard which he bade me delyver to one mellor, and for motley and lynyng for Robert Lache 11s. 3d.		
Of Old Mr. Davenport of henburye 5s. 4d for A coate cloth which hugh swyndells had It was delyvered to lockett.		
Of Mr. Davenport of goytt 25s which I was contracted to have Receaved coales for. it was 31s. I have received 6 quarters of coales in part of payement.		
Of Mr. Davenport more for velvett for A sadle and gryene leese	20	0
Of Robert haryson 51s 8d. received at one tyme 20s. at an other tyme 12s. in part thereof.		
Of Mr. Thomas Duncalfe	36	0
Of John Smyth Whereof I have had som in dyinge	9	0
Of Thomas Robinson of heaton	16	2
Of William holt Sir Ric buckley man	4	0
Of Mr. Ric hide	2	0
Of Thomas hexam of marple.	6	0
Of William hexam	3	6
Of Rob Ward	6	0
Of Rauffe newton	16	1
I owe Rauffe newton 3s that he paid for John my sonne		
Of Thomas bruck cowper		8
Of Alex collyer		8
Of Robery Redich 4s 2d. and costs of the Court 10d.		
Of Thurston Partington	6	10
Of george Chorlton the elder of purs	19	0

Debts appearinge unpayd by and in his Dett booke

Of Rauffe birch	5	4
Of Ric Smale the younger	5	0
Of John birch of bramall	5	4
Of Andrewe Rodes	9	4
Of Ric Johnson of Etchalls	7	0
Of Ellice Cruft	17	10
Of Wm. heginbothom sonne of Robert heginbotham of Derbishire	4	6
Of humfrey bridge		14
Sum	42 19 10 [sic]	

56 Stockport Probate Records

Witnesses: James fearne, James Willymson the yonger, George Redich.

Inventory: James Willyamson of Stockport, Alderman.   Taken: 2 June 1607.
Of: goodes catells and detts.
Prisers: Edmond Shelmerdyne, Thomas Andrewe, James Ferne and James Wyllyamson.

	£	s	d
one barren cowe		40	0
one nagg		30	0

In the shoppe

	£	s	d
5 yardes three quarters tufted tafytie		30	0
2 yardes Suger tafytie		16	0
5 elnes and an halffe tafytie		50	0
one halffe peece Red durance		17	0
21 yardes myndgled durance		21	0
Ten yardes buffyne		10	0
14 yardes of wismille fustyan		21	0
53 yardes holmes fustyne		52	0
9 yardes white tuft		5	0
4 grosse Silk buttons and some od		6	8
one quarter gross threade and hare buttons		4	0
od pewter buttons and other buttons			12
three ounce and an halffe coloured silke		4	0
Tufted Satute [sic] lace		6	0
7 ounces firrett Silke		2	6
halffe a pound and halffe an ounce gulowne lace . . .		13	4
5 ounces of Statute galowne lace		3	4
5 ounces bobbyn lace		6	0
halffe a pound tuft lace and velvet lace		8	0
halffe a pound cheynet lace		10	0
1 gross and one halffe grosse statut lace		9	0
2 ounce and an halffe pearled silke lace		2	0
in capp lace and Ribbyn			18
in garteringe 15 pound			12
2 li crewle and crewle lace		5	0
white statute lace and other colours		4	6
1 pound 2 ounces coloured threade			16
3 lb 3 quarters frynge		6	8
6 dosen longe Silke buttons		2	0
clothe for bowltinge clothes		2	0
1 yardes greene durance			12
10 lb girdells and 14 crupps		5	0
2 yardes blewe kersey		5	0

18 yardes 3 quarters red clothe	27	0
4 yardes tawnye and greene kersey	9	0
12 yardes coloured halffe thicke	16	0
6 yardes beyse in Remlantes	9	0
5 yardes and an halffe white kersey	11	0
5 yardes and an halffe kersey with a black list	6	4
one peece white kersey	22	6
Russett and halffe thicke 18 yardes	19	6
in little remlantes of fryce and cloth 7 yardes	8	0
16 yards white cotton and kelter	10	8
3 white cottons	22	0
in Tassells	4	0
in pennars		4
one chist in the shoppe	5	0
bordes and boxes in the shoppe	10	0
Scales and weightes		6

in the parlour

one fetherbed 2 pillowes 2 bolsters	30	0
1 coveringe 1 coverlett and 3 blankettes ould ones	10	0
6 Quisshens	10	0
one paire bedstockes	2	4
2 Coffers and one arke	5	0
one lyttle cubbord and other bordes	4	0
3 sheetes 3 bordes clothes 2 towells one pyllowe beare 2 napkins one Syffe clothe 1 shurt and three shurt bandes	22	6

in the howse and butterye

in pewter 51 lb	25	6
in brasse pott mettall 12 lb in panne mettall 12 lb	8	0
1 brasse pan and one brasse pott	40	0
one furnace	5	4
in iron ware a fyre Iron a Spitt tonnges pot hookes gowbertes a frying panne 2 hackinge knyves and Rakentree	4	0
2 growte stonndes 2 brewing keyres	10	0
[illegible] ales stonndes	2	0
2 esshons one pige 4 kannes	2	0
one brendrett	2	0
one forme and 8 bordes in the buttrie		16
the cubbord and bord in the howse	40	0
the Short bord in the howse	3	4
the longe forme 1 buffett stoole 3 cheyres	3	0

In the hieghe chamber

one bord 2 formes 3 olde cheyres	10	0

58 Stockport Probate Records

one fether bedd 1 bolster 2 pillowes and one chaff bedd caste .	13	4
2 cover lettes 1 cadow 1 blankett	[illegible]	
one paire old sheets		18
one paire bedstockes		8

In the Inner highe chamber

2 pare bedstockes 1 greate arke one cheyre one kneydinge troghe and others 3 old lowmes and somme od beddinge . .	8	0

Remeyninge in Thomas Williamson howse

2 brasse pottes 1 cheyre 2 buffett stooles 2 kannes one pigge one Rownd table one paire bedstockes one broken buffett stoole and one bord	13	0
his bodylie apparell	50	0
Sum	46 4	5

His outward dettes as appeare by his last will and testament admont in the whole to the somme of £10 – 22d besydes 26s – 8d turned over. His inward dettes as appeare by the same his last will and testament admount in the whole to the somme of [a line straggles through the text to the sum of £42 19 10 below.] his dettes Remayninge due by his dett book and sett downe in the same will and testament Admount in the whole to the Somme of £42 19 10.

Office endorsement: probate to executors.

27. ALEXANDER LOWE OF STOCKPORT, MERCER.
S.Pr. [31 March?] 1608.
Will, letters, numbers and signs in old hand in the left hand margin of the document have been omitted. Health: Sick in body.   W.T. 26 February 1607/8.

I commend my sowle in to the handes of Allmightye God my maker and Continuall preserver, hoping by the merritts of Jesus Christe to be one of the number of those that shalbe saved and my bodye to be buryed in the Church of Stockport in or neare unto my Seate or place wheare I was usually wonte to sitt, Firste Concerning my landes and Tennements which yt hathe pleased Allmightie God to indue me withall the most parte of them are alreadye Conveyed and established by mee by severall Deedes and Conveyances, And according to the same my will and mynd ys That they shall Remayne for ever Reserving unto Elizabeth my Wyeffe a full Thirdd parte of the sayd landes and Tennements for and during the terme of her naturall lyeffe; Item I gyve and bequeathe the Under Roome of the howse wherein the Schoole ys nowe kepte to and for the use of the Schoole to be kepte theere for ever. The Scholmaster thereof for the tyme beinge yelding and paying yearely unto my heires and some of Sixe shillings

Eight pence Rente, The which sayd house I doe so gyve and bequeath uppon the Reservacion of the Rent afforsayd For and in Consideracion of my Forme in the Churche and Libertie for free buryall for mee and my heires for ever, Item I gyve and bequeathe unto Oswald Mosley of Manchester Clothier and to his heires for ever who hathe maried one of my grand Children my house in the Hillgate wherein William Torkington or his assignee or assignees doth now inhabit and dwell togeather with all grownds Commodities and proffetts to the sayd howse belonginge Reserving unto the sayd William Torkington and his assignes suche estate as I have alreadie made him, And Concerninge my moveable goods and Chattells my will and mynde ys That they shall be devided in to three equall partes my debtes being first paid and discharged of my wholle goods whereof one equall parte I gyve and bequeathe unto Elizabeth my sayd wyeffe another parte I gyve and bequeathe unto Robert Robynsonn of Manchester, who hathe marryed the other of my Grandchildren in satisfacion of a Covenant heretofore made unto him And the Thirdd parte I Reserve unto my selffe to be disposed as here after followeth And for my Funerall expences my will and mynde is That the same shall be taken out of my sayd Thirdd parte wherein I doe require myne Executor hereafter named to be the rather moderate, that so the more maye remayne to such good uses as I doe hereafter Declare by this my last will, Item I doe gyve and bequeathe unto the sayd Oswold Mosley my grandchild or to him that shall have the medyate Remaynder of my lands Called the Mooresyde Howse with thappurtenances all the Implements of howsehould stuffe As Bedstidds, Tables, Presses, Stooles, Chayres, Formes, Irons, Forfyer and other suche like Implements as shall be Remayning therein at the tyme of my Decease Item whereas there is Sixscore pounds due unto mee by Roger Harper and Johnn Barrett Payable at Certen Dayes and tymes agreed uponn betweene us, My mynde and will ys That the Somme of Fortye pounds being a Thirdd parte of the sayd Sixscore pounds shall be and remayne to the augmentacion and increase of the wages of the Schoolemaster of Stockport for the tyme beinge, for ever, to be hadd and receaved at suche dayes and tymes as the same shall bee due, And further I do will and bequeath the sume of Tenn pounds for and towards the augmenting of the Schoolmasters wages afforesayd to make upp the sayd sume of Fortye pounds the Full sume of Fyftie pounds All the sayd Sume to be Imployed and used for the benefit of the Schoolemaster afforesayde by the Parsonn of Stockporte the Maior of Stockport and the most Auncyent Alderman thereof for the tyme beinge Item I gyve and bequeath for and towards the Reparacion of the Steeple of the Churche of Stockport the sume of Tenn pounds Item I gyve and bequeathe the sume of Twentye pounds to be lett out and Ymployed by the Parsonn Maior, and the most Auncyent Alderman of the Towne of Stockport for the tyme beinge to and for the use and benifite of the poore of the sayd Towne for ever Item my mynd and will is further And hereby I do bequeath the sume of Thirtty poundes to be used and ymployed by myne executore and by my loving frends Rowland Mosley Esquire and Rychard Gerrard Parsonn of Stockport to suche Charitable use or uses as I have made knowne to them or some of them

And yf yt shall happen the saide some of Thirttie Pounds or any parte thereof to Remayne and be unspent after the full ymployement and use before mencioned Then my will ys That the sayd sume of Thirttie pounds or suche parte thereof as shall Remayne and bee unspent as aforesayd shall be used and ymployed to suche other Charitable use or uses as to myne Executor and to the sayd Rowland Moseley and Rychard Gerrard shall be thought meete and Convenient Item Whereas Sir William Davenport of Bromhall Knight owethe mee a Certayne sume of monney as may appeare by Reconings betweene us I am contented and pleased and my will ys, That Fortye Poundes of that monney shall Remayne in the hands of the said Sir William Davenport to bee bestowed upponn any of his Sonnes as he shall thincke meete Provyded allwayes and upon a condicion that the sayd Sir William Davenport his executors or assignes shall faythefully and truly within Three monthes next after my decease paye or Cause to be paide to myne Executore or his assignes all suche sume and sumes of monney as shall Remayne and bee due to mee and myne executor over and above the sayd some of Forty Poundes otherwyse the sayd legacye to be voyde and of non effect Item I gyve and bequeathe unto the sayd Rychard Gerrard Parsonn of Stockport Twenty shillings hoping he will preache at my buryall Item I gyve and bequeathe unto Robert Bate my servant Twentie shillings over and above his wages Item I gyve and bequeathe unto Margaret Asheton my servant mayde Twentie shillings likewise over and above her wages Item I gyve and bequeathe unto William Peereson Twentie shillings and to George Newtonn other Twentie shillings Item I gyve and bequeathe to Elizabeth Byrche, my half sister, Fortye shillings And for the Residue of my Thirdd parte of goods Remayning unbequeathed be yt moore or lesse My will and mynde ys that it shall remayne and bee for and towards the maynetenance of an usher to teache under the Scholemaster of Stockport for ever, And to that use and nonn other I do gyve and bequeathe the same And Further my mynde ys That the sayd sume of monney That shall soe Remayne whatsoever yt bee shall be putt for the uses Imployed and bestowed to the use beforesaid by the Parsonn Maior, and most auncyent Aldermann of the sayd Towne of Stockporte for thetyme being for ever.

Executor: testator's 'well beloved Sonne and Frend' Oswald Mosley of Manchester the younger.
Witnesses: Ri. Gerard and Tho. Simkin.
Office endorsement: probate to executor.

28. JOHN ROBOTHOM OF STOCKPORT, HUSBANDMAN.

I.Pr. 12 April 1609.
Will, sick in body.   W.T. 10 April 1609.

I comend my soule unto almightie god my maker and Redeemer and my bodie to the earthe from whence itt came and to bee buried in the Church or Churchyard of Stockporte where it shall please my verie good Landlord George Elcocke to thinke good: Item I give and bequeathe to my Landlord his Daughter Alice Elcocke one litle Coffer the fyer Iron and the table in the house all which shee shall have after the Decease of Katherin my wyffe: Item, the residue of all my goods unbequeathed I doe wholie give them to Katherin my wyffe my funerall beinge Discharged.

Executor: testator's wife Katherin.
Supervisor: testator's landlord George Elcock of Stockport, yeoman.
Witnesses: Elizabeth Seddon and John Lowe.

Debts which I do owe	£	s	d
To Willm Dickinsonn Aldermann		2	6
To Willm Dickinsonn in the padacar			16
[Sum	3	10]	

Inventory: John Robothom. Date taken: 19 April 1609.
Of: goods.
Prisers: John Lowe, John Cottrell, Christopher Piggott and Edward Warren.

	£	s	d
2 brasse potts and 2 leads		5	0
in pann mettell		2	6
in pewter		5	0
in Iron ware		3	0
in trene ware		6	8
4 litle bords and one forme		4	0
in chaires and stooles			12
in woorke loomes		4	0
in chests and bords		12	0
in flaxe		7	0
in beddinge and bedstocks		16	0
in Bacon		8	0
2 wheeles			6
in qushens			8
1 litle sheepe		2	0
in his Apparell		14	0
Sum	4	11	4

Office endorsement: probate to executor.

29. ISABELL TORKYNTON OF STOCKPORT, WIDOW.
S.Pr. 27 March 1610.
Will, first lines damaged. Health: visited with sicknes and weaknes and infirmities in my bodie. W.T. [damaged] 7 James I.

I commend my soule to Allmightie god my maker and redeemer and my bodie to bee buried in the parisch Church of Stockport in the south syde of the same Church neare unto my late husband Allex Torkynton Item It is my will and mynd and I doe geeve and bequeathe unto John Bradley Otes Bradley and George Bradley Twentie poundes in money to bee equally devided Amongst them Item I doe geve unto John Birche of Levenshulme tenn poundes in money A brase panne my best silver spoone A pewter kann A spitt A payre of [damaged] A fyre Iron and the table in the house. Item I geeve to the wyffe of the said John my best gowne, Item I geeve To Ales Birche daughter of the said John Berche my greatest brasse pott my trunckell bedd one fether bedd and furniture Item I geeve to Allex Birche and George Birche sonnes of the foresaid John Birche forty shillinges in money Item I gyve to the wyffe of Willm Nicholson Alderman A malt Arke and A payre of Bedstocks Standinge in the high Chamber and fyve shillinges in money Item I gyve to [*erasure*] my ould lanlady fyve shillinges in money Item I gyve to Issabell Shuttelworth my god daughter a silver spoone A cupborde A standinge bedd with the furniture A pewter pynte kanne A frynge panne and A greate leadd Item I geeve to the wiffe of Addam Mottershedd of Macclesfeild tow pewter disshes and A Chist standinge at my bedd syde Item I geve to the wyffe of John Roodes of Bramhall my silver pynne and hookes Item I geeve to Ellen Lynnen A lyttell brasse potte and A pewter dishe Item I gyve to George Bradley my brothers sonne a lytell Arke and A paire of sheetes Item I geeve to Otes Bradley A drippinge panne Item I geeve to Mr Arther Storer fyve shillings in money Item I gyve to Alderman Nicholson A chiste standinge in the syde of the house, Item I geeve to Ellen Redyche towe shillinges in money and all my worke daye petycotes Item I gyve to Elliz: Bradleye my god daughter my ould goune Item I gyve to the wyffe of Abraham my neighboure the [*erasure*] carpenter A [*erasure*] lytell leade and A pewter dyshe. Item I gyve to th wyffe of Raphe Tayleor tow shillinges in money And to Edward Warren other towe shillinges in money Item It is [my] mynd and will that there bee bestowed to the vallue of Six poundes att my funerall. All the rest and residue of all my goodes Chattells and deptes whatsoever I doe geeve and bequeathe unto John Birche and Willam Diconson sonne of Robt Diconson deaceassed equally betweene them.

Executors: the said John Bradley and John Birche.
Witnesses: Willm Diconson, Raphe Diconson and Edward Warren.

Inventory: Ellizabeth [sic] Torkynton, widow. Taken: [25?] March 1610.
Of: goodes cattells and depts.
Prisers: Thomas Ouldam, Rauphe Diconson, John Diconson and John Bradley.

	£	s	d
In beddinge in the parler is a Cadowe towe blanketts a fedderbedd a shorte bedd tow boulsters and A pillowe together with the teaster and the beddstockes	3	13	4
in the Chamber above a fether bedd a bouster towe mattreses 3 blanketts a coveringe and tow paire of bed stockes	3	0	0
in the same chamber a greate Arke and 3 litellons a greate coffer and tow littellons and other od ymplements		30	0
A meate borde		6	8
A greate coffer in the parler		8	4
tow lytell coffers		8	0
a cupbord		16	0
in pewter dishes and other pewter		26	8
in brasse tow potts		12	0
3 kettells a chaffinge dishe a morter a scellat and a Chandeler		16	0
2 leades		5	0
a fryinge panne and A drippinge pann		3	4
an Axe and other Iron ware		8	0
3 Cheares and stooles and alyttell round bord		3	4
treene ware		2	6
woollen aparrell for her bodie	3	0	0
quishens		4	0
Lynnins and naparie ware		50	0

Debts by bill and bound owinge to the testator

Thomas Benison and Edward Thorneyley	17	12	0
Katheren Houlden Anthonie Nicolson and Willm Wharmeby	11	0	0
Raphe Nicolson	5	0	0
John Breatland Robt Worth and Reynold Hollinworth	5	5	0
Edward Ryle and John Boland	4	8	0
two sylver spoones a sylver pynn and hookes		20	0
Sum	63	7	2

Office endorsement: probate to John Birche an executor.

30. HENRY HOULME OF STOCKPORT MERCER.

S.Pr. 25 June 1610.
Inventory of: wares, goodes and chattels. Taken: 22 September 1609.
Prisers: Peter Hey, Robart Bordman, John Barrett and John Redich [all] of the same towne.

	£	s	d
one Standing bed with a whyt Cadowle one fetherbed two blanketes one Boulster and one pillow	2	10[?]	

one other paire of Bedstockes one green Cadowle one mattris
   two pillowes and one blankett 26 8
one other paire of bedstockes one fetherbed one boulster two
   blanketes and one Covering 2 0 0
one Littell pair of bedstockes one Coverlet two blanketes and
   one boulster and one Chafbed 23 4
one faire Standing bed and Cortayns for the same one Cadoule
   one fetherbed one Chafbed one boulster with fethers and
   thother with Chaffe two blanketes and one pillow . . . 6 0 0
one faire presse two Chistes one littell table one trunke and
   one Close Stoole within the parler 30 0
Three Chistes above in the Chamber 20 0
one presse within the Buttree 10 0
Three tables in the house one forme fyve Cheares fyve Stooles
   and one Round table and one carpet 22 0
Fyve Quishens 10 0
the Seeling in the house 2 6 8
In Sheetes Pillowbears and other Linens 4 1 6
one Lead in a fornes foure pottes three skelletes 2 Cettell panes
   one driping pan three Brasse Candelstickes one frying pan one
   Chaffing dish one skimer 2 0 0
In Pewter 21 0
In treen ware with one spininge wheele and earthen pottes . .   18 6
In Iron ware 19 0
In Bordes Ladders and such Lyke thinges 8 0
One Cowe 2 13 4
One Swyne 10 0
In Corne and Haye 3 0 0
In Torfes and Coles 3 4
In bookes 5 0
In Silver spoones and other plate 3 16 0

In the Shope
In Grocery 10 0
In Seyes and serges 33 0
In Lane Cambrick and other od wares 5 12 6
In Scales and waightes one morter and pestell 10 0
In Chists Pylbordes and other forneture in the shope with one
   paire of scales 10 0
In Redy monney with two litell Ringes 10 7
In the defuncts Aparrell with one ould saddell and brydell . .   33 4

                                               Sum 50 13 9
                                            [*recte* 51 17 1]

Debtes owing unto the said Henry

George Blomiley		23	4
Mr Allexander Elcoke		6	8
Thomas Elcoke		6	6
uxor Mr Lawrenc Wright		4	0
uxor Henry Barrlow		2	0
Thomas Anderson			9
Francis Shrigley			7
Mr Hyde de Longlee		23	4
Georg Eliord		3	4
Georg Elcoke		10	0
John Grantham		20	0
Anthony Houlme		5	0
uxor John Cooke			3
the executors of widow Seele		10	0
	Sum 5	15	9

Debtes owing by the said Henry

unto Mr James Brearley of London		41	0
more		10	0
	[Sum 2	11	0]

Office endorsement: probate to deceased's relict Emma.

31. JOHN BENESSON OF STOCKPORT.   I.Pr. 6 July 1610.
Inventory of: goods and chattels.   Taken: 2 June 1610.
Prisers: John Redich, Martin Wood, ⟨John Burg,⟩ Henry Rydings, Robart Cheetam.

	£	s	d
In Apparrell for his body both Linen and wollen with hat stockings and shooes		12	0
In debtes owing unto the said John first Allexander Boswill[1]		29	8
	Sum	41	8

Debtes owing by the said John Bennesson

unto Raph Oldham		22	7
unto uxor John Swindels for 2 sherts		4	6
unto Georg Siddall		4	0
unto John Burgis			8
unto Henry Rydings		2	0

66   Stockport Probate Records

unto Martin Wood	6
unto Edward Garnet	12
unto Alles Wharmby	3
Sum	35 6

1. Buried 2 June 1610 John Benneson servant to Alexander Bossoyell of Stockport, Gent.

Office endorsement: commission to Thomas Chetham of Bredbury, 6 July 1610.

32. ROBERT FALLOWES OF STOCKPORT.
I.Pr. 14 September 1610.
Will, sick.   W.T. 24 August 1610.

First I geeve my soule into the hands of Almighty god that gave it, verely and stedfastly beleeving to bee saved by the death and merit of Chryst Jesus my Saviour and redeemer, and my body to bee buryed in the churchyard at Stopporth: And touching those goods that God hath in his mercie bestowed upon mee, my will is, that they shalbe disposed of as foloweth: First I geeve and bequeath unto Robert Fallows my sonn one lead and lykewyse all my work lomes and work tooles, which I use for my handy craft Item my will and mynd is that Alice Fallowes my wyfe Robert Fallowes my sonn and Joane Fallowes my doughter shall dwell and bee altogether (if god geve thym lyfe) Untill my sayd sonn and doughter come to their Age, And then my will is, That after my debts bee payd and funerall expences discharged, all my goods mouvable and unmouvable shalbe equally devyded betweext Alice Fallowes my wyfe Robert my sonn and Joane my doughter.

Executrix: testator's wife Alice. Mk. and S.
Witnesses: Thomas Normansell, Adam Syddall and Robert Sydall.

Debts which I Robert Fallowes do Owe	£	s	d
Imprimis to Mr Gerrard my master		20	0
Item to Ann Reddish		20	0
Item to Robert Wynnington		20	0
Item to Adam Syddall		40	0
Item to Roger Harper		5	2
Item to Margerie Fallowes		8	0
Item to John Jackson of Brynnington		14	9
Sum	6	7	11

Debts owing unto mee Robert Fallows		
Imprimis of Robert Gee		16
Item of William Radcliff		18

Item of Kathryn Etchuls of offerton		16
Item of Tho. Goddard		11
Sum	5	1

Inventory: Robert Fallowes of Stockport.   Taken: 4 September 1610.
Of: goods and cattells.
Prisers: Robert Sydall, Adam Sydall, Tho. Newton and James Buerdsell.

	£	s	d
two kyne	6	0	0
in hay		30	0
in wollen yarne		11	0
towe leads			18
foure brasse potts		13	4
towe skelletts			12
in pewter		13	4
in drinking potts and ticknall mettall			18
in Tymber		30	0
in yron ware		4	0
in treene ware		10	0
in Alepottes			18
in flax		22	0
in Arks and coffers		6	8
in lynnens		35	3
in bedding		50	0
in Quishins		3	4
in chayres stooles and one board		5	0
sowe and piggs		26	8
in Apparell		26	8
[Sum	20	12	9]

Office endorsement: probate to executor.

33. MARGARET MARSLAND OF STOCKPORT, WIDOW.

I.Pr. 23 November 1610.
Inventory of: goodes and Cattells.   Taken: 20 November 1610.
Prisers: Peter hays, James Buerdstell, Raph Allen and Tho. Symkyn.

	£	s	d
One coverlett one bolster and one bedstock		2	0
one Gowne and two old peticoa [damaged]		6	0
in lynnens			12

one spyning wheele		8
one long table in the howse and towe [damaged] . . .		20
one Chayre three stooles and a kneding trough		12
one lead and one skellet	2	0
foure old Quisshins		4
a frying pann, one spitt and a hacking knyfe		12
one fyreyron		12
in pewter		18
in trene ware		8
one syde of a bedd and bothom		4
one young henn		3
one wiskett		1
one old spade		2
one ladder		4
one hetchill trest and a swingle foot		2
one payre of blades and a foot [damaged]		1

[Sum 1 0 3]

Office endorsement: probate to [damaged] Henshawe.

34. JAMES DANIEL OF STOCKPORT, WEBSTER.

I.Pr. 4 January 1610/11.
Will: some fading and damage. Health: [sick] in body.   W.T. 29 May 1609.

First I commend my soule into the hands of Almighty god who of his grace and infynyte mercie gave it mee, And my body to the earth whereout it was taken, hoping by the merits of Christ Jesus to bee one of that number that shalbe saved. Imprimis for my smale lands and Burgage in Stopport aforsayd nowe in my Tenure and occupation I geeve the same wholly unto Allexander Daniell my brother and to his hayres and assignes for ever upon condycion that Joane Daniell my wyfe, shall and may have and enioye one croft or parcell of land, the letle croft, all the Roomes and high chambers over the fyer howse, all the thresshing bay in the barne half the turfcoat and half the garden for and during the terme of hir naturall lyfe so that she keepe hir selfe sole and unmaryed, And doe pay the one half of the cheefe Rents and service due and payable for the same. And after the decease of the sayd allexander danyell my brother, leaving no Issue male behynd hym lawfully begotten at the tyme of his death. Then my mynd and will is that William daniell the sonne of Raph daniell late of Stopporth afor sayd deceased and the Issue male of his body lawf[ully – damaged] begotten, shall and may have hold and enioy all my sayd Lands and Burgage formerly mentioned and everie part and parcell [damaged] and their proper use and uses for ever. And for default of such Issue male of the sayd William then to the [damaged] of the sayd William and to the Issue male of his body lawfully to bee begotten for ever [damaged] then to the use and behoofe of John daniell brother of the sayd William and frannces and to the Issue male of his body lawfully to bee begotten for ever And for default of such Issue, then to the hayres of mee the sayd James daniell for ever. And whereas their is towe tacks of grownd joyntly betweene my brother Allexander and mee, thone lying in bramall thother neer unto the blacklach for certen years yet to come And also certayne goods and Chattells in lyke manner betweene us, my mynd and Will is (having the consent and allowance of my sayd brother Allexander thereunto) that Joane daniell my sayd wyf shall have and recyve the proffits and commodityes of the sayd Tacks and parcells of grownd and also shall have recyve and take the sayd goods and Chattells to hir only use and behoff for ever And whereas I have one other Tack of grownd for certayne yeares lying in Adswodd, I geeve and bequeath all the Right interest and demannd which I have of and in the same, unto Joane daniell my sayd wyfe. Item I geeve and bequeath unto my brother Allexander daniell 40s. of lawfull money And all weaving lomes reeds with [damaged] appurtenances. Item I geeve and bequeath unto Edward Roger and William Bancroft the sonnes of Allexander bancroft of Adswodd evrie one of theym 3s. 4d. Item I geeve and bequeath unto Margeret Heyron the doughter of godfrey heyron 3s. 4d. The residue of all my goods chattells and debts after my debts payd my funerall expences performed and these my legacies [damaged] in this my present testament fulfilled I wholly geeve and bequeath to my wyfe.

Executors: testator's brother Alexander Daniel and testator's wife.
Witnesses: damaged, concludes with Tho. Simkin.

Inventory: James Daniell of Stockport, webster.   Taken: 2 January 1610/11.
Of: goods and Cattales moveable and unmoveable.
Prisers: Godfry Heyrod, Hugh Heyrod, Allexander Bancroft, Roger [Swinston?] and John Cusworth.

	£	s	d
in barly thresshed and unthresshed		40	0
in Rye		20	0
in oots		5	0
in hay		10	0
towe kyne	4	0	0
towe sheepe		4	0
in bedding	3	0	0
in lynnens		20	0
in lynnen yarne		10	0
in pewter and brasse		40	0
in Arks and chests		10	0
in bedstocks stooles and chaires		10	0
in boards forms and one table		6	0

70   Stockport Probate Records

in treene ware		10	0
in lomes and Reeds warp stock and Rings		10	0
ladders		2	0
in salt flesh		10	0
a swyne lyving		4	0
in yron ware		10	0
in Apparell		20	0
upon [damaged] william chedle	7	0	0
towe bills of debt	8	16	0
in tacke of ground in any place	3	0	0
in [damaged] his chest		14	0
in [damaged] trunck			12
[Sum	38	12	0]

Office endorsement: probate to executors.

35. WILLIAM SWYNDELLS OF STOCKPORT, HUSBANDMAN.

S.Pr. 19 February 1610/11.
Will.   W.T. 15 December 1610.

Beinge desyrous to bestowe those goodes whiche the Lord in mercye hathe vouchsafed me, nowe in the tyme of my healthe, and knowinge death to be Certaine to everye lyvinge Creature, but the tyme thereof uncertayne, doe make and ordeyne this my laste will and Testament in manner and forme followinge. First I Comend my soule into the handes of Almightye God my maker and Continuall preserver, hopinge in the merites of Jesus Christ to be one of the number of those that shalbe saved, and my bodye to the earthe whereoute it was taken. Item my mynd and Will ys That all suche debts as of Righte and in Conscience I doe owe to anye person or persons shalbe deducted, payd and discharged oute of my whole goodes: And Lykewyse my funerall expences unto what sume soever they shall amounte unto, or growe to be (whiche I desyre to be moderate) shalbe deducted and payd oute of my whole goodes alsoe. Item I give and bequethe unto my worthy master Mr. John Arderne of Hawarden in the Countye of Chester Esquier twoe Angells in gould. Item I give and bequeth unto Mr. Henrye Arderne sonne and heire apparent of the sayd John Arderne twoe Angells in gould. Item I give and bequeth unto William Swindells my sonne Thirtye poundes of lawfull Englishe money in full satisfaction to him of his Childes parte and portion of all my sayd goodes, Chattells and debts. Item I give and bequethe unto William Swyndells my Grannd Chylde, Tenne poundes of lawfull Englishe money. Item I give and bequethe unto my Cosen Robert Swyndells of the Heald, William Swindells of Godley, William Swyndells and Alice Swyndells of Romiley, everye one of them Fyve shillinges. Item I will, leave and bequeth unto all suche poore people as shall resorte unto my buryall, everye one of them Twoe pence. Item I give and bequethe For and towardes the makinge of the Bridge neare unto my house, Comonlye Called the New Bridge Tenne Shillinges. Item I give, leave and bequethe For and towardes the makinge and Repayringe of the Steeple of the parishe Churche of Stockport in the Countye of Chester; Tenne Shillinges. Item I give and bequeth unto everye one of my Godchildren, Twoe Shillinges. The Rest and Residue of all my sayd goodes, Chattells and debtes whatsoever, after my debtes payd, my funerall expences performed, and theise my legacies in this my presente Testament Conteyned, fulfilled and accomplished; I wholelye give and bequeth unto John Swyndells my sonne. And I desyre my sonne John to give of his owne goodes to my sonne Edward Fourtye shillinges; And the Reason why I doe not give anye portion of my goodes to the sayd Edward ys; because I have alreadye given him his full Childes parte of my goodes in my lyfe tyme.

Executor: testator's son John Swyndells.

Provyded alwayes That if my sayd sonne William Swyndells be alreadye dead, and leave wyfe and Children or anye Chylde behinde him lawfullye begotten Then I give and bequethe the sayd sume of Thirtye poundes to his sayd wyfe, Chylde or Children withoute fraud or further delaye. Mk.

Witnesses: John Sydebothom, Raphe Ouldham and Tho. Simkin.

Inventory: William Swyndells of Stockport, husbandman.
                                    Taken: 6 February 1610/11.
Of: goodes and chattells.
Prisers: John Sydebotham and Thomas Simkin.

	£	s	d
in readye money	48	0	0
Receyved in debts in the decedents lyfe tyme	22	11	7
A tacke of ground taken of one Hughe Kenyon for fourteene yeares: fyve thereof yett unexpyred	5	0	0
Three Closses taken of one Roger Leighe for fourteene yeares: seaven whereof yet unexpyred from the first daye of Marche next	11	18	0
Three parcells of land taken of one William Thornelye for tenne yeares: Three yeares of the same yett unexpyred from the first daie of May next	9	0	0
one parcell of land taken of one Anthonye Mottershed for Twentye and one yeares Tenne yeares whereof yett unexpyred	10	0	0
owinge by John Higham nowe of Hyde and John Higham of Werneth as appeareth by theire bound	7	0	0
owinge by Robert Williamson and William Rocrofte as appeareth by theire Bill		29	0

more owinge by the sayd John Higham of Hyde 4 0 0
his apparrell 3 6 8

                                                                Sum 114 5 3
                                                            [recte 122 5 3]

Office endorsement: probate to executor.

36. JOHN WHITACHERS OF STOCKPORT, SHOEMAKER.
                                                               S.Pr. 23 April 1612.
Will, sick in body.   W.T. 24 January 1611/12.

First I geve and surrender up my soule into the handes of Almightie God that gave yt, verily and stedfastlye beleevinge to be saved by the death and passion of his sonne Jesus Christe my Lord and Saviour, and to be one of his elect and chosen children and my bodie to be buryed in the Churchyard of Stockport. And Concerninge those goodes which Almightye God of his mercye hath bestowed upon mee, my mynd ys I have [sic] them to be distributed as followethe. First I geve unto Margerye Whitachers my wyfe the Summe of Twentye poundes in monye, to be taken up out of my whole goodes. Item I geve unto the sayd Margery my wyfe one Bedsteed in the parlour next to the streete, with the clothes and furniture thereof; Item I geve unto my sayd wyfe one cloke. Item I geve unto my sayd wyfe the biggest chiste standinge in the sayd parlour. Item I geve uto my sayd wyfe my brewinge kayre with potts and stounds thereunto belonginge. Item I give and bequeath unto George Whitachers my sonne the summe of Tenne poundes in monye to be taken up out of the residue of my goodes. Item I geve unto my sayd sonne one bedsteed in the high Chamber with the clothes and furniture thereof. Item I geve unto my sayd sonne one brasse potte, the best which I have but one, sixe pewter dishes of the middle sorte, one great brasse pan, and one brandreth after the death of my sayd wyfe, for my will ys that my sayd wyfe shall have and enjoye the sayd pan and brandreth as her owne duringe her naturall lyfe. Item I geve unto my sayd sonne all the workeloomes and worktooles, belonginge and appertayninge to my trade and occupacon. Item I geve unto my sayd wyfe and sonne one presse in the parlour next the streete, to be used joyntly betwixt them, and after the death of my wyfe then to remayne to my sonne. Item I geve unto my sayd sonne one Bible. Item I geve unto him one litle chiste standinge in the parlour aforesayd. Item I geve unto Margerie my sayd wyfe my best brasse potte, and sixe of my best pewter dishes. Item I geve unto Anne Whitachers the daughter of George my sonne Twentie shillinges in Monye. Item I geve unto Edward Rhodes sonne of Alexander Rhodes my sonneinlawe Twentie shillinges in monye. Item I geve unto John Rhodes sonne of the sayd Alexander Twentie shillinges. Item I geve unto Marie Whitachers daughter of the sayd George Twentie shillinges. Item I geve unto every one of my Cosin John Burdsells children of Marple 12d. Item I geve unto John Burdsell sonne of James Burdsell of Stockport 12d. Item I geve unto John Potter sonne of George Potter 12d. Item I geve unto Margerye Burdsell daughter of Thomas Burdsell 12d. And concerninge the residue of my goodes mooveable and unmooveable, my will and mynde ys that after my funerall expences be discharged, and debtes and Legacyes payd, they shalbe devyded amongste Margerie Whitachers my sayd wyfe, George Whitachers my sayd sonne and Margerie Rhodes my daughter, wyfe unto Alexander Rhodes aforesayd by even and equall portions.

Executors: testator's wife Margerie and John Burdsell of Marple. Mk. and S.
Witnesses: Thos. Normansell, George Whitachers and James Burdsell.

Debts owinge unto mee John Whitachers	£	s	d
Imprimis of James Kemp of Ecchills of lent monye	2	0	0
Item of Edward Broocks of Stockporte		13	4
Item of the wyfeof Thomas Dande		4	0
Item of Wllm Higinbothome of Marple Tanner	2	6	8
Item of John Gibbon of Edgley	2	8	0
Item of Wllm. Marsland of Wernith		20	0
Item of Lawrence Goole of Stockporte		17	0
Item of Widowe Moores of Marple		20	0
Item of Mr. Alexander Bosvyle of Stockporte		35	0
[Sum	12	4	0]

Inventory: John Whitachers of Stockport, shoemaker.
Taken: 11 March 1611/12.
Of: goodes and cattals.
Prisers: Robert Dodge, Francys Robinson, James Burdsell, George Whitachers and Tho. Burdsell.

	£	s	d
one Bedde with the furniture in the Chamber next the streete pryced to	3	0	0
one Bedd in the highe Chamber with furniture		50	0
one Bed in the Buttrye with furniture		30	0
7 payre of sheetes 12 napkins one boardcloth one towell and 3 pillowe beeres		39	8
wollen cloth one pillowe beere and a Ringe		22	0
one peece of whyte clothe		3	4
in Brasse		36	8
in pewter		38	3
one morter pestill one brasse candlesticke and one plate		4	6
2 leades			20
in Iron ware		11	6

74   Stockport Probate Records

in Tryne ware		20	0
in earthen ware		3	8
Coffers Arkes 2 Barrells one presse and one Turnill		41	8
7 wiskettes one sacke and pokes		3	4
one disboard and other boardes		17	0
in Chayres stooles and quishions		4	6
in dishes spounes and other thinges			16
3 houpes of wheate and one pecke of Rye		22	6
2 houpes of Barlye		6	8
half a houpe of Rye		3	0
in instruments that belonge to a shoemaker		6	8
in Leader and shoes	4	13	4
2 swyne and piggs		32	0
in torves coles and fyrewood		6	8
his apparell		30	0
in Debts as appeareth by specialltyes	118	16	2
owinge for shoes	4	6	8
in Debts nominated in the will	12	4	0
		164	15	9
	[recte	164	16	9]
in readie monye		24	0	0
	[Sum	188	16	9]

Office endorsement: probate to executors.

37. HUGH MOTTRAM OF THE TOWNSHIP OF STOCKPORT, WHEELWRIGHT. S.Pr. 13 May 1612.
Will, ould aged and troubled with Gods loving correction.   W.T. 3 May 1611.

Knowinge death to be certayne to everie livinge creature, but the hower thereof unknowen wishing that love and good agreement may bee had and continued amongst all men after my deceasse, but especially amongst my owne wyfe and children doe ordayne and make this my laste will and testament in maner and forme followinge First and principallie I doe committ my soule to God the Father Almieghtie, by whose Sons precious bloud shedding, I doe truste to be saved, and to inheryt his everlastinge kingdome, And my bodie I doe committ to the earthe whereof yt came, to be buryed in the parish churchyord of Stockporte, in such maner as my frends shall think convenient And for order and for distribution of all such wordlie goods as God of his goodnes hath blessed mee withall Firste I doe devyse and my will yt is I doe geve unto my sonne Hugh Mottram the Summe of Sixe pounds thirteen shillings fower pence, for and in the consideration of his filiall and childs parte of all my goods whatsoever. And in lyke maner I doe devyse geve and bequeath unto my sonne Raph Mottram the summe of other six poundes thirteen shillings fower pence of lyke lawfull monye of England, And the same to be payd and delivered unto them, and unto either of them, at such tymes as my executors herein named can conveniently come by the same And all the rest of all my goods whatsoever yt is my will that the same shall be equally devyded between Margaret my wyfe, and Willm Mottram my sonne, savinge that yt is my will that Margaret my sayd wyfe shall have the full use of all my houshold goods duringe her naturall life and after her deceasse my sonne William Mottram he to have one half of the same as then yt shalbe founde.

Executors: Peter Mottram of Adlington and William Mottram of Prestburie. H. and S.
Witnesses [after list of debts]:
Raph Hooleye, wheelright and Lawrence Fallowes.

These are the debts owinge unto me the day & yeare aforesayd without specialltye.

	s	d
Imprimis of Thurstan Rowsson alias Matley for making one payre of wheles at my owne table	4	0
Jeffrey Taylor of Chorlton wheelewright for one cowe hyre .	8	6
Raph Didsburye of Bredburie lefte of a recknoing [sic] . .	24	0

And all the rest of debts owing unto me are in spetiallty.

Inventory: Hugh Mottram of Stockport.   Taken: 30 April 1612.
Of: goods and cattalls.
Prisers: George Newton, John Hopwood and William Mottram.

	£	s	d
one cowe prysed to		48	0
Haye		16	0
twoe fetherbeds twoe boulsters & three pillowes . . .	4	0	0
7 Coverletes and 5 blankets		53	0
2 mattresses		6	8
13 payer of sheets & other linnens	3	10	0
in wollen clothe		10	0
in newe linnen clothe		20	0
cheese and one ark		40	0
2 payre of bedstocks		10	0
in Corne	3	6	0
in malte and meale		20	0
in Brasse		20	0
one turnill & 6 sacks		10	0
in pewter		12	0

2 leades		3	4
in Iron ware		8	0
in tryen ware		10	0
in earthen potts		2	0
one bord a cupbord & other loose bords		30	0
in Chayres & Stooles		2	6
in salte beefe		5	0
in Qushions		2	6
in Spokes & other tymber		20	0
in Workloomes		14	0
in fuell		10	0
his apparell		50	0
in tacks of ground	17	0	0
in debts by specialties[1]	112	0	0
in debts without spetialtye		12	6
Sum	161	11	6

1. 92 in r.h. margin struck out.

Office endorsement: probate to William Mottram.

38. ELLEN TAYLIOR OF STOCKPORT, WIDOW. S.Pr. 26 May 1612.
Will, damaged. Health, sick.   W.T. 1 March 1611/12.

I commend my soule into the hands of Allmightie God my maker and continuall preserver, hopinge in the merites of Jesus Christ to be one of the number of those that shalbe saved, and my bodye to the earthe wheirout yt was taken. Item my mynd and will is that all suche debtes as of right and in conscience I doe owe to anie person or persons and lykwyse my funerall expences whatsoever they shalbe, shalbe paid and discharged out of my whole goodes. Item I give and bequeath unto my cosen George Vaudrey two silver spoones and to my cosen Richard Vaudrey other two silver spoones and to my cosen Ane Vaudrey the wyffe of the said George my best hatte save one lyned with velvett. Item I give and bequeath unto Ellen Vaudrey daughter of the said George one partlett. and to Margery Vaudrey her sister one paire of satin sleves. Item I give and bequeath unto Margreat Hardman my best hatt. Item I give and bequeath unto Anthonye Taylior of Northburye twentie shillings which hee oweth me. Item I give and bequeath unto William Taylior brother of the said Anthonie, one bed standinge and beinge in the high chamber as yt now ys with thappurtenances and furneture to the same belonginge, Item I give and bequeath unto Elizabeth Taylior sister of the said Anthonye and William six pownds twelfe shillings which Thomas Garnett of Stockport oweth me as appeareth by his will. Item I give and bequeath unto every one of my Godchildren twelve pence, the Rest and Residue of all and singular my goodes, chattells, cattels and debts of what name nature sort qualitie or condicon soever the same be or wheresoever the same remayneth or be or shall or may be found I wholly give and bequeath unto Allice Taylior sister of the said Elizabeth for and towards her preferment.

Executor: Allice Taylior, sister of Elizabeth Taylior.
Overseers: William Banckroft and Anthonie Taylior. Mk. and S.
Witnesses: John Boland, John Barrett, Thomas Elcok and Thos. Simkin.

Inventory: Ellen Taylior of Stockport, widow. Two inventories.
Taken: 25 May 1612.
Of: goods and chattels. The second inventory is dated only 1612, and has no prisers' names.
Prisers of May inventory: Thomas Elcoke, John Barrett, John Winne and Allexander Mosse.

	£	s	d
Two Kyne	4	13	4
One Sawe		18	0
In Pullen		2	4
One Standinge bed in the parler with all furneture their to belonginge	3	13	4
One Standinge bed in the Chamber with all furneture therto belonginge	2	6	8
One Trokell bed with furneture	1	10	0
One Cobborde in the house		13	4
One bench with seelinge therto		13	4
One Longe Table and two short ones in the house		13	4
Two other Tables		5	0
Formes, Cheares and stooles		5	0
In quishens		10	0
In Chists		16	0
In Pewter	1	13	4
In Brass	2	0	0
one fyregrate with other Iron ware		6	0
In TreeneWare		13	4
In glasses, pots and other earthen ware		3	4
In Corne and Mault		20	0
In Flesh and Butter		13	4
in fuell		10	0
one Byble with other books		6	8
in Flax and Yorne		12	0
in Nappery Ware	3	13	4
In pooakes and bags			12

78   Stockport Probate Records

	£	s	d
In specialties	11	5	8
in silver spoones	1	6	8
In Redy Coyne		15	0
the defuncts apparrell	5	0	0

[Sum 46 19 4]

[The other inventory is written on a separate sheet of paper and in different hands].

	£	s	d
2 Cowes	4	16	8
one heffer		26	8
four Caulves	4	0	0
7 sheepe and a lambe		24	0
an ould mare and a nagge		33	4
six swynes		26[1]	
three geese and a gander and seaven younge ones		5	2
2 turkies		3	0
29 newe Bushells of Malte	3	16	0
Barlie 21 newe Bushell	3	10	0
foure newe bushell of Wheate		21	4
2 newe Bushell of Rye		8	0
3 newe Bushells of oates		5	0
2 ould waines with plowes and all things belonginge to them		20	0
a ladder		2	6
3 peeces of tymber		15	0

[Inventory continued in new hand]

	£	s	d
all treene wares in the house [erasure]		43	0
brasse		28	0
pewter with three brasen Candle sticks		36	0
Ellen his bed with furnitures	5	0	0
Anne his bed with furniture	3	0	0

Given unto the [said] Ellen and Anne by the Mothers will and not unto John his use

	£	s	d
two feather beds with bedstocks and two worser beds with the Close on them	3	6	8
sheats		45	0
naperie wares		24	0
two webbs of clothe with yorne		23	4
quishions 11 course quishions		4	0
three Coffers and a tye		13	4
foure silver spoones		14	0
a grate, a broche golberts a fryeing pann with acorns [sic]		15	0

6 ould sacks with a windowe sheate	5	0
her beste gowne a peticoate with a hatte given to Anne	40	0
a gowne and a peticoate given unto Ellen	30	0
in Lynnen apparell	10	0
in newe Cloath	30	0
flaxe		16
a hatte	4	0
a spade and a lytle pykell		8
[erasure] tables cheares with all things belonginge	20	0
hive of bees	4	0
bacon	18	0
leade	30	0
mucke	6	8
coales	3	4
a cupboard given to John Taylier	13[2]	4
	[erasure]	
[Sum 60	1	4]

1. Erasure in pence column.
2. The sum 13s 4d was interlined over an erasure of an earlier amount.

Office endorsement, on will: probate to executor.

39. MARGARETT HURST [OF STOCKPORT, buried 9 April 1613. Office endorsement gives status as spinster]. I.Pr. 22 April 1613.
Inventory of: goods. [No date taken given.]
Prisers: Allexander Mosse and Thos. Typpinge.

	£	s	d
one bedd		23	4
in brasse and pewter		3	10
one lead		2	6
in treene ware			5
one piggen			4
in lynnens		5	0
towe peticoats		10	0
one Silk hatt			10
one Coffer and an Ark		4	0
one Chayre			4
[Sum	2	10	7]

Office endorsement: probate to Katherine Hurst.

40. DOROTHY ELCOCKE OF STOCKPORT, WIDOW.

S.Pr. 28 Sept. 1613.
Will: damaged. W.T. 12 May 1609.

Beinge often tymes sickly and consideringe wh [damaged] that death beinge most certaine cometh at most uncertaine houres and tyme And myndinge therefore by the help of God to [damaged] some order for such temperall goodes as the lord of his goodnes hath lent me to the end that when death shall apeare I may [damaged] be troubled with anie wordley Affares doe make and declare this my present testament contayninge herein my laste will in maner and forme followinge that ys to say first and principalley I comend my soule into the handes of the most blessed and gloriouse [damaged] in whom I doe unfainedley belive trustinge most Assuredley through the merites death and passione of our Lord and Savoure [damaged] Christe that all my sines are forgiven me and my bodie to be buried at the discrecion of [damaged] Executor hereunder named Item I give devise and bequeathe unto my sonne Allexander Elcocke two angells of gould to make him a Ringe to weare for my sacke in full discharge of his childes parte of all my goodes to be paid unto him whith in two munthes after my deceasse Item I give devise and bequeath to my sonne Richard Elcocke Two angels of goulde to make him a Ringe to weare for my sacke in full discharge of his childes part of all my goodes to be paid him by my executor within two monthes after my decease Item I give devise and bequeath to William Elcocke my god sonne sonne of the said Allexander Elcocke one Kowe calfe Item I give devise and bequeath to Dorithie Elcocke daughter of Thomas Elcocke one broode shite and three pillowe beares agreable to the same. Item I give and bequeath to Marie Elcocke daughter of Thomas Elcocke one fyne payre of flaxon shits and two pillowe beares Item I give devise and bequeath to Frances Elcocke sonne of the said Thomas one Eue and one lambe Item I give devise and bequeath to Anne Elcocke my daughter in law wyffe of Thomas Elcocke my sonne all my best apparell of lynnen and woollen Item I give devise and bequeath to Dorithie Manninge my workday goune my workeday petiecoate and a white petecoate Item I give devise and bequeath to my cosen Margrite Hardman my beste purse The rest and ressedue of all my goodes catels and chatells after my depts and legacies paide and my funerall expenses discharged I doe wholey give devise and bequeath unto my sonne Thomas Elcocke.

Executor: testator's son Thomas Elcocke.
Supervisor: testator's 'lovinge sonne Allexander Elcocke'. H. and S. [No witnesses].

Inventory: Dorithey Elcocke of Stockport. Taken: 1 May 1613.
Of: goods detets [sic] Catles and Chatells. Three hands are used.
Prisers: William Dickinson, William [?D]ickinson [and] Sampson Hunt, aldermen, and John Barret, burges.

Stockport Probate Records   81

In the ould parler
	£	s	d
6 paire of flaxson Shites at	3	0	0
13 paire course Shites at	3	5	0
4 fine table clothes at	1	1	0
4 Course table clothes at		12	0
5 rounde table clothes at		5	0
29 table napkines at		13	4
14 pillowbeares at	2	0	0
2 Course pillowbeares five towels and a walet with 3 Cubbord clothes at		10	0
one featherbeade 2 boulsters 2 pillowes at	2	0	0
one materis 3 blanckets and one Cadowe at	1	8	0
one Standinge bede with seyled Cettels Curtens and vallens and rodes at	1	0	0
a truckle bed 4 blanckets 2 coverlides with one Chaffe bed and 2 pillowes at	1	8	0
9 Cushens 2 window Curtaines with a Rode and a stille glasse at		6	0
2 Round tables 7 Joynt stoules with a truncke and 2 boxes at	1	2	0
in the Chimnie 4 bares of Iyron with one paire of tonges at		2	4
one presse at	1	6	4
painted clothes at		6	8
	20	4	8

In the new parler
	£	s	d
one feather bed one boulster 2 pillowes at	1	13	4
one Cadow one blancket one materis	1	4	0
one standinge bed Curtayns with a paynted cloth		13	4
one truckle bed at		2	6
one presse 2 Chistes and one Desk with a truncke	1	4	0
a stoule and a cheare at		1	0
a bason and eweure and 7 peauter Candelsticks 6 salts 2 peauter Cups 5 Tunes 2 Canes of peauter 2 bottels 3 floure potes 2 sace panes at	1	10	8
4 brase Candelstickes at		7	0
2 Casse of Trenchers at		2	6
glasses paynted Cups and basens at		2	0
one hundreth and three pound of peauter at	3	7	3
5 tables with pickters in them at		5	0
	10	12	7

In the chamber over the new parler
	£	s	d
one standinge bed and Settels at		13	4

a chafbed 2 boulsters 2 blanckets one coverlide 17 0
2 sitting whiles with boourdes tressels and other things . . 5 0
a womans Sadell and furniture at 10 0

                                                                                                                                2 5 4

in Corne
40 houps of barlie at 10 0 0
wheate and Rey 6 houps at 2 4 0
5 bushells of oates at 4 0 0
straw and haiie at 6 8
2 shovels and a barne racke 5 sives a window shite and three
    sackes at 8 0
one lader at 4

                                                                                                                        16 19 0

in Catele
4 keyne 3 sterks a heffer and a bullocke at 14 3 4
5 eweus 5 lames and 10 yonge shipe at 2 19 0

                                                                                                                        17 2 4

In the butterie
3 tables 2 boourdes with shilffes at 17 0
one great brasse pane at 1 13 4
4 pootes and a possnet at 1 19 0
one chafing dish 2 skellits 2 skummers one brasse ladle 1 fryinge
    panne at 8 0
2 spits one tostinge Iyron a paire of snuffers and a paire of
    gooberts with other Iyron ware at 6 0
5 barrels 1 Turnill 2 Chournes 2 booukes 2 eshen 3 doson of
    Trenchers 4 chesforths 7 tinnes 6 basters with other trine ware
    at 2 0 0
glasses and potes at 2 0
a cubbord and a skonce at 6 8
in Jugges and pots 2 6

                                                                                                                      7 14 6

In the Hall
two tables at 12 0
3 table clothes and two window Curtaines at 10 0
7 sett Cushens at 7 0
9 Courser Cushines at 2 6

6 Joynt stoules and three Cheares at		10	0
2 silled formes with another forme at		6	0
one fyre Iyron 1 Rucketrie 1 bare of Iyron one paire of Tonges at		7	6
a mape with other painted papers at		3	0
	2	18	0

litelle butiere

Two Cubbords and Shilffes at		8	0

litelle parler courtside

one silled bed with a settells at	1	0	0
2 bedes at		6	8
in Dunge		10	0

In the kitchen

one borde and 2 knedinge troughes at		4	0
a truckle bed at		3	4
in silver sponnes and a gould Ringe at	1	10	0
Redie Coyne at	1	4	0
in aparell	10	0	0
	15	6	0
[Sum	93	1	5]

Office endorsement: probate to executors.

41. ROBERT GARDNER OF STOCKPORT, COWPER.

S.Pr. 1 April 1614.
Will, sick.   W.T. 15 June 1611.

First I give and bequeth my soule into the hanndes of Almightie God trustinge to be saved by the Deathe and passion of Christe Jesus, and my bodie to Christian buriall: And as touching those my Worldlie goodes; First my Will is; That Elizabeth my nowe wyfe shall have the whole halfe of all my goodes: And the other halfe I Reserve to my selfe to paye my Debtes, to discharge my funerall expences, and to discharge suche and those Legacies as herein I shall give and bequeth: My Will is that my Debtes be paid if I owe anye: Item, I give and bequeth to Robert Burghe my Godsonne 2s 6d. Item I give to Robert Hordron my Godsonne Twoe shillinges Sixe pence; Item I give to Robert Wynne Twoe shillinges sixe pence. Item I give to the Daughter of Marie Tounge Twoe shillinges Sixe pence. Item I give to my brother Hughe Gardner Twelve pence.

Item I give to my Sisters everie one of them Twelve pence apeece: And alsoe I give and bequeth all the Remainder of my goodes whatsoever, theise before said beinge discharged according to my Will; to my said Wyfe.

Executrix: testator's wife Elizabeth. H. and S.
Witnesses: John Redich, John Winne and Edward Brodhurst.

Inventory: Robert Gardner of Stockport, Cowper.   Taken: 9 March 1613/14.
Of: goods and chattells.
Prisers: Roger Harper, John Barrett, George Newton and Thomas Newton.

	£	s	d
In readie money	9	0	0
one silver spoone and other ould silver		11	0
in Pewter		53	4
in Panne brasse		50	0
in Pott brasse		33	6
in yron Ware		30	0
in Divers odd things in an highe Chamber		10	0
in one highe Chamber on the southe syde of the house one paire of Bedstockes with furniture to the same		30	0
in one Parlour one highe bed and a lowe bed with furniture to them	8	10	0
in Linnen	4	0	0
his apparrell		40	0
chushens		7	0
in Chests and Arkes		26	8
in Tables and Stooles in the Parlour		16	0
one Cupbord, tables, Chaires and stooles in the house		50	0
in one litle Buttrie; one Table and Shilves		10	0
one Leade		2	0
Brewinge vessell in the Brewhouse		35	0
one Tubb of salte Beefe		5	0
Wheate and Malte and flower		53	4
Ale and Beare		26	0
Treene ware, earthen vessell and drinking glasses		6	8
Butter and Cheese		6	0
one paire of Scales and twoe Ladders		2	0
Fewell		10	0
Sum	46	17	6
[*recte*	47	3	6]

Debts owing by the decedent
to Richard Fletcher for Malte		26	8
to Mistress Hulme for Wheate		14	0
Sum		40	8

42. EDWARD BIBBYE OF STOCKPORT, LINEN WEBSTER.
C.Pr. 13 May 1614.
Will: sick.
W.T. 7 May 1614.

I soe [sic] and bequeath my soule into the hannds of Almighty god and into the hannds of his sonn Jesus Christ my alone savyer and redeemer by whous merits death and blood sheading I doubt not but to bee saved and by no other way or meane whatsoever and my body to christian buriall in the parish Church of Stopporth or elswhere it shall please god to apoynt. also I geeve and bequeath unto Nicholas Bibbie of Openshaw 12d also I geeve and bequeath unto Alice Harrison latewyfe of William harrison late of Stopporth deceased 10s The rest of all my goods moveable and unmoveable my Funerall expences discharged I geeve and bequeath unto John Jackson and James Jackson his sonn.

Executors: testator's 'welbeloved Frends Thomas Mottershed and Richard Smyth Caryer' both of Stockport. H and S.
Witnesses [after list of debts]: Godfrey Bancroft, hercules Jackson and William Nicolson.

debts owing unto mee Edward bibbye	£	s	d
Imprimis John Chetman of Stockporth Mason	3	0	0
Item John Lowe lat of Stopporth		30	0
Cowps of Altringam		20	0
Item Hugh Smyth of levensulme for a dublet and 8 yards of sackcloth		8	4
Item more owing by the sayd Hugh Smyth			16
Item Tho Mottershed		2	8
Item owing by Richard blakborne a Chist which he borowed of me the Chist is worth		3	0
Item Willm Morris is to geeve me a pair of goode new shoes for an old Reckning betweext us for which shoes I am to geeve hym 6d			

debts which I owe
Unto Georg Ridgway		2	8

Inventory: Edward Bibbie of Stockport. Taken: 9 May 1614.
Of: goods chatles and cattles.
Prisers: [names given in preamble, marks and signatures at foot]: Frances Hankinson, mk., John Daniell, signs and Richard Fletcher, mk.

	£	s	d
his Bedstead one blankett 1 Coverlett 1 bedhilling 3 sheets 1 bolster 1 old Chaffbed		13	0

86   Stockport Probate Records

in wodden ware	12
in Reades	12
pullis and shutles	12
Treddles and waights	10
in Temples and healdstones	12
An arke	16
1 oger and wimble	2
1 lome and stopps	3 4
1 Chist	4 0
2 Cheares and a stoole	8
3 brasse pans and a skellett in waight 8lbs	5 0
1 brasse pott in waight 6 lb	2 0
1 dozen of Trenchers	2
10 Spoones of pewter	4
1 yearthen pott	1
his bodilie Aparell	10 0
in debts inward as appeareth by the will	[blank]
Sum	2 5 0
[recte	2 4 11]

Office endorsement: executors renounced, probate to John Jackson of Stockport.

43. CHRISTOPHER PIGGOT OF STOCKPORT, HABERDASHER.

C.Pr. 1 July 1614.
Will, aged.   W.T. 22 February 1606/7.

Dreading the uncertayne tyme of Gods visitacion knowing death to bee certayne to every Creature and the tyme thereof unknowne to thend love and Frendship shall and may bee hadd betweene my wyff daughter and Frends after my decease doe make and declare this present testament herein contayning my last will in manner and forme folowing: First and principally I doe comend my soule into the hands of Almighty God my maker redeemer and only savyer by the merits of whose sonns most precious bludd sheading I trust to bee saved and to Inheritt his eternall kingdome And my body and bones I comytt to christian buriall in the parish Churchyard of Stockporth before mencioned in such place as my Executors and frends think meete and convenyent. And for the order and distribucion of my goods and debts It is my will and mynd as hereafter folowes First that all such debts as I owe of right or conscyence to any person or persons my Funerall expencs and the probacon of this my last will and testament shalbe paid deducted and performed of my wholl goods: And after the same bee discharged then it is my will that the Residue of all my seyd goods and debts shalbe devyded into towe equall and just parts One part whereof I geeve and bequeath unto Margret my wyff And th' other part I will, geve and bequeath unto Margret my daughter. And I make and constitute the said Margret my wyff and Margret my daughter my full and lawfull Executors to execute and performe this my last will and testament in all respects according to my mynd and the trust I repose in them. And I doe geeve the goodewill of my howse with itt Appurtenances wherein I nowe dwell unto the sayd Margret my daughter from and after my naturall decease by the lycence and goodewill of my goode master and landslord Robt. Dokenfeld Esquyre And I doe utterley Revoke Renounce and disanull all former wills legacies bequeaths and Executors by mee heretofore made bequeathed named or Appoynted.

Witnesses: John Reddich George Reddich.

Debts owing by the testator	£	s	d
to Mr Alderman Dickenson		2	0
to Frannces Robynson		2	0
to George Whittikers for a paire of shoes		2	4
to his wyff			7
to George Sharman			6
to Raph Mosse and his wyfe			10
Sum		8	5
[recte		8	3]

Debts owing to mee			
Inprimis Jo. Williamson as appeareth by a bill		20	0
more as appeareth by the same bill therein underwritten		3	4
Willm. Chedle		2	9
Roland Griffyn in money			7
and for towe hattbands			8
Anthony Percevall for work			7
John Hudson of Heaton			9
[Sum	1	8	8]

Inventory: Christopher Piggot. Taken: 6 June 1614.
Of: goods.
Prisers: Georg Jennings, Henry Rydings, George Whittikers and Tho. Whittakers.

	£	s	d
in pewter		20	0
in brasse		2	6
in potts and panns		3	0
in lead			6
in Iron ware		4	0

88 Stockport Probate Records

an axe and a knyfe		12
in ironware more		18
a wodden candlestick		2
a lanterne and a pair of cards and a grater		6
for Instruments	2	0
in woll		2
in hatt and bands	2	6
for stuff in the shopp	4	0
for wodd		12
for boards and seeling	10	0
Apparrel	12	0
for the bedd and bedding	26	8
for treene ware		16
in Manure		18
Sum 4	14	4

Office endorsement: probate to executors.

44. RAPH ASHTON OF STOCKPORT, MASON. S.Pr. 13 July 1614.
Inventory of: goods cattalls and chatells. Taken: 8 May 1614.
Prisers: Thomas Benison, Godfray Heron, James Burdsill and Randle Thorneley.

	£	s	d
one Bed and one Cupbord	1	10	0
in Coffers Arkes and one Table	1	0	0
in pewter and Brasse		14	8
in Tryen ware		8	0
in Bedding and linnens	2	10	0
in Bords and fyrewood	1	3	4
one swyne pryce		8	0
in Iron ware		16	0
in chaires and stooles		1	4
in malt		5	0
in quuishions		2	0
one Fornace	1	0	0
in money debts and Specialtyes	58	17	0
in money more		19	7
Sum	70	11	11
[recte	69	14	11]

Office endorsement: probate to executors.

45. RICHARD GERRARD, PARSON OF STOCKPORT.

S.Pr. [no day and month given] 1614.
Will: [The preamble is unusual and is given in full]. W.T. 10 May 1614.

In the name of the Blessed trinitye, God the father, God the Sonne, and God the holye Ghoste three distincke persons and one God of all moste infinite Maistye, by whose goodnes I Rychard Gerrard parson of the Churche of Stockporte in the Countye of Chester. was made and hitherto have beene graciouslye preserved, the same greate and glorious name firste beinge called uppon for direction I the sayde Rychard Gerrard doe make and ordeyne, this my last will and Testament in maner and Forme Followinge That is to saye First I doe willinglye and Cheerefullye Commend my soule into the hands of Almightye god, who gave yt and whoe will save yt and preserve yt to ever-lastinge lyffe by his mercye in Christe Jesus, and my bodye I doe Commend and bequeath to Christian buriall, when and where and in what sorte yt shall seeme good to myne executour And for my goods, first I give and bequeath all writing of Court Rowles and other things belonginge to the libertye of the Parsons of Stockporte for the houldinge of the Courte, unto my Successor the Parson that shall be whosoever leavinge to him to use the same, as he shall thincke good. And for my Worldlye goods as they stand I doe herebye give and bequeath unto everye of My children Twentye Shillings a peece, as a legacye to everye of them, And all the rest and residue of my goods and Chattells, I doe whollye give theym to Ursula Gerrard my naturall and lovinge Wiffe, [Gerrard then proceeds to dispose of his lease of the rectory of Hanslope in Buckinghamshire, calendared as follows: The will *recites* a *lease* by (1) the Mayor and City of Lincoln, 10 December 17Eliz. I [1574] *to* (2) Robert Monnson, Justice of Common Pleas of *Premises* Rectory, parsonage and manor of Hanslope, plus appurtenances specified, in Buckinghamshire. *Term* 99 years from end of a lease [made by (1)?] to (3) Sir Robert Lane of Horton, Northants, knt [date and terms not specified]. *Rent* £80 p.a. *Further recites* the eventual assignment of the lease to (4) Wm Gerrard of Harrow on the Hill, Middlesex. *Further recites* that (4), 25 July 40 Eliz I [1598] assigned to (5) Sir Richard Molyneux, (6) Sir Peter Leigh, (7) Ed. Ratcliffe, (8) Thos. Gerrard and (9) Felix Gerrard gents, all (4)'s term of years unexpired in the moiety of the premises. *Further recites* that (4), 29 June 4 James I [1606] assigned to (5–9) and to the testator the other moiety of the premises. *Further recites* that (5–9), 21 August 40 Eliz I [1598] and 2 July 3 James I [1605] assigned the profits of the said premises to the testator and such persons as the testator should by deed or will in writing appoint. *And finally recites* that (8) is now dead.
Now by virtue of the above deeds the testator assigns the profits of all the premises to Ursula Gerrard his wife, her executors and administrators, she paying the costs of conveyance and assurance by (5–9).]¹ hopinge that she will by meanes thereof raise Mayneteynance to her selff, and Conveynient porcons and estates for my Children, Whom I leave to her goodnes beinge theire naturall mother to be delte withall as they shall give cause And whereas I have trusted my Cosyn Hamnet Hyde esquier and my neighboure and good freind Henrye

Bradshawe to take the purchase of certen lands in Stockporte from Rychard Browne and others to be Conveyed to such as I should appointe I doe hartelye authorize and will and require theym, to Convey the same lands to my said wiffe and her heires by such reasonable assurances as she or her Councell learned in the lawes Shall devise or appointe And for all gratuities to servants or freinds I reserve the same to my wiffe, to be delte in as her estate maye well afford.

Executrix: testator's wife, Ursula Gerrard. H. and S.
Witnesses: Hamnet Hyde, John Hyde deane [of] M[acclesfield], Thomas Normansell and William Byam.
Office endorsement: probate to executrix.

1. For details of this property see *V.C.H. Bucks*, IV, p. 361 and J.W.F. Hill, *Tudor and Stuart Lincoln* (Cambridge, 1956), pp. 52–53, 73.

46. HENRIE SCLATER OF STOCKPORT, HUSBANDMAN.

S.Pr 14 July 1614.
Will: sick.
W.T. 25 March 1614.

Firste I commend my soule into the handes of Almightie God my maker and Continuall preserver hopinge in the merites of Jesus Christe my Savior to be one of the number of those that shalbe saved; And my bodye to the Earthe whereoute it was taken, And as for those goodes which the Lord in mercie hathe given me, my mynd and will is; That they shalbe bestowed as hereafter followeth, That is to witt; That they shalbe devyded into Three equall parts one parte whereof I give devise and bequeth unto Anne nowe my wyfe, another parte unto my twoe Children, and to suche other my Chyld or Children as shall hereafter happen to beborne. And the Third equall parte of my said goods I reserve for and towards the payinge and discharginge of my debts and of my funerall expences whatsoever they maye be: The Reste and Residue of which said Third parte of myne, I wholelye give and bequeth unto my twoe Children, or to such other my Child or Children as shall happen hereafter to be borne.

Executors: testator's wife Anne and Thomas Ouldham of Heaton Norris 'my neighbour'.
Overseer: Nicholas Lees.
Witnesses: George Bradley, Richard Hudson and Tho. Simkin.

Debts owinge to the Testator	£	s	d
Imprimis owinge by John Sydebotham of the Hill Topp	22	0	0
Item by William Smithe of Brinnington	8	16	0
Item by George Sclater my brother and Nicholas Lees my brother in law	13	7	0
Item by Alexander Mosse Butcher	3	0	16

Receyved of this sume	22	0
Item owinge by John Robinson of Brinnington	30	0
Item by John Wilson	23	1

Debts owinge by the Testator

Imprimus owinge to my Master	23	0
Item more to my Master	30	0

Inventory: Henrie Sclater of Stockport, husbandman.

Taken: 26 April 1614.

Of: goods and chattells.
Prisers: John Robinson, Peter Heyes, Richard Hudson and James Fell.

	£	s	d
one Cowe		50	0
his apparrell and one purse	3	0	0
one Cupbord and table and three stooles, alsoe a longe table, a forme, Chayres, stooles and treene ware, Brasse and Pewter one greate Arke twoe staves and twoe pickforks . . .	4	0	0
one payre of Bedstockes and tymber at the house in the lane .		30	0
eighteen Jystes at the house in the towne		8	0
one Standinge bed one trucklebed and Coverlett, three blanketts two boulsters, two pillowes and a Chaff bed	3	0	0
one paire of bedstockes and twoe Chaff beds		6	8
Sheetes, pillowbeares, towells and other Lynnens . . .		40	0
one Longe Table and a Forme		3	0
Seaven Chestes		23	4
Nagers and Chizells		3	0
in Sheepe and a tacke of ground	3	9	0
owinge by John Sydebotham of the Hill Toppe	20	0	0
owinge by William Smithe of Brinnington	8	9	0
owinge by George Sclater and Nicholas Lees	12	7	0
owing by John Wilson		23	5
Sum	63	12	5

Office endorsement: probate to executors.

47. MARY ALLEN OF STOCKPORT. [Buried 13 July 1614.]

C.Pr. 15 July 1614.

Inventory of: goods. [Date taken not given.]
Prisers: Nicholas Blomeley and Robt. Boardman.

		s	d
towe coates	. . . .	2	0
one blankett	. . . .	2	0
3 sheetes	. . . .	4	0
one bolster case one pillowe	. . . .	2	0
one gowne and savegard	. . . .	2	0
in other old lynnens	. . . .	2	0
a paire of hose	. . . .		2

[Sum 14 2]

Office endorsement: probate to Edward Kemp and Francis Newcom of Stockport.

48. JEROM WARREN OF STOCKPORT, TAYLIOR.
C.Pr. 19 August 1614.
Will, sick.   W.T. 15 August 1614.

First I geeve and bequeath my soule into the hannds of Almighty God my Maker. And into the hands of his sonn Jesus Christ my alone Savyour and Redeemer by whoes merits death and blude sheading I doubt not but to bee saved everlastingly and by no other way or meanes whatsoever And my Body to Christian Buriall in the parish Church of Stockporth or where els it shall please god to appoynt: And for my worldly goods Chattels and Cattells I geeve and bequeath in manner and forme folowing. First I geeve and bequeath to Ann Cowley towe pewter disshes Item I geeve and bequeath unto my Aunt Jane Whyte a Coate Mr. Davenporth of the Myles end gave me. Also I geeve and bequeath unto Mrs. Katheryn Davenporth a psalm book and to her sister Mrs. Ann a prayer booke. Also I geeve and bequeath unto William Cowley a whyt dublett a Shert and a hatt. Also I geeve and bequeath unto my Brother Gregorie a fryze Jerkyn a dublett my best hose and a paire of Stockings. I geeve unto Robert Cottrell a litle black staff and unto William Dickenson my withen staff. Also I geeve unto John Shalcrosse a bearing staff. Also I geeve unto Edward Crooke younger a shurtband of Cambricke. And the rest of my goods I geeve and bequeath unto my Aunt Jane Whyt.

Executor: James Kelsall, gent.

Debts due unto mee Jerome Warren and at this present owing
by William Fletcher of Stockport taylore 7s.6d
Francis Elcock oweth me 2s.4d. if hee make clayme to a litle chist
and Georg Elcock my landlord 4s.8d. forgeven.

Debts which I the sayd Jerome Warren doe owe.
Unto Thomas Williamson 10s.0d.
Unto Richard Glover 14d.

Witnesses: Robt. Cottrell, John Shawcrosse, Edward Brook and Willm. Nicolsin.

Inventory: Jerom Warren, taylior.   Taken: 18 August 1614.
Of: goods chattells and cattells.
Prisers: no names given, though the names are said to be underwritten.

	£	s	d
in pewter disshes weight 15 pound		10	0
one skellett an old pann and a hacking knyfe			12
one lead			12
one paire of sheets			20
one paire of beddstocks			8
1 frying pann & fyre Iron			12
towe hatts		3	4
1 Mattress a blankett towe Coverletts a bolster		5	0
in bodely Apparell one black [erasure] nitt dublett		4	6
a greene Jerkyn		3	0
a fryze Jerkyn a Dublett his best hose and a paire of stockings		8	0
a whyt Dublett and old shurt		6	8
towe paire of shoes			12
one paire of old whyte hose			20
a horsemans coate		13	0
Sum	3	10	3
[recte	3	1	6]

Office endorsement: probate to executor.

49. RICHARD KENYON, CLERK, LATE RECTOR OF STOCKPORT.
C. Account exhibited 15 November 1615.

[Calendar] Accountant: Richard Fogge, gent.

Accounts exhibited: 15th November 1615, before Dr. David Yale, Chancellor of Chester.

	£	s	d
Charge: Sum of inventory	137	2	2
Debt due by Robert Duckenfeld of Duckenfeld esquire	4	1	8
Total	141	3	10

Discharge:
various sums spent on the administration as follows:

funeral charges	13	1	5
mortuarie fee to late Bishop of Chester and things due in that behalf specified in the Inventory	13	6	8
fees for letters of administration of deceased's goods . . .	1	4	0
Exhibiting the inventory		2	4
drawing these accounts		3	4
for a copy of them		1	0
Proctors fee [illegible] November 2		5	2
Exhibiting the account and for the act this day [15 Nov.] . .			8
Proctors fee this day		1	0
	28	5	7

Rest of goods retained by Fogge to offset against debts owed him by the deceased
[112 18 3]

50. [WILLIAM NORTON] OF STOCKPORT, [buried 26 February 1615/16.]
C.Pr. 8 March 1615/16.

Inventory of: goods and chattels. Document is damaged throughout; deceased's name from Office endorsement.   Taken: [?] February 1615/16.
Prisers: Thomas Garnette, [Fr]ancis Robinson, William Flechar and Allexander Rodes.

	£	s	d
Firste one Cadda [damaged]		3	4
one Coverlete			12
one payre of shettes		4	6
a bouster and a pilowe			12
towe payre of bedstockes		5	0
in oulde bedinge			8
one Cettell		10	3
one leade			12
one fryinge [sic] a spitte a payre of tonges a payre of pott hockes a tostinge yeren a fyer yren a backe spittell and a shreadinge knyfe		5	0
in putter			6
in tryne Ware			12
in pigenes nogenes a cane a [damaged] ll a Deshen and a bage breade			[damaged]
a hachett a spade and a pyck [damaged]			10
towe littell tables		2	0

three Cheres and three stool [damaged]		[damaged]
a pice of woode and three [damaged] des		[damaged]
in yertthen ware		[damaged]
a baxston		[damaged]
a narke and a saffe		[damaged]
a littell whille and a pay [damaged] of Cardes		[damaged]
his towles in the shope		[damaged]
a sive and towe basketes		[damaged]
in woolen yorne		[damaged]
in mucke		[damaged]
a payre of tentores		[damaged]
his bodilye aparell		13 4
in triflinge thinges		4

Office endorsement: probate to deceased's relict Jane Norton.

51. [EDWARD HALL OF STOCKPORT, buried 21 March 1615/16].
C.Pr. 29 March 1616.
Inventory badly damaged, deceased's name taken from Office endorsement. Date taken and prisers' names lost, together with an unknown portion of the document.

	£	s	d
in Iron [damaged] grate and other Iron		[damaged]	
one [damaged] leade [damaged]		6	8
brewing vessells Barrells Eshins piggins Canns and other treen-ware		15	0
in earthen Ware			16
in Coffers		20	0
in bedstockes		6	8
in bedding		25	0
in lynnins		26	0
in fower quishins and one turnell		2	0
the defuncts his apparell		5	0
one lease of the howse of the late decedent	6	0	0

Debts owing unto the decedent

Allexander Moss		9	0
Robert Hough		6	5
Jo. Colyer		6	3
Francis Elcock		4	0
Olyver Dodge		3	4

Office endorsement: probate to Matilda Hall, relict of Edward.

96 Stockport Probate Records

52. BLANNCH THOMSTON OF STOCKPORT, WIDOW.

I.Pr. 19 July 1616.

Will, the right hand side of the will is damaged. Her status as widow comes from the office endorsement; the date of the will is lost.
Health: sick. The will mentions the testator's sons John and Raff, and her daughters Margaret and Kathreyn.

Executors: Olyver Dodge and John Browne.
Witness: Oliver Dodge.

Inventory: Blannch Thomston of Stockport.   Taken 28 June [1616].
Of: goods.
Prisers: William Swyndels and Raph Bruck.

	£	s	d
for hir wollen cloaths		16	6
one old hatt			6
one silk hatt			12
in lynnens		3	0
[Sum	1	1	0]

Office endorsement: probate to executors.

53. EDWARD DOUGHTYE OF STOCKPORT, [CLERK, LATE RECTOR OF STOCKPORT].

S.Pr., Inventory exhibited, 14 January 1616/17.
Inventory of: goods and chattells within the Countye of Chester.
Taken: 8 October 1616.
Prisers: Roger Harper, James Burdsell, Thomas Newton and John Boland.

	£	s	d
in corne & hay	63	0	0
twoe bedsteeds		15	0
One truncke & one litle pinchett		5	0
in linnins	3	12	0
Three bedsteeds	2	0	0
in bedding	10	0	0
In plate	10	0	0
One Cupbord & one presse		36	0
4 tables & one Forme		40	0
2 cheares & 2 stooles		4	0
Six Quishions & one table Covering		15	0
In potte brasse & panne brasse		40	0
In pewter		20	0

		£	s	d
In bricke & one cheesepresse			6	8
In maynor & fuell			4	0
One sowe & sixe piggs			30	0
In duckes			2	0
In iron Ware			20	0
In tryen ware barrills bords shelves & earthen pans			20	0
In Butter & cheese		4	10	0
‹in Butter & Cheese›				
his apparell		8	0	0
Twoe bookes			10	0
One ould whyte gelding		2	0	0
In debts owing unto him		26	0	0
Sum		142	9	8

Accounts: for Edward Doughtie, clerk, late Parson of the Parish Church of Stockport.   Presented 15 January 1616/7.

The true and perfect Accompte of Thomas Andrewe Administrator of the goods and cattells of Edward Doughtie Clerk late Parson of the parishe church of Stockport ‹deceased› in the countie and dioces of Chester deceased of and concerninge the administracion of the goods and cattells of the said decedent made and exhibited by vertue of his oath before the Right Worshipfull Mr. David Yale doctor of the lawes and Chancellor of the Dioces of Chester the 14th daie of Januarie Anno Domini juxta computacionam ecclesia Anglicane 1616 as followeth.

The said accomptant doth acknowledge that all and singuler the goods and cattells of the said decedent mencioned in an Inventorie therof taken and remaininge in record came to this accomptants hands wherewith he doth charge himselfe the same extending to the summe of

	£	s	d
	142	9	8

Payments and disbursments made by this accomptant for and Concerninge the said decedent as followeth wereof he Craveth allowance

	£	s	d
Imprimis paid for the severall expences of the said decedent		10	0
Item paid for letteres of administracion of the goods and cattells of the said decedent and for a commission to take [damaged] accomptants oath and bond [damaged] at Stockport		[damaged]	4
Item spent in travellinge Charges in comminge to Chester to fetch the said letters of administracion and Commission		10	0
Item paid [erasure] to the lord bishoppe of Chester for his mortuarie	12	0	0
Item paid to Mr. Arthur Storer, preacher at Stockport for wages due to him by the decedent	5	5	6

98   Stockport Probate Records

Item paid to Mr. Thomas Normansell Clerke curate of Stockport for wages due to him by the decedent	15	0	0
Item paid to James Burdsell a debt due to him by the decedent and recovered of this accomptant in the hundred court of Macclesfield the summe of £9 and Charges spent in the same court 13s 2d in toto	9	13	2
Item paid by this accomptant to Mr. Willm Whittington a debt due to him by the decedent and recovered of this accomptant in the towne court of Macclesfield the summe of £12 and charges spent in the same court [damaged] in toto . .	12	5	10
[damaged] paid by this accomptant [damaged] Edmond Jodrell esquire a debt due to him by the decedent and recovered of this accomptant in the towne court of Macclesfield the summ of £20 and charges spent in the same court 5–6d in toto	20	5	6
Item paid by this accomptant to James Burdsell Thomas Newton Willm. Daniell Alexander Rodes and Robt. Bordman a debt due to them by the decedent and recovered of this accomptant in the towne Court of Macclesfield the summe of £20 and charges spent in the same Court 5–6d in toto	20	5	6
Item paid by this accomptant to Thomas Normansell Peter Hey Thomas Simkin Raphe Oldham and Robt. Wood a debt due to them by the decedent and recovered of this accomptant in the towne court of Macclesfield the summe of £20 and charges spent in the same court 5–6d in toto	20	5	6
Item this accomptant craveth [damaged] allowance of the summe of £4 due to this accomptant by the said decedent for his wages	4	0	0
Item paid by this accomptant to Stephen Willms. for wages due to him by the decedent	1	13	4
Item paid by this accomptant to Miles Partridge for wages due to him by the decedent	1	13	4
Item paid by this accomptant to Ellenor Shawe for wages due to her by the decedent	1	6	8
Item paid by this accomptant to Margaret Smith for wages due to her by the decedent		13	4
Item this accomptant craveth allowance of £10 which was due to him this accomptant by the said decedent for victualls used in the said decedents house in his lifetime and for divers other things which he this accomptant brought into the said decedents house in the decedents lifetime and for which he this accomptant was ingaged for in the towne of Stockport and other places neere there unto adioyninge the summe of .	10	0	0
Item paid for drawinge of these accomptes		3	4
Item paid for exhibiting of the same			4

Item paid for ‹the› a copie of these accomptes	3	4
Item paid for the quietus est upon the said accomptes and for the seale of the same	10	8
Item this accomptant craveth allowance [damaged] for and towards his travelling charges in comming to Chester to make his said accomptes	6	8

[The Latin conclusion is difficult to construe but may be summarised as follows:]

Sum of receipts	142	9	8
Sum of payments	147	2	4
Excess of payments over receipts	4	12	8

54. ISSABELL HIBEART OF STOCKPORT, [Inv: widow].

I.Pr. 25 October 1616.
Will, sick. W.T. 7 September 1616.

First and principallye I bequeath my soule into the handes of almightie god my maker and Redeemer, And my bodie to the earth to be buried in decent manner att the parish Church of Stockport, Accordinge to the discretion of my Friends; And as Concerninge such Worldlye goods as god hath lent mee, my mynde and will is, That my forth bringing and finerall expences shalbe taken of my whole goods; Imprimis I give and bequeath unto Mester Robeart duckenfield esquire my Landlorde one foulded Table, Item I give and bequeath unto Robeart Hibbeart one Chafbead, Item I give and bequeath unto Allexander Summister in money 12d, Item my mynde and will is and I further give and bequeath unto Katheren Hurst my sister all and singuler my sed goods; my debts and finerall Expenses and theise Legasies above payd discharged of what nature kynde or propertie soever the bee or wheresoever the Remayne.

Executors: Charles Sydebothom and testator's sister Katheren Hurst.
Overseer: Edward Ashton alias Wylde. H. and S.
Witnesses: William Bradlie, John Bramma and Peter Sydebotham with others.

Inventory: Isabell Hibbart of Stockport, widow. [Buried 21 October 1616]. No date given.
Of: goods.
Prisers: Georg Newton, John Boland, Raph Oldham and Robte Hibbart.

	£	s	d
in pewter		26	8
in brasse		24	0
one fyre yron and shov and other Iron ware		16	0
one fornes and one brade		11	0
in treene ware		30	0
in potts and glasses		7	0

one Chist one Arke and other boards in the buttries	12	0
one folden table in the howse	10	0
in the two Chambers above in wodden ware and other tryfling things	10	0
in the great Chamber above in bedding boards and other Implemets	12	0
in the howse boards forms and Chaires	6	0
in the high Chamber without one ladder hay and other Implemets	5	0
in fuell	12	0
in the litle parlor one bedsteede and bedding	40	0
in sheets and other lynnens	34	0
two Chists in the litle parlor	8	0
in Malt meale and greats	4	0
in hir apparrell	26	8
Sum	14 14	4

Office endorsement: probate to executors.

55. ELIS CROSSLEY OF STOCKPORT, WOLLEN WEBSTER. [buried 6 December 1616]. I.Pr. 13 December 1616.
Will: no statement re health, but of good and perfect remembrance.
W.T. [damaged] February 1615/16.

First and principally I do comytt my soule Unto the Father Almighty by the meritt of whoes sonns most precious bludshed for our salvation I Doe trust to bee saved and to inheritt his everlasting Kyngdome and my body I Doe remytt to the earth whereof it came and to bee buryed in the Church or Churchyard of Stockporth And for distribucon of all such worldly goods as god hath bestowed Upon mee, First I Doe Devyse and it is my will and I geeve and bequeath unto Tho Crosley six pence, And I geeve unto Robt Whewhall six pence, Also I geeve Unto John Crosley six pence And in lyke manner I doe geeve unto Charles Crosley six pence, these foure legacies I doe geve unto my Cosyns aforsyd as a full part of my goods Chattels and Cattels that I am willing to bestowe: all the Rest of my goods Chattels and Cattels I geve and bequeath Unto Katheryn Crosley my wyfe, she the sayd Katheryn paying all my Debts Discharging the legaces the Funerall expencs and the Probacon of this my last will and Testament.

Executor: testator's wife Katheryn.
Supervisors: testator's servant John Clough and James Fynsonn. H. and S.
Witnesses: Willm. Cowley and James Fynsonn.

Inventory: Elis Crossley of Stockport. [Date taken not given.]
Of: goods, cattells and chattells.
Prisers: [names at foot] John Wharmby, John Nicolsonne and George Elcocke.

	£	s	d
in beddinge		23	4
in sheets		10	0
in Loome and reeds and warpstocke		10	0
two Arks and one Coffer		3	4
in treene ware and one Dishe bourd		6	8
two little bottls, one little leade and one skellett		3	4
in pewter		3	4
in butter		5	4
in Cheeses		1	4
in earthen potts			6
in Iron ware		3	4
in Chayres and stooles		1	0
one little bourd		1	0
two payre of bed stocks		3	4
in whyte lynne		1	0
in fuell		2	0
in whyte yearne		20	0
in gray yearne		7	0
one wiskett			2
in quishons		1	0
his Apparell		10	0
Sum	5	17	0

Office endorsement: probate to executors.

56. SISLEY HUITTE OF STOCKPORT, WIDOW.

I.Pr. 17 January 1616/17.
Will, troubled with weaknes and Infermetie of bodie.   W.T. 20 April 1615.

I Comend my soule into the handes of almightie god my maker and Continually preserver hopinge by Christ to be on of those ‹shall› that shall be saved and my bodie to the earth and for thos small goodes which the lord hath in his merce vochsaved me my mind and will is to bestowe them wholly on John Millington of the aforesaid towe and Countie After that my funerall exspences whatsoever the shall amount to shall be payd and discharged out of them then the rest and residue of my goodes whatsoever I give to the sayd John Millington.

Executor: John Millington.

Witnesses: Nicollas Elcock, Godferat Herode and Frances Hall.

Inventory: Sisley Huitte of Stockport, widow.   Taken: 11 January 1616/17.
Of: goodes and cattalls.
Prisers: Frances Shrigley, Nicollas Elcock and George Marsland.

	s	d
in pewter and Brass and treene ware and Iron ware	6	0
her Apparell and Bedinge .	4	4
Sum	10	4

Office endorsement: [Cyslie Huett] probate to executor.

57. LAWRANCE RIGBIE OF STOCKPORT.

I.Pr. 14 February 1616/17.
Will, [no statement about health of body or mind.]   W.T. 3 February 1616/17.

I Committ my soule into the hanndes of Almightie god and my bodye to bee buried in the parishe Churcheyard of stockport Item my will and mynd [damaged] that all suche debtes as of Right and Concience I [*interlined* : doe] owe to [damaged] person or persons bee paid out of my whole goodes Item [damaged] expenses discharged I give unto John Lumbston and to h [damaged] Catteren Lumbston eather of them 5s Item I give to my dough [damaged] Elizabethe Rigbie 6s 8d if shee Come for itt within tenn [damaged] after my deacease and if she Come not in that tyme then Allis Cotterell to have itt. Item the Rest of my goodes debtes and Chattel [damaged] and whatsoever to be devided into three partes and Ellin Cottere [damaged] have a third parte and her sister Allis Cotterell to have the other two partes.

Executors: John Swindels and John Lumbston.
Witnesses: Raphe Brucke and William Swindels.

Debts owinge to mee	s	d
Imprimis Sir William Davenport	18	0
Item John Swindels .	48	0
Item John Lumbston	42	0

Inventory: Lawrance Rigbie of Stockport.   Taken: 11 February 1616/17.
Of: goods debts and chattels.
Prisers: John Sydbothom of Bredbury, husbandman and Robert Ridgway of Stoc[kport] husbandman.

	£	s	d
a debte owinge by Sir William Davenport		18	0
a debte owinge by John Swindels		48	0
a debte owinge by John Lumbston		42	0
in Bedstockes and Bedinge		8	0
in Iron ware			12
in apparell		10	0
Sum	6	7	0

Office endorsement: probate to executors.

58. JOHN ROBINSON OF STOCKPORT, YEOMAN.

S.Pr. 30 April 1617.
Will, sick.   W.T. 13 January 1616/17.

Knowinge that nothinge is more Certeyne then death, and nothinge more uncerteyn then the houre thereof; willinge therefore (after the example of good kinge Ezechias) to sett my house and goodes in order, to thend peace and quietnes may be had and embraced amongst my wyfe and Children after my decease Doe therefore make and ordeyne this my last will and Testament, in manner and forme followinge first and Principallie I Comend my soule into the handes of Almightie God my maker and Creatour and to his onelie sonn Jesus Christ my saviour and Redeemer, and to the holie ghost my sanctifyer, trustinge in the holie, blessed and glorious Trinitie to be made an heire in the Kingdome of Heaven, as my undoubted trust and beleefe in this behalf is And as concerninge my bodie, I Comend the same unto the earth whereof it was first fashioned, hopinge that at the last daye, it shall rise agayne a glorious bodie, and be made partaker with the saintes and elect in the kingdome of heaven, and I will that the same shalbe buried in the parish Church of Stockport, at the discretion of my Executor hereafter named. And as Concerninge suche Temporall goodes, as god hath endowed me withall, my will and mynd is (that after my debtes paid, and funeralls discharged) the same shalbe devyded into Three equall partes and portions, The first parte whereof I give and bequeath to Jane my welbeloved wyfe, according to the custome of the Countrie: Item the seacond parte of my said goodes, Cattells and Chattells I give and bequeath to my eldest sonne Francis Robinson. And whereas heretofore there were Certayne goodes given to my Children and others, by the last will and Testament of James Taylier my brotherinlawe deceased, whereof I am Executour For the which goodes Robert Hardman and his wyfe, have Comensed and brought divers suites agaynst me, for tryall whereof the said Cause is referred to the Comon lawe: By reason of which suites all the said goodes are wasted and spent; If therefore the said Robert Hardman and his wyfe, doe not or shall not Recover the same, Then I give to everie one of my Children Twentie poundes in leu thereof and in full discharge and satisfaction of theire Childes partes and filiall portion of my goodes: (if the Third parte of my goodes Called the Testators parte will extend thereunto Item I give and bequeath unto the said Francis Robinson, my eldest sonne, and the heires Males of his bodie Lawfullie begotten and to be begotten: All my Landes, Tenementes and hereditamentes whatsoever: And for default of such issue, then I give and bequeath all the said Landes, Tenementes, and hereditamentes afforesaid whatsoever, to Alexander Robinson my seacond sonne and to the heires Males of his bodie lawfullie begotten and to be begotten: And for default of such issue: then I give and bequeath all and singuler my said Landes, Tenementes and hereditamentes whatsoever to Richard Robinson my Third sonne and to the heires Males of his bodie lawfullie begotten and to be begotten: And for default of such issue, Then the same Landes, Tenementes, hereditamentes and premisses to be and Remayne to the Right heires of me the said John Robinson for ever: Item I give unto my said sonne Francis Robinson and his Assignes: All the estate, terme and interest which I have of in and to a Certeyne Barne in Stockport, Comonlie Called Horderne Barne, and of in and to the landes and groundes thereunto belonginge, which said Barne and groundes I hould by Lease from George Elcocke, for a Certeyne terme yett to Come, as by the said Lease doth and may appeare. Item I give and bequeath to everie one to whome I am grandefather unto an Ewe sheepe, and to everie one, to whome I am Godfather unto the summe of Twelve pence in money and I will that theise last Legacies shalbe taken out of my whole goodes before anye Division be made thereof. Item my will and mynd is, That if the said Robert Hardman and his wyfe doe not Recover the money so given by the said James Taylier (as aforesaid) That then my Executor hereafter named shall give and pay to the Children of Robert Vaudrey of Sale, my brotherin Lawe deceased, the some of Fyve poundes to be equallie devyded amongst them (if the said Third parte of my goodes called the Testators parte will amounte and extend thereunto).

Executor: testator's eldest son Francis Robinson. H. and S.

Debtes due to the Testator without specialtie. [First Column]	£	s	d
William Bennet for one Cowe hire for 3 yeares 2 past at Anuntiation nexte		30	0
William Higginson of Lyndall for one Cowe hyre at Martlemas nexte		20	0
Franncis Shrigley for halfe hoope of wheate		2	8
Mr. Boswell for wooll 21s whereof I received of his wyfe Foure shillinges		17	0
For 20 stone of hey		5	0
Margerie Warren for one hoope of wheate and one halfe hoope .		12	0
Laurence Bradley of Poynton for 3 stone of Hempe . . .		11	0

Robert Daniell of the Shawe heathe for 2 stone of Hempe and 2 lbs of Flaxe	9	1
Robert Radcliffe of Combstall for 1 stone of Hempe	4	0
William Squyre for the rest of a reckoninge	18	9
John Pristnall of Widford for 2 stone of hempe and one stone of Flaxe	15	0
Ales Dixson and James Lamkin alias Dixson for one stone of hempe	4	0
The same James Lent money	5	0
Edward Hudson of the Hilgate for 4 stone of Hempe and halfe a stone of Flaxe	19	1
Grace Benetson for 2 stone of hempe	8	0
Thomas Bancrofte of Deane Rowe for 2 stone of Hempe	8	10
Laurence Ryle and John Bradley for one stone of Hempe	4	0
Thomas Lingard of Macclesfeild	4	0
Raph Hulme and Thomas Hulme for 2 stone of Hempe	8	0
John Etchilles for one stone of hempe for Thomas Etchilles of Wilmeslowe	4	0
John Wakefeild for one stone of Flaxe	7	0
Robert Rydinges for halfe a stone of Flaxe	3	4
Laurence Wood and Henrie his sonne for one stone of Hempe	4	0
Thomas Osbaston of Adlington for one stone of Hempe	3	8
John Swindells of Lyme 4 lbs of Flax	2	0
Hugh Stanley for a rest of Flax	13	6
Mr. James Kelsall for a rest of Flaxe received by his wyfe	36	4
Ellen Burges for 4 lbs of Flaxe for William Burges	2	2
John Burges for halfe a stone of Flaxe for Robte Janney of Rungey	3	11
Robert Barlowe in his handes upon a leavie agaynst Jenkin Hudson	5	11½
the Testator paid to Hugh Ouldfeild and Robert Burges the summe of 10s 5d apeece upon Condition that they shold attach Richard Burges of the Houghe and if they should not attach him they should repaye backe agayne either of them Fyve shillinges		
Lent to Gyles Asmall of Shawheath	1	0
to John Shaw for a payre of shoes	2	6
James Hunt for 200 and halfe of Iron	40	0
Alexander Mosse butcher of ould debte whereof I forgive him 20s	3 0	0
more of Lent money	20	0
more for halfe a hyde	6	8
more for a Cade hogg	6	0
Robert Hough for a Remayner of Sixe sheepe	22	6
Mr. Alexander Hollinworth for one hoope and halfe of wheate		

12s and 1 hoope of Barley 6s 18 0
William Bridge, for 1 hoope of Barley 6 0

                 Sum 23 13 11½

Debtes due to the Testator without specialtie [Second Column]

John Hudson of the watersyde, oweth for barley but how much I refer to himselfe			
Thomas Rodes of Werneth for 2 hoopes of Barley		12	0
Robert Siddall for two Cow hyres loose at May day nexte		20	0
William Brentnough for 3 hoopes of Barley		18	0
Mr. Laurence Wright which I lent him about 4 yeares since and sent it him by his man John Wharmby	5	0	0
William Hardey of Sale for [*interlined*: a] Cow hyre		9	0
John Barlowe Junior for one Cowe, loose in Januarie come 2 yeares, after 10s a yeare			
John Barlow for an other Cowe loose at the Annuntiation nexte for 3 yeares		25	0
William Bretchgirdle for 2 kyne 3 yeares whereof one is past and the end is at Candlemas	3	0	0
Thomas Worthington for 2 kyne at Martynmas next		40	0
an ould Reckoninge, which he hath broken me promise for		7	0
Edmund Peeres for one Cow he sent me home		20	0
for another Cowe which he still keepes lose at Martinmas next		20	0
Thomas Burges 1 Cowe hyre 3 yeares		21	0
William Brentnough for lent money at yeares end		22	0
Paul Nicholson for hyre of one Cowe at Martlemas nexte		7	0
Roger Lee for hyre for one Cowe for 3 yeares 2 yeares to Come at the Anuntiation next		20	0
Robert Lee de Ladibridge for 3 yeares hyre of one Cowe, lose at the Anuntiation and due everie yeares end		30	0
Robert Downes and Richard Hurst his suretie for 1 Cowe for two yeares past		20	0
Richard Hurst for one Cowe, at May day nexte		8	0
John Hampson for One Cowe at our Ladie day		10	0
Laurence Seele for one Cowe at our Ladie day nexte		10	0
William Henshawe for Rent of Cowsells wyfes house at our Ladie day cominge		13	4
Humfrey Kirke, for one Cowe hyre at Anuntiacion		10	0
John Pycrofte for one Cowe hyre		10	0
John Browne for a heyffer 3 yeares loose at May day come two yeares 8s per Annum		24	0
William Patricke, a heyffer for 3 yeares 2 yeares past at our Ladie day nexte		30	0

lent to Olliver Dodge for to lose a horse that was pledged to

Hugh Ashton	30	0	
Richard Smith for 2 quarter of Coles since he dwelled at Nangreave	4	4	
more to the same Richard Smith for Barley at severall tymes by a hoope and a halfe hoope at a tyme and never paid penye as much as comes to	24	0	
Laurence Seele for Straw		12	
lent to Edmund Hulme	10	0	
more to the same Edmund Hulme for an execusion for William Jannye that he undertooke to paye	8	4	
Thomas Bordman for 1 stone and halfe of Flax and 6s 8d of Lent money	18	5	
Raph Jackson for a rest of flax	5	0	
Elnor Alcocke of Fulshaw widowe, for a Cowe hyre and 2s left unpaid of another yeare	12	0	
Elizabeth Matley for 2 lbs of Flaxe		13	
Raph Johnson, a rest of 2 stone of hempe	5	5	
Bartholomewe Wharmbie, for a rest of Reckoninge	6	8	
Hugh Burges, a rest for his daughter Ellen	12	8	
Richard Coppocke for 1 stone of hempe for Elizabeth Wood	4	4	
Thomas Robinson for 2 stone of hempe, rest of reckoninge	9	2	
Alexander Rocrofte of Styall for rest of a Reckoninge		20	
Reynold Foden for 1 stone of hempe	3	6	
Robert Pownall of Bromhall for one stone of hempe	4	2	
more for one Cowe hire 3 yeares	24	0	
Laurence Hall of Poynton for one stone of Hempe	3	9	
Thomas Fynney for 1 stone of hempe for Raphe Hollinworth	5	8	
Henrie Massie of Hale for 2 stone of hempe	8	0	
William Orred of Poynton for 1 stone of hempe	3	8	
Sum	38	13	2

Debtes due to the Testatour without specialtie [Third Column]

John Bowker the rest of a reckoninge		2	2
John Yonge of Kettleshulme for 5 stone of hempe		18	0
Thomas Williamson for 1 stone of hempe for Katherin Bradley		3	8
Raph Cheetham of Woodley for 2 stone of Hempe		7	0
Uxor John Gibbon left unpaid at our last reckoninge			12
Edward Smallwood of Gamesworth for hempe	3	0	16
Edward Coughen of Woodford for 3 stone of hempe		11	0
Nicholas Higgenbotham of Disley for one stone of hempe		3	6
Raph Toft of Cloudwood for 4 stone of hempe		13	4
Raph Bradley for 1 stone of hempe for uxor John Wood		3	6
Robert Rowbothome of the hake for 4 stone of hempe		13	4
Ellen Smith for a stone of hempe and a rest of a Reckoninge		4	3

John Coughen for one stone of hempe 4 0
James WolsenCrofte for 3 stone of hempe 11 0
George Hooley for 1 stone of hempe 3 6
John Greene for 1 stone of hempe 4 0
Christopher Fowler for 2 stone of hempe 7 4
Marie Wood a rest for hempe 2 0
Sibell Allen for one stone of hempe 3 8
William Thornecroft of Rhodes for 14 stone of hempe . . 53 8
Reynold Meykin for 2 stone of hempe 7 0
John Redich for 2 loades of hey 15s whereof he stopped for grasse for the Cubler 9s 4d 5 8
Mr. Alexander Elcocke, oweth upon a reckoninge 50 0
he oweth for 28 loades of dunge, which was not reckoned .
Mr. Richard Lee of Baguley 16 6
Thomas Elcocke for flax 4 stone and 8 lbs and 7s of a reckoninge . 41 8
spent in a Jorney to London, agaynst my Ladie Chomley which Mr. George Honford promised to repaye 3 7 10
more to Phillip Downes at Chester Assizes 10 0
more received by John Wither 20 0
lent to John Dickinson of London sonne of Elizabeth Vadrey the some of 5 0 0
Edward Williamson alias Deane for a syeth 3 0
John Brooke of Cheadle for a syeth 3 0
Edward Thorneley for 4 sythes for his maister Sr Peter Leigh . 12 0
Mr. James Kelsall for 2 sythes 6 0
John Spouner and Thomas Harrop last unpayd of a Reckoninge . 3 0

Sum 28 17 11
[*recte* 28 16 11]

Sealed signed and published as the last will and Testament of the above named John Robinson in the presence of us.
George Parker Raph Ouldham James Burdsell William Hartley
somma totalis horum debitor 91 5 0½ [*recte* 91 4 0½]

Inventory: John Robinson of Stockport, yeoman. Taken: 28 April 1617.
Of: goods and chattels. The inventory comprised three pages of goods, and two pages of debts owed to the deceased. The second page of debts was added as an afterthought, and was not totalled. The prisers supplied totals for each page of the inventory, except the last.

Prisers: Anthonie Nicholson, William Torkinton, Raph Ouldham, James Burdsell and Richard Brooke.

	£	s	d
in readie money	5	14	2
his apparell	5	0	18
11 yardes of wollen Cloth or thereaboutes		22	6
2 Tables and 6 Buffett Stooles in the Hall		20	0
One Cupbord in the Hall		12	0
4 Chayres in the Hall		2	6
3 loose bordes in the hall and 2 litle Stooles			18
Bordes and Shilves in the Buttrie		2	6
one Round table and a Bord in the Chamber above . . .			18
one standinge Bed in the same Chamber		20	0
one Truckle bedstead in the same Chamber		5	0
one great Chest, one litle one and one ould Arke . . .		12	4
one Fetherbed, one Boulster, one pillowe, one Coverlett 3 Blankettes and one Mattresse		46	8
one other Fetherbed 2 boulsters 1 pillowe 1 Coverlett and a Blankett upon the Trucklebed		28	4
in Napperie Ware		35	6
one Bed in another Chamber		20	4
one Standinge bed and a Trucklebed in the Chamber or Parlour above in the house		25	0
more beddinge belonginge to the same Parlour upon the Trucklebed		20	6
7 yardes of Wollen Cloth made of Lambes Wooll . . .		11	6
the Beddinge in the litle Parlour beneath in the house . .		26	8
one Bedstead and beddinge in an outhouse		10	4
one great Coffer and 3 base bordes in the Shoppe . . .		10	0
Ballances and waightes		7	6
in Pewter 43 lb waight		33	4
one dripinge pan		3	4
in Brasse		40	10
in earthen pottes and Treene Ware		6	8
in wooll and sheepe skines		18	0
in Beeffe and Bacon		54	0
one Fatt Swyne		30	0
malte and the Arke		7	0
in Iron ware at the house		8	0
2 hoopes and 3 peckes of French wheate and barlie . . .		6	0
12 hoopes of Barley		52	0
3 Bushells of windowed otes		44	0
8 Silver Spoones of the better sort		53	4
broken Silver Spoones		20	0
Mucke and Meanor		3	0
in hay		4	0
2 peeces of Timber		10	0

110   Stockport Probate Records

in Barlie		17	0
2 Acres of hay grasse		50	0
a Turkie Cocke		2	0

[End of Page 1] Sum Page 51   0   4
[*recte* 50 18 4]

[Page 2]

Sixe Stirckes	8	2	0
67 Sheepe	21	0	0
8 litle drawen oxen	21	0	0
3 plowes with the plowe Irons and one ould Slead		10	6
One yonge sorrell Geldinge	5	6	8
One ould Geldinge		20	0
One yonge Colte		46	8
10 Kyne and 4 Calves in his owne keepinge	33	6	8
One payre of shod wheeles and 2 old Cole waynes		46	8
Some odd Sclate		2	0
One Tumbrell with the wheeles		5	0
7 yokes 2 payre of Clevesses and 3 Teames		21	0
One Bucklinge Teame		2	0
12 other yonge beastes in his owne keepinge	22	5	0
one double Harrowe and Three ould single harrowes		13	4
4 axes 2 billes 2 mattockes 2 Shovelles and one spade		6	8
2 Iron wedges 2 axletree pinnes 2 Spokeshaves one payre of pinsers and a hammer		3	0
One hand Sawe			4
4 Ould Sythes			16
2 Ould Muckehookes			6
2 Culters a litle old share and a broken Forke		2	6
2 Longettes with a Teather			6
3 payre of ould weedinge tonges			4
2 ould Hackney sadles and a brydle		5	6
2 old broken pichforkes			6
a litle ould Iron with an old Arke			8
old broken wheeles, an old broken wayne other old wood with some wheele timber		16	0
a packsadle and a Carte sadle		5	0
Certeyne sawne bordes		6	0
Certeyne old wood lyinge in the Feild syde		4	0
an Hopper wiskett			3
a fewe speakes and 2 shelbreades		2	0
in wheate and Rye	16	0	0
a Cabb of Otes	8	13	4
3 hoopes of Barlie		13	0
2 wiskettes 2 sives and 2 axletrees			18

5 more axletrees		2	6
in Hey		6	0
One load of Stone			12
in donge and Meanor at the newe barne		30	0
in Timber at the Crosse lache		50	0
7 Capons and 5 hennes		9	6
4 geese		4	0
One bay of barley and some more and that is in the Chaffe ricke at Horderon barne	20	10	0
in hay		5	0
a sheepes skinne and a forke			22
in hey and mucke in Adswood		20	0
in mucke and Meanor		2	6
in mucke at the head of the hillgate		7	6
Sum Page 174 18 9			

[Page 3]

in Otes in the hilgate barne		7	10	0
in hay			20	0
Ladder and a bad sheepes skinne				8
Mucke and Meanor			2	0
Tymber in the paddocke Karre			40	0
One Other wayne and a payre of shod wheeles with an old Cartrope			43	4
Bull hyde			10	0
Stirke skyne			3	0
2 Calves skinnes			2	0
One Cowe Hyde			9	0
2 Kyne in the Custodie of William Bretchgirdle the one prised to		3	3	4
the other to			36	8
One in the handes of William Cash of Styall		3	0	0
One Cowe in the handes of Thomas Burges of Styall			36	8
One Cowe in the handes of Edmund Peares of Deane Rowe			40	0
2 kyne in the handes of Thomas Worthington of Morley Steyre		5	6	8
One Cowe in the Handes of William Bennett of Hanford			56	8
one Cowe in the Handes of William Higginson of Fulshawe			50	0
One Cowe in the Handes of Robert Downes of Etchills			53	4
One Cowe in the handes of Robert Leigh of Adswood			46	8
One Cowe in the handes of Laurence Seele		3	0	0
One Cowe in the hands of John Browne of More Syde			46	8
2 kyne in the Handes of William Cheadle of Edgley		5	13	4
2 kyne in the Handes of Robert Siddall of Fallowfeild		6	13	4
One Cowe in the handes of John Picrofte of Stockport			46	8
2 kine in the handes of Roger Lee of the Right Banck		4	13	4
William Hyde als Patricke hath one Cowe in his hands			53	4
One Cowe in the keepinge of John Hamson of the Hilgate			53	4

John Barlowe of Ashton upon Mersey Bancke and his Sonne,
have either of them twoe kyne in their keepinge . . . 10 13 4
kyne in the keepinge of Alexander Collier 5 3 4
One Cowe in the keepinge of Paul Nicholson of Redich . . 3 0 0

By leases
One lease from William Bridge 37 0 0
One lease from Rabert Leigh 10 0 0
One lease from Mr Robert Tatton 34 0
from George Milnes Certeyn leases in Revertion . . . 54 0 0

Corne sowne at Georg Milnes 45 0
Corne sowne at Robert Lees 34 6
Corne sowen upon the land, in Adswood 40 0
                      Sum Page 199 2

[Page 4]
Debts Owinge to the Testator appearinge to be due by bound
by Mr William Davenport of the Myles end 100 0 0
by Otes Bordman 44 0
by Reginald Ryle 11 0 0
by Thomas Lynney 43 0
by George Parker gent 30 0
by Robert Gilliver 5 10 0
by John Gibbon 8 16 0
by James Coppocke 5 10 0
by Roger Brundreth 43 0
by James Rowson 4 7 0
by Robert Collier . . . . 12[?] 2 0¹
by Richard Fawkner . . . . 5 [?] 0
by Robert Collier 4 10 0
by Roger Lees . . . . [?] [?] 0
by Robert Lee . . . . 4 [?] 0
by William Brentnall . . . . 3 [?] 0
by Raph Ouldham 4 2 0
by Thomas Blackshaw . . . . 5 [?] 0
by John Jackson 5 10 0
by Francis Bretland . . . . 10 [?] 0
by Richard Cockson . . . . 3[?] 0 0
by James Heald . . . . 5 [?] 6
by William Ashton 3 0 0
by William Cash . . . . [?]
by John Dickinson . . . . [?]
by John Barlowe . . . . [?] 18[?] 0
William Bridge . . . . [?]

	£	s	d
by George Chadwicke	10	4	0
by Alexander Collier	7	10	0
by Alexander Collier	3	2	0
by Alexander Knott	4	8	0
by Alexander Knott	3	6	0
by Brian Cleyton		22	0
by Elizabeth Stanfeild		36	10
by William Stanfeild		32	0
by William Cheadle	3	0	0
by William Cheadle	10	0	0
by the same William Cheadle by 2 notes under his hand		53	0
William Warren gent.	6	10	0
by Edmund Peereson		22	0
by Edmund Peerson		23	0
by John Henshall	3	6	0
by William Hall		35	3
by James Wolsencroft		33	4
more by the same James Wolsencroft		33	4

Debtes Owinge to the Testator appearinge to be due by Bill

	£	s	d
by John Torkinton	6	12	0
by Alexander Bibbie		24	0
by John Richardson	3	6	0
by Randul Baylis		10	3
by Raph Clayton		22	0
by William Wilkinson		33	0
by Richard Hankenson		44	0
by Randull Ridgway		22	0
by Raph Newton	4	18	0
by Thomas Blomiley		22	0
by John Bennetson		22	0
by John Henshall		22	0
by Edward Higham		22	0
by Thomas Burges	7	6	0
by Laurence Latham	3	0	0
by John Warren	3	6	0
by Paule Nicholson	6	9	0
by Robert Arstall		44	0
by John Hollingworth		12	0
by James Renshaw		35	0
John Williamson		30	0
George Charlton	3	0	0

Sum Page 386. 7. 6.

The totall Some of this Parte [?] Inventary is   811   6   8

114 *Stockport Probate Records*

One Caliver and a head peece and furniture hereto belonginge   8   0

[Page 5]
More appearinge to be due to the Testatour by Bill

by Arnold Ryle	4	8	0
by John Cashe	3	12	11
by Henrie Coppocke	3	6	0
by Raphe Walker		44	0
by Robert Radcliffe		[illegible]	
by Henrie Goodyeare		[illegible]	
by William Harrison		11	0
by Thomas Bancrofte		11	0
by Edward Brooke		14	0
by Thomas Nicholson	5	12	0
by John Kelsal	3	6	0
by Alexander Kempe		44	0
by Hugh Greene		44	0
by Laurence Wood		4	0
by John Ryle		45	0
by Laurence Bradley		11	0
by Raph Ouldham as appeareth by a note	11	0	0
by William Nicholson		40	0
by Hugh Haye		46	8
more by Hugh Hay	3	6	0
by Edward Browne	4	2	6
more by Edward Browne		18	0
by Edward Mottershed		22	0
more by Edward Mottershed	3	0	0
by Richard Burges		22	8
more by Richard Burges	13	0	0
by John Sinderland		40	0
by Jeffrey Alcocke		52	4
by Hugh Clarke		23	4
by George Hollinworth		52	2
by William Higham		4	6
by Raph Downes and his Sureties	3	0	0

1. This and the next sixteen entries, down to and including William Bridge, are illegible.

Office endorsement: probate to deceased's son Francis Robinson, sole executor.

59. EDWARD BENNISON OF STOCKPORT, TAILOR.

S.Pr. 29 October 1617.
Inventory of: goods chattels and debts. Taken: 21 October 1617.
Prisers: George Newton, John Fallowes, William Mottram and John Hopwoode.

	£	s	d
his wearinge apparell	5	7	0
in Catle	9	0	0
one Swyne		15	0
in Sheepe	4	0	0
one Silver Spoone		6	0
in Barlie	2	6	0
in oates		48	0
in hey		30	0
in hempe and Flax		2	0
in fuell		5	0
in timber		5	0
in ladders		4	0
in geese and other pulleyn		7	0
for a lease of two severall peices of ground for one yeare	6	0	0
in the house a Cupbord a dishbourd Formes twoe chaires with other thinges		40	0
a great arke		13	4
six coffers and other arkes		40	0
in wooll		32	0
in woollen yarne and broken wooll		13	0
in beddinge and bedstocks	4	0	0
one Tornell with other implements of houshold stuffe		6	0
in pann brasse		13	4
in pott brasse		11	0
for one leade		4	4
in pewter		8	0
in earthen potts			12
in Iron ware		10	0
for twoe paire of cardes and one crate			18
in wooden ware		10	0
in Cheese and bacon		5	0
in lynnen		31	0
Sum	43	0	2
[recte	48	14	6]

Debtes owing to the Testator
by Raphe Ouldham 44 0 0

116   Stockport Probate Records

by Mr. Richard Warren		5	0	0
by William Sydebothom		3	0	0
in new lynnen cloth			4	0
	Sum	52	4	0

Sum	95	4	2
[*recte* 100	18	6]

Office endorsement gives: Edward Benetson of 'Stockport Moreside'. Probate to executors.

60. JANE ROBINSON OF STOCKPORT, WIDOW.   S.Pr. 26 October 1618.
Will, sick.   W.T. 4 June 1618.

Knowinge that nothinge is more certen then death, nor any thinge more uncerten then the howre thereofe, doe therefore make and ordeyne this my last will and Testament in manner and forme followinge, that is to saie First and principallye I commend my soule into the handes of Almightie god my maker and Creator, to Jesus Christ my saviour and Redeemer, and to the holy ghost my sanctifier, beseeching the holy, blessed and glorious Trinitie to have mercie upon my soule, and my bodie to be buried in the parish Church or Churchyord of Stockporte, at the discretion of my Executors hereafter named Item my will and mynd is, that all such debtes as of right I owe to any person or persons whatsoever, shalbe paid and dischardged out of my whole goodes and Chattells without any delaie, and alsoe my funerall Charges likewise to be paid out of the same Item I give and bequeath unto Franncis Robinson my eldest sonne, Fourtie shillinges of lawfull English money, as a Remembrannce of my love and motherly affecction towards him Item I give and bequeath unto Alexander Robinson my second sonne, the summe of Tenn poundes of like lawfull English money, in like remembrannce of my motherlie love and affecction towardes him Item I give and bequeath unto Richard Robinson my youngest sonne, the some of like lawfull English money, in like remembrannce of my motherlie love and affecction towardes him, And likewise I give unto my said sonne Richard Robinson, one standinge bedsteed and the great chest without a locke standinge in the Chamber where Nicholas Elcocke and his wyefe doe nowe lye and alsoe one fetherbed two blancketts one boulster, one pillowe and my best Coverlett Item I give and bequeath unto my daughter Jane Mills widowe, the great bedstidd in the parlour wherein I nowe lye, and all the beddinge and furniture thereunto belonginge, And I likewise give unto the said Jane my pyde Cowe, one pan, Eighteene poundes of Lynnen yerne which I have nowe in my howse and one great Chest in the parlour next the shopp Item I give and bequeath to my sonne in lawe Raphe Kenion of Newton Fortie shillinges of lawfull english money, and to my daughter Margerie his wyefe, one bedsteed standinge in the great Chamber, one fetherbed, one blanckett, one boulster and one Coverlett Item I give and bequeath to John Kenion and Elizabeth Kenion, the Children of the said Raphe and Margerie Kenion the summe of Twentie poundes to be equally devyded betweene them, that is to say tenn poundes apeice, Item my will intent and mynd is that Margerie Hardman my sister, shall have use possesse and enioy, one Chaffe bed, one boulster, one Blanckett and one Coverlett wherein and whereupon shee usually lyeth, duringe her liefe, And that after her decease the same shalbe and Remayne to the use of Isabell grantham my sister the wyefe of John Grantham, and to the use of the Children of the said Isabell after her decease Item my will is that my Executors hereafter named, shall at their discretions give unto the said Margerie Hardman the summe of Twentie shillings of lawfull English money, for and towardes her releife, at such times and in such manner as shalbe thought fitt by my Executors. Item I doe give and bequeath unto Isabell Grantham my said sister my blacke morninge gowne, a blacke petticoate and my hatt lyned with velvet Item I give and bequeath unto Willm Grantham, George Grantham, Raphe Grantham, James Grantham and Ales Grantham Children of the said Isabell my sister and John Grantham her husband, the some of Thirtie shillinges of good and lawfull money of England to bee equally devyded amongst them Item I give and bequeath unto my god daughter and grandchild Margarett Robinson daughter of my said sonne Frannces Robinson, the some of tenn poundes and my Browne Cowe, and to everie other child of the said Frances, nowe livinge, I give and bequeath to each of them Fortie shillinges Item I give and bequeath to my god daughter and grandchild Marie Robinson daughter of my said sonne Alexander Robinson the some of Tenn poundes of lawfull English money, and to everie other Child of the said Alexander nowe livinge I give and bequeath to each of them Fortie shillinges in money Item I give and bequeath to such Child, as the wyefe of my sonne Richard Robinson is nowe with Child withall whether it be sonne or daughter (if it fortune to live one Yeare after my decease) the some of Fyve poundes, or in default thereof to the mother of the same Child after the decease thereof Item I give and bequeath unto my grandchild Marie Mills the some of Tenn poundes of lawfull English money Item I give and bequeath unto my grandchild Robert Mills the some of Fourtie shillinges and to Anne Mills his sister the some of Fyve poundes Item I give and bequeathe to my daughters in lawe, Anne Robinson, Marie Robinson and Margerie Robinson, and unto everie one of them twentie shillinges a peice Item I give and bequeath unto my god sonne John Robinson Alehowsekeeper the some of two shillinges, and to everie one of his brothers and sisters sonnes and daughters of Ambrose Robinson deceased to each of them twelve pence a peice, and to Henry Dickenson sonne of Henry Dickenson smith 12d Item I give and bequeath to John Cottrell the sonne of Robert Cotterell of Stockport aforesaid twelve pence Item I give and bequeath to each of the Children of George Elcocke of Stockport twelve pence a peice, and to Martha Robinson the daughter of John Robinson of Brinington twelve pence Item I give unto my sonne Franncis Robinson, All my oates nowe growinge or lately sowed in Adswood (for his Costes and paynes in soweinge thereof) Item I give and bequeath unto my daughters, Jane Mills and Margerie Kenion all my wheate and other Corne nowe growinge in the hilgate feild, horderne and in the parke Item I give and bequeath unto Theophilus, Willm, Ales, and Anne sonns and daughters of Anthony Nicholson of Reddich in the Countie of Lancaster yoman the some of Fourtie shillings to be equally devyded amongst them Item I give and bequeath unto Thomas and John sonns of James Beurdsell of Stockport aforesaid yoman the some of Twentie shillinges to be equally devyded betweene them, And if any of the infants before mencioned, shall fortune to dye before they or any of them accomplish the full age of one and twentie yeares or be maried, then my will mynd and intent is, that his her or their porcon soe dyinge shalbe equally devyded amongst his her or their brothers and sisters, which shall survive, anythinge herein conteyned to the contrarie thereof in anywise notwithstandinge Item my will is that the parentes of the infants before named shall have the government of their severall childrens Legacies before by theise presentes to them given, untill the accomplish the severall ages of Twentie and one Yeares or be married which shall first happen Item I give and bequeath unto Sara Elcocke and Margarett Dale to either of them three shillinges foure pence Item I give and bequeath unto Franncis Robinson and Anne his wyefe, two of my best silver spoones, To Alexander Robinson my sonne and Marie his wyeffe other two of my best silver spoones, to my sonne Richard Robinson and Margerie his wyefe, other two of my best silver spoones Item I give and bequeath to my daughter Jane Mills, two of the best of the courser and worser sorte of silver spoones, and to Raphe Kenion and Margerie his wyefe the other foure, And to the said Margerie I give and bequeath my best hatt Item I give and bequeath unto my sister Margerie Hardman, my ould redd pett coate, And all the rest and residue of my [cloths] as woollen and Lynnen I give and bequeath unto the said Jane Mills my daughter Item I give and bequeath unto my said daughter Jane Mills three poundes, and to my daughter Margerie Kenion the some of Fourtie shillinges Item I give and bequeath unto my grandchild Anne Mills the great Cupboard in the howse Item I give and bequeath unto my said daughter Jane Mills, one Moytie or halfe parte of all my howsehould stuffe before by this my last will and Testament not given or bequeathed Item the other Moytie or halfe parte beinge all the rest or residue of my howsehould stuffe not formerlie bequeathed, I give and bequeath unto the said Richard Robinson my sonne and the said Margerie Kenion my daughter, to be equally devyded betweene them Item all the rest and residue of my goods, Cattells and Chattells whatsoever, not formerlie given or bequeathed, my debtes and funerall charges beinge paid and dischardged, I give and bequeath unto my said Children Franncis Robinson, Alexander Robinson, Richard Robinson, Margerie Kenion and Jane Mills to be equally devyded amongst them Provided alwaies and it is my will and mynd, that yf any of my Executors hereafter named or any other person or persons whatsoever, unto whom I have given or bequeathed any thinge in or by this my last will and Testament, shall at any tyme or tymes hereafter from and after my decease, attempt, doe, Comitt, or cause or suffer to be attempted, done, or Comitted any Acte or acts, thinge or thinges, devyse or devyses whatsoever by suites in lawe, or otherwise howsoever with a purpose or intent, to gett obteyne or recover any parte or parcell of my goodes or Cattells or Chattells more then is ment or intended to be given or bequeathed, in and accordinge to the true meaninge of this my said last will and testament, unto him, her or them soe attemptinge comittinge or doinge the same, Then such person or persons, that soe shall attempt, doe or Comitt any such Acte or Acts, thinge or thinges in manner and forme as aforesaid shall not have receave, perceave or take any benefitt proffitt advantage or comoditie whatsoever, by force vertue or meanes of this my last will and Testament, of any Legacie therein given or bequeathed, any guifte, Legacie or bequest herein conteyned to the contrarie thereof in anywise notwithstandinge.

Executors: the said Franncis Robinson, Alexander Robinson, Richard Robinson and Raphe Kenion.
Overseers: Robert Cottrell of Stockport, vintner, Samuell Siddall of Stockport, woollen draper, James Buerdsell of Stockport, yeoman and Nicholas Elcocke of Stockport woollen draper. H.& S.
[No witnesses.]

And it is further my will and mynd, that my Executors shall give unto the poore people of the Towne of Stockport, at my funerall, the some of Three poundes sixe shillinges eight pence to be distributed amongst them at the discretion of my Executors a fore named.

Inventory: Jane Robinson of Stockport, widow. Taken: 8 October 1618.
Of: goods and chattels.
Prisers: George Siddall, Willm Warburton, Thomas Newton, John Robinson and George Whittikers.

	£	s	d
two loades of Haye		26	8
Two Kyne	6	0	0
one hogge		16	0
Coales		12	0
fyre Wood		4	0
one greate Malt Arke		4	0
Barlie unthrashed		46	8
Wheate unthrashed		20	0
14 pewter dishes and other Pewter		20	0
4 brasse potts, one posnett, one pann and two brasse Candle-sticks		26	8

Iron Ware		6	8
one Cupboard		13	4
Three tables in the howse		20	0
sixe buffett stooles and other stooles and Chayres		13	4
Treene ware		5	0
Earthen ware		2	0
Two great Chestes		24	0
Three little Chestes		10	0
One dozen of silver spoones	3	0	0
seventeene Yardes of new Lynnen Clothe		14	2
sixe payre of sheetes and one odd one		32	0
for boardclothes Napkins and other Lynnens		10	0
all her apparell Lynnens and Woollen	4	0	0
one standinge bed, and furniture uppon it in the greate Chamber above	3	10	0
one standinge bed and furniture upon it in the oate Chamber [sic]		53	4
one Coverlett, a chaffe bed and a boulster, and one blanckett		13	4
one standinge bed, and all the furniture upon it in the parlor belowe	4	0	0
one Truccle bed and it furniture		15	0
other lowe bed and it furniture		15	0
one Lanthorne			6
fower ould quishions			16
the Compost and dunge aboute the howse		12	0
Shelves and odd boardes		3	4
all odd implements			12
for certen Irish yorne		22	3
Sum	43	13	7

Debts due to the decedent

Franncis Robinson by specialtie	100	0	0
more the same Franncis, without specialtie	20	0	0
Richard Robinson, by a bill or Memorandum	20	0	0
Raphe Kenion, by a bill or Memorandum	20	0	0
Sum	160	0	0
Sum	203	13	7

Renunciation of Executorship. Dated: 11 September 1618.

Alexander Robinson of Adswood, yeoman, one of the sons of the deceased, and appointed as one of her executors, renounces his executorship, saving to himself and his wife and children all legacies etc. Signed: Alexander Robinson.

Witnesses: Rafe Kanyan, William Warburton and William Hartley [all signed].
Office endorsement: probate granted to Richard Robinson and Robert Kenion, two of the executors nominated, with reservation for Francis Robinson, also nominated.

61. MARY ARDERNE OF STOCKPORT, WIDOW. S.Pr. [year only given] 1619.
Will, sick. Document endorsed as a copy made by Jo. Bickerton, notary public.
W.T. 21 March 1618/19.

First and principally I give and bequeath my soule unto almightie god my maker and Creator And unto Jesus Christe my saviour and Redeemer through whose bitter Death and passion I trust to inheratt the kingdome of heaven Item I give and bequeath my bodie to be buried in the parishe Church of Stockport Item for my worldly goods and Chattells my will is that they shalbe disposed of in such manner and forme as is hereafter lymitted and appointed that is to saie; First I give and bequeath unto my sonne John Arderne the somme of fourtie pounds of lawful Englishe money Item I give and bequeath unto my sonne Robert Arderne fortie pounds more in money Item I give and bequeath unto my sonne Raphe Twentie poundes more in money Item my will is that my Executors hereafter named shall keepe and deteyne Twentie poundes more out of my whole estate in their hands to ymploye yt to the best benefitt they maye or Cann and the same to dispose of to and for the reliefe of my said sonne Raphe att the discrecion of them my said Executors hereunder named Item I give and bequeath unto my ‹nephew› neice Mary Arderne the Daughter of Henry Arderne of Hawarden in the said Countie of Chester Esquire the somme of Fortie pounds more in money to be ymployed for her best advantage at the disrecion of my Executors hereunder named untill she shall accomplishe the age of one and Twentie yeares or be Married [erasure] which shall first happen Item I give and bequeath unto my sonne Henrie Arderne Esquire all such househould stuffe as remayneth at Hawarden and are particulerly expressed in one note hereinclosed and also all my husbandrie wares at Bredburie Hall Item I give and bequeath unto Mary Holland the Daughter of my brother Edward Holland Esquire five pounds in money Item I give and bequeath unto Marie Millington my neice five pounds more in money Item I give and bequeath unto John Arderne my granchilde the sonne of my sonne Robert Arderne one Cowe which is in the hands of the said Robert and all such increase of the same Cowe as in right shall belonge to me at my decease Item I give and bequeath unto Alice Arderne the daughter of my said sonne Raphe Arderne the somme of Tenne pounds in money to be ymployed for her best advantage at the discrecion of my said Executors untill she shall accomplishe the full age of one and Twentie Yeares or be married which shall first happen Item my will is that in Case my sister Leckonbie survive me Then shee shall have my taffetie Cloake Item I give and bequeath unto my Daughter Marburie one little guilt boule and my best gown with my best Kirtle and my best petticoate Item I give and bequeath unto Mr Storer the preacher 20s in money Item I give and bequeath unto the poore people of the towne of Stockport Fortie shillings to be distributed amongst them at the Discrecion of my Executors Item my will is that my Executors shall not disburse more then Twentie pounds in my funerall Charges Item I give and bequeath unto every one of my Executors hereunder named a peice of gould of 22s for their paines in the executinge of this my said will Item the remainder of all my goodes Chattells and other things not before by this my said last will and testament bequeathed I give and bequeath unto my sonnes John Arderne Robert Arderne Raphe Arderne and to Marie Arderne my Neice before named equally to be devided amongst them Item my will and mynde is that all such somes of money as are hereunder particulerlie mencioned to be taken in my name onely in trust to the use of Certaine persons hereunder numarated shalbe Disposed of to such persons as the same severall somes appear to be Due (accordinge to the trust reposed in mee) any bond or obligacion made in my name to the Contrarie notwithstandinge.

Executors: Edward Holland of Heaton, Lancs, Esquire, Raphe Arderne of Cruckiley, Cheshire, Gent. and William Whittington of Stockport, Gent. H. and S. Testator signs.
Witnesses: William Callier, mk., Alexander Johnes, mk., Raphe Seddon.

A note of Such Debts as are Due to the testator in trust for such as are hereunder named

	£	s	d
Imprimis by John Swindells ‹upon› bond to the use of my neice Marie Arderne and John Arderne my nephewe Children of my sonne Henry Arderne	13	4	0
Item by William Smith of Brinnington by bond to the use of the parties above named	11	0	0
Item by John Gibbons without spetialtie to the use of the parties above named	8	16	0
Item by John Cumberbach to the use of Margarett Arderne Daughter of Henry Arderne Esquire given by Mistress Huland	7	18	0
	per bond		
Item by Thomas Johnson alias Faulkener and others to the use of my sonne Raphe by bond	66	0	0

Debts Due to the Testator

	£	s	d
By John Swindells of Romeley by bond	5	0	0
By Thomas Hill by bond to be paid the 27th of July next	11	0	0
By Richard Brooke without spetialtie	30	0	0
By Mr Davenport of Henburie	14	0	0
	per bond		

Memorandum that the note of goods [erasure] belonginge and In this will mencioned to be given to ‹Mr› Henrye Arderne Esqyr was not affixid to the originall nor therein inclosed as was and is therein mencioned but by the administrator it was affirmed that he never knewe of such [erasure] nor had none [erasure]
  Jo: Bickerton.

Inventory: Marie Arderne, widow, late wife of John Arderne of Hawarden in the county of Chester, esquire. Taken: 10 May 1619.
Of: debts goods and chattels.
Prisers: [names at end] Ambrose Nicholson, Ric. Hudson, Willm. Hibbert and Wm. Booth.

	£	s	d
in readie money	3	10	0
more receaved since her death	15	0	0
‹in plate ounces at the ounce›			
In the dyninge chamber			
one drawinge table and the frame for the same	1	0	0
one cupbord		5	0
two chairs covered with set worke	1	0	0
sixe buffet stooles covered with set worke		18	0
one little stoole covered with set worke		3	0
two buffett stools covered with nield worke		2	0
one throwne chaire		2	0
11 buffett stooles uncovered		12	0
one little lowe stoole uncovered			12
‹one little lowe stoole uncovered›			
a Carpet of set Worke for the cupboard affor said		3	4
five set worke quishions of the better sort		12	0
foure old set worke Cushions of a worser sort		8	0
a paire of tables		4	0
In the kittchen			
Imprimis 7 brasse potts waighinge 5 score 9 pound at 5^d and 8^d the pounde	3	4	11
a boyler		16	0
five brasse pannes 47 lbs	2	6	8
fifteene pewter dishes of severall sorts three sawcers and one pye plate	1	0	0
five broaches		5	0
one drippinge pan		3	4
two chopping knives and one strikinge knife			12
one broilinge plate			6

foure skelletts	5	0
three ladles		18
one fleshe hooke and an iron Candle sticke		4
three wodden lossetts		12
one Rainge or grate one paire of Racks one barre of iron to hange the potts on three irons hanginge upon the same to hange potts at two paire of pot hookes one fire shovell one paire of tongues and one fire potter	26	8
one frieing pan		16
one brasse morter and a pestle	11	8
one knedinge troughe	3	4

More in the kitchen

five flitches of Bacon one of them havinge a great peece cut out	1	14	0
one hanginge brundrett one grid iron and a standing brundrett		2	0
two graters			8
one salt pye			4
one little basting ladle			7
one Iron chafing dishe			4
one hanginge tostinge Iron			2

In the brewhouse

five brewing keeres and one cooler	2	4	0
two Eshens and three piggins one trough for the wort to runne into		7	0

In the buttrie

three pewter flagons		5	0
five pewter candlesticks		3	4
one bason and Ewer		6	0
one pewter voider		3	0
six brasse candlesticks		4	0
two pewter salts			6
one pewter quart and one pynt		2	0
two dosen of trenchers			8
7 woodden Cannes		2	0
11 stone bottles		4	0
greate glasse bottle covered with leather			12
8 barrells and two hogsheads	1	10	0
two Rundletts			6
two Tun dishes			16
two chists		5	0
one old scraping knife			2

In the hall
one longe table upon a frame		6	8
little square table		5	0
two Formes			16
one chest		3	4
2 grates		12	0

In the Wett larder
three beefe tubbes		16	0
one bord to laie beef on			6

In the milke house
8 butter tubbes		1	0
half a dosen kimnels and three basons		3	0

In the little parlor
two feather bedds two bolsters one pillowe five blanketts two coverletts and two wooll beds	7	0	0
one little square table		3	4
one cupbord		13	4
foure curtaines before the windowes		3	0
curtaines and valence for one bed	1	0	0
one seeled paire of bedstocks with a tester	3	6	8
one truckle bed		5	0
one little clocke	1	6	8
two little coffers		5	0
one fyre shovell one paire of tongues			12

In the little chamber at the staire head
one feather bed one boulster one pillowe one Wooll bed three blanketts one Cadowe one Canopie one Cupbord cloth of set worke one paire of bed stocks one chaire covered with cloth one cupbord one screene and a halbert	5	10	0

In the chambers at the staire head
one paire of bedstocks		4	0
Stillatorie		5	0
trunke bound with Iron		13	4
one old trunke		3	4
one sumpter sadle		6	0
five strawe basketts			20
syde Saddle with the furniture for the same and a pillion		[blank]	

In the lower parlor
one malt Arke		6	8

126 Stockport Probate Records

one meale Arke	1	0	0
little Chest		2	0
one great Turmell		4	0
one hacking saddle		6	8
one churne		4	0
one hetchell		3	4
a little table upon a frame		2	0
one paire of bedstocks one feather bed one Wooll bed – two bolsters foure blanketts	2	16	0

In the great Chamber

two feather bedds one Wooll bed one Chaffe bed foure blanketts four pillowes two bed Coverings one Canopie two bolsters	7	0	0
the Curtaines and – Curtaine Rodds before the windowes		6	8
one Chaire one Chist and a round table		12	0

In the Chamber over the old parlor

one paire of bedstocks one feather bed one Wooll bed two bolsters two coverletts and one blankett	2	6	8
two heare seeves		2	0

In the kittchen Chamber

two paire of bedstocks		4	0
two Chaffebeds		4	0
two bolsters		2	0
three blanketts		4	0
two Coverletts		5	0
salt tubbe and a tubbe to make Candles in		2	0

Cattle at Breadburie

two steares of foure yere old	6	10	0
11 stirkes or twinters whereof foure of them are oxe beasts	28	6	8
8 yereings whereof two oxe and six Cow beasts	10	0	0
9 melch kine	17	6	8
Seaven suckinge [erasure] Calves	3	0	0
two kyne at hyre one in Bramhall at Humfrey Birkenshawes and an other at Willm Tailers in Breadburie	6	10	0
one two yere old bull	2	0	0
one boare one sowe and three pigges	2	16	0
one old bay mare and a colt of three yere old	8	0	0
three pullen Capons, twelve hennes and one Cocke foure geese and a gander and 24 goslings foure duckes and one drake ten chickens	1	5	0

At Bredburie

for barley	24	0	0
for wheate and Rye	12	0	0
for oates	20	0	0
for Corne upon the ground	64	0	0
2 basens and ewres		16	0
in pewter	3	4	0
4 Chamber potts		4	0
a payer of bellowes			12
a seller of botles		6	8
2 hanginge Candlesticks		2	0
a brasse morter		2	6
a Chaffeinge Dishe		2	6
an alblaster Morter			18
a Case of trenchers			12
a Wheele		2	6
a payre of wafer tonges		2	0
a backspitle 2 payer of tonges		2	0
a Wolbedd 2 boulsters 3 blanketts a white Cadow		24	0
2 Carpetts		43	4
Curtaines for a Canabie		8	0
a Canabie		20	0
Waighes and Waightes		3	4
a Close Stoole		2	0
a Canabie with Curtaynes and a window		4	10
Cushen	4	10	0
in Linnen Cloth		16	0
a hue Cloake and savegard		10	0
2 Curtaines of linesey Wolsey		10	0
Curtaynes blew and yellowe		10	0
a Coate of tuftaffitie		20	0
greene Carpett		10	0
in honey		4	0
a payer of stokeings		2	0
flackes 9 poundes		9	0
yarne 6 pounds and half		10	0
a baskett and a boxe			12
a greate Coffer in the Clossett a deske 2 little trunckes		20	0
in flaxe	4	8	0
one dozen of spoones called the 12 Apposles 24 ouz and quarter att 5s the ouz	6	1	9
12 other spoones wayeinge 18 ouz and three quarters att 4s 10d the ouz.	4	10	7
two white bowles wayeinge 25 ouz and three quarters att 4s 10d ouz	6	4	5

128   *Stockport Probate Records*

a silver poringer wayeinge 5 ouz and 3 quarters at 4s 10 the ouz		27	9½
3 guylte bowles and a cover wayeinge 47 ouz att 5s 2d the ouz	12	2	10
a guylte double Salte wayeinge 16 ouz att 5s 2d the ouz	4	2	8
a guylte bowle wayeinge 5 ouz att 5s 2d the ouz		25	10
lynnens in a trunke bound with iron	5	11	0
7 towells		30	0
one payer of sheetes		11	0
an other payer of sheetes		26	8
an other payer		10	0
table clothes		9	0
one table cloth		10	0
one payer of sheetes		24	0
a table cloth		30	0
one payer of sheetes		14	0
9 yards of linen cloth		21	0
one payer of sheetes		20	0
one table Cloth		5	6
one table cloth		12	0
one table cloth		8	0
a daper table cloth		20	0
a table cloth		5	0
a table cloth		4	0
a table cloth		4	0
two Cupboard Clothes		10	0
2 Cupboard Cloathes		13	4
one dozen of napkins		8	0
two dozen		30	0
pillowberes 6 payer		18	0
curtaines white and blew		8	0

Linnens in the butterie

5 payer of sheets		16	8
4 payer		23	0
4 payer		30	0
5 pillow beres		12	6
a table Cloth		3	4
one other		3	0
one other			12
one other		2	6
one other			12
a Cupboard Cloth			12
a table Cloth		2	6
two table Clothes			20
one other			12
a table cloth			12

a Cubbard Cloth			12
one other			6
a towell			6
two towells			12
a nother			6
one dozen of napkins		8	0
one dozen		5	0
one wallett			8
a towell			6
a sheete		3	4
a sheete			8
two payer of sheetes		6	0

At Bredburie

one hogshead			6
one barrell			6
six Chesfortes		2	0
a leather sumpter		5	0
two brasse potts		10	5
one fryeinge pann			12
one chaffebed 1 boulster		2	6
3 coverletts 2 blanketts one boulster		9	0
one brundrett one grate		5	0
2 cheares			12
a kan a wiskett one pewter dishe			12
Measures		3	0
a brasse pann		5	0
a Cupboard		5	0
a longe board and a forme		3	0
a pannell		2	0
a barre of iron and two potrackes		2	0
a cheese presse		3	4
a knedtrough			18
a greate arke		13	4
three payer of bed stocks		6	8
the deceadents apparell valued to fortie marks	26	13	4
Sum	410	10	1½

Office endorsement: probate to Robert Arderne.

62. WILLIAM DICKINSON OF STOCKPORT.
Will, sick.

S.Pr. 20 May 1619.
W.T. 30 April 1619.

First I commend my soule into the handes of Almightie God, verily beleeving to be saved by the death of Christe my saviour and redeemer, and my bodie to the earth from whence it came. And touching those goodes that god hath bestowed uppon mee, my Will is that they be disposed of as followeth. Imprimis whereas Sir William Davenport oweth me £118 and odd money, I geve and bequeath unto Elizabeth my Wyffe the one half of the said debte. Item I geve unto my said wyffe one Hundred poundes which I Covenanted to give her at the tyme of our mariage. Item I geve unto Ellyn Dickenson Marie Dickenson and Margaret Dickenson my daughters all my debtes that are owing unto mee equally to be devyded amongst them. Item I geve unto Robert Dickenson my brothers sonne twentie poundes. Item I geve unto my Sister Jane Kenyon all the debt she oweth mee. Item I geve unto the said Elizabeth my Wyffe one other Hundred poundes worth of my goodes; and the rest of my goodes to my said Children. [No executor nominated].

Witnesses: Tho. Normansell, William Ardernne, Adam Mottershed and Raphe Dickenson. [Witnesses appear to have signed this copy.]

Inventory: William Dickenson of Stockport, alderman. Taken: 11 May 1619.
Of: goods and chattels. Some damage to document.
Prisers: Adam Mottes[ed], William Ardern, Samuell Siddell, James Burdsell and Thomas Andrew.

	£	s	d
his apparell	13	6	8
in silver and gould	22	19	6
in Fyer wood and Turves		13	4
twoe Hackney saddles and bridles		10	0
sixe bordes and twoe postes in the stable		5	4
one Coffer for to put oates in		3	6
three shovels, twoe Axes, three Awgers, one hacke and twoe Curricombes		5	6
twoe Swine troughes		2	0

Kitchin Chamber

	£	s	d
one Saltinge tubbe		3	0
twoe Saltinge turnelles with Covers		10	0
one olde Coffer without a Cover		1	0
one great Bowke		7	0
one Cradle		2	6
twoe sitting wheeles and Swistes		3	0
one Chest and one little table		4	0

hanginge shelves		2	0
one hopper		7	0
malte	2	0	0

Chamber over the lower Flower
one Chest without a Cover		4	0
fower good bordes		4	0
one Spininge wheell		1	4

Chamber over thee Hall
twoe great arkes for malte	1	3	0
one seatt		1	6
sixteen bordes		8	9
twoe sides of bedstockes		1	6
one Shelfe for a Cubbord		2	0
one peece of Timber			6
one Closse stoolls one little Chaier and one olde buffet stoole .		1	3
all other odde Implementes		3	0

Clossett Chamber
one Crabpresse		2	0
one little Coffer			8
one Chest		7	0
one olde Saddle and pillion with furniter		7	0
one olde Tressell			6

Chamber over the parler
Barley		16	0
wheat and Rye		6	0
twoe wiskettes, one halfe hoope and one tubbe . . .		2	6
in yorne		4	0
in Sackes and pokes		5	0

Chamber over the butterie
one Standinge bed	1	0	0
one truckell bed		6	0
one [*interlined* : longe] Chest		8	0
one heighe great Chest		7	0
one little Chest and ane olde Forme		1	0
Meale and groates		3	0

In the Oriell
one greatt Chest		3	0
Packclothes and Cordes		7	0

Kittchen
in Treen ware	1	0	0
in bordes and shelves		3	0
one Furnace		8	0

The butterie without
one Chesse presse		3	0
in treene ware		16	0
sixe barrelles		16	0
one Coffer		6	0
one knedinge turnell and a little borde		4	0
in bordes and shelves		5	0
in Earthen ware		3	0

In the Halle
Twentie twoe Cushions	1	2	0
one great seeled Chest		10	0
a square table		7	0
one paier of tables		1	6
one longe table and twoe Formes		14	0
one deske		4	0
twoe little tables		10	0
three Cheares and twoe stooles		2	0
the seelinge in the hall	4	10	0
bookes		13	0
Iron ware of the better sorte and the worse		10	0
in pane mettle 72 pounds weight	3	12	0
in potte mettle 244 pounds weight	5	0	0
in Pewter	9	0	0

In the butterie in the house
two Cubbordes		17	0
one great Chest		5	0
treen ware and glasses		7	0
glasse case, bordes and shelves		7	0

In the parlor beneath
sixe sett Cushions		18	0
five other Cushions and a pillowe		10	0
twoe mappes		2	0
one Cubbord		17	0
one longe table		16	6
a Closse stoole		6	0
one Chest		8	0
a little Chest and a deske		8	0

one standing bed and a seatt to it 2 5 0
Curtens Rodes and hanginges to the foresaid bed . . . 1 0 0
one bed Covering and blanckettes 7 0 0
one Fetherbed three bowlsters and three pillowes . . . 2 15 0
one Flocke bed and Chaffe bed 10 0
one Truckell bed 16 8
one Cadowe, one Coverlett, and one Blanckett . . . 1 0 0
one Chaffe bed 2 6
twoe Fetherbedes, six pillowes and one bowlster . . . 2 15 0

The parlor belowe
one warminge pane 5 0
three little hand baskettes 1 0
sixe buffett stooles 6 0
sixe buffett stooles Covered 18 0
twoe Framed Cheares and stooles 7 0
one sett Carpett 15 0
fower olde Carpettes 7 0
the seelinge 4 10 0

In the Closett
one seeld bed 15 0
one Fetherbed, twoe pillowes, and one boulster . . . 1 4 0
one Chaffebed and one boulster 5 0
one Coverlett and twoe blanckettes 8 0

In the parler above
three presses and seelinge 2 10 0
[*interlined* : one] seeld bed, seate and hanginges 1 10 0
one Cadowe and fower blanckettes 1 6 0
sixe boxes 14 0
one little truncke and one Chest 6 0
one Chaier and twoe stooles 8 0
one great Chest 8 0
one Fetherbed, three bowlsters, and one pillowe . . . 2 15 0
one white Cadowe, and twoe blanckettes 14 0
one truckell bed and one Chaffe bed 10 0
one Cubbord tabell 5 0
one Fetherbed and twoe boulsters 1 14 0

In the Clothe house
one bed and appurtenances 6 0
bordes 3 0

In the mens Chamber

two Coverlets and two blanketes		8	0
One Fetherbed and a boulster	1	10	0
One old Chaffbed and a boulster		2	0
One Coverlett and fower blanketes		14	0
One Chaffbed and boulster		2	0
One fetherbed and two boulsters	1	10	0
Beeffe and Porke		13	9
two Flitches of Bakon	1	0	0

In Linens

Eleven new paire of Sheetes	3	17	0
seaven paire of other sheetes at Eight shillings the paire	2	16	0
three other paire at six shillings Eight penc a paire	1	0	0
two other paire	1	0	0
other two paire	1	0	0
one other paire		10	0
Eight paire of Sheetes	5	6	8
fower other paire of sheetes	3	0	0
two paire of Sheetes	1	7	0
One Sheete	1	0	0
Eighteene paire of other sheetes	6	0	0
two paire at		18	0
fower paire and one od sheete	1	0	0
two paire of Sheetes		10	0
three paire of Sheetes		15	0
one Boulster Case		2	6
three dossen of Napkins		15	0
One dossen of Napkins		6	0
One dossen of Napkins		7	0
One dossen more		5	0
One dossen more		10	0
One dossen more		8	0
Seaven Napkins		7	0
fower Sivecloaths		7	0
Seaven diaper Napkins		4	0
Neene Napkins		3	0
fower wrought Pillobeares	1	0	0
other six pillobeares		12	0
three other Pillobeares		4	0
seaven other Pillobeares		10	6
fower other at		8	0
Eight Towells		9	6
three Fyne towells		8	0
two Brod table Cloathes		16	0

Seaventiene table Cloathes	3	4	4
one duble silver salt	5	2	6
One New silver boule	2	2	6
One [erasure] parcel gilt Beaker	2	14	0
One brod Boule one pot with a Cover	4	12	0
two Ould salts and Covers	4	3	0
Neenteene silver spoones	4	14	0
Tenn silver Spoones gilt at the end	5	2	6
Three Kyne	10	10	0
One per of great Scales and beame		2	0
Compost		6	8
One Hogge	1	6	0
in od implementes	1	10	0
one great Chiste in Manchester		10	0

In Woodes House and grownd

One Mare Fower Geldinges and three geires	24	10	0
two Akers of Oates	6	13	4
two Akers of Barley	10	0	0
in Wallinge stone		3	4
Fower dores		2	0
two Bordes in the stable		1	0
two peeces of walle timber in the stable		1	8
two Longe Bordes		2	0
14 Bordes		5	0
fower harrowes		16	0
one hundred of Lattes		1	8
spurs and ould timber in the Barne		12	0
six peeces of timber Lyinge on the More		5	0
one tree Lyinge on the more		10	0
Oates at daniells	2	0	0
Mucke in the hilgate		6	8
Corne in the hilgate Barne	7	10	0
Windoe sheetes		2	6
three sives one wisket three Rakes and one Pecke on shovell		1	6
Corne in the Woobutes	1	0	0
One browne Cow in the Woobutes	3	5	0
in Linen Cloth at Congleton	18	10	0
fyftie peeces of Cloth	47	0	0

debts due by specialties

by Sir William Davenport knight	25	0	0
more by the said Sir William Davenport	34	8	0
more by the said Sir William Davenport	25	0	0
more by the said Sir William Davenport	34	8	0

136 Stockport Probate Records

by William Davenport esquire	50	0	0
by the same William Davenport esquire	50	0	0
by the same William Davenport esq	10	0	0
Thomas Roades of Bramhall	20	0	0
Margerie Warren and Edward her sonne	3	0	0
Peeter Ashton	6	10	0
assignements		[blank]	
ground which the testator held of Thomas Williamson	10	10	0
yorne at the bleachinge	1	2	0

Debtes due to the testator without specialtie

by Mr Robert Downes		8	0
by James Baguley		5	0
by Thomas Cooke	1	0	0
by Edward Bowerhouse of the Bridgend		1	6
by George Elcocke		15	0
by George Barrett		1	6
by Raphe Wooffendyne			6
by Hughe Kenyon	1	0	6
by John Ouldham of Chester		2	0
by Jane Robinson my wieves daughter		5	0
by Mr John Warren the lord of the towne	54	18	4
by Allexander Smith		3	0
by John Grantham of the Milnegate	2	0	0
by Edward Kempe		2	0
by Kateren Pigott		2	4
by Raphe Baylie		15	0
by Mr George Parker	2	0	0
by John Dickenson Robert sonne	5	0	0
by Mr Winington	4	0	0
by Thomas Boardman of the hilgate		2	6
by George Wood of Bramhall		10	0
by George Browne of Poynton		4	11
by Mr John Warren		9	8
by Mr Alderman Hunt		3	4
by George Hollinworth		10	8
by Sir Edward Warren	62	18	4
by Mr John Warren of Poynton	2	0	0
by John Williamson of this towne		13	4
by Mr John Davenport of Wabanckhill		13	4
by Thomas Rowson	1	0	0
by Alice Allicocke		1	0
by Margerie Grantham		3	0
by Robert Cottrell		2	0
by John that built the steeple		10	0

by John Fallowes wief 2 0
by Mr Urmeston 6 8
by Nicholas Smith of derbieshire 2 0
by John Warren of this towne 16 2
by Mr John Warren 7 0 0
by Richard Wilson 1 5 4
by John Roades of Bramhall 6 8
by William Ashton weaver 1 0
by Thomas Harrop 1 0
by Raphe Bowerhouse 5 0
by Jane Chorlton of Withington my wieves sister . . . 1 2 0
by Nicholas Blomeley 5 0
by Mr William Gerrard 1 0 0
by George Browne 6 8
by Randle Hankinson 4 0
by Hughe Stanley 2 16 2
by Edward Brooke 5 0
by George Hopwood 7 8
by Mr Normansell 6 0 0
by John Sandes 9 5
by Thomas Greens 3 0 0
by John Hadfeild 3 0
by John Barrett 1 10 0
by Edward Chorlton 13 4
by John Fallowes 3 5
by John Sydebothom 16 0
by John Brodhurste of Maclesfeld 1 6 8
by Mr Laurence Wright 3 0 0
by Mr Woodward 1 0 0
by Thomas Kelleys wief 2 4
by George Gorton 5 0
by John Rudson 12 0
by John Sanndes and Robert Shawe 6 0
by Anne Hough 2 0
by Robert Heyldes wief 2 4 0
by John Daniell 10 8
by Thomas Cheetam 3 4
by Thomas Stanley of Cheadle Hulme 1 0

[two columns: 1.h. col:]
by Richard Mottershedes wief 5 0
by Robert Rydinges 1 6
by Henry Daniell 15 0
by Frannces Shrigley 1 2 0
by John David for George Elcocke 1 0 0

138 Stockport Probate Records

by Hugh Daniell		11	6
by Robert Hough	2	0	0
by George Potter		7	3
by Thomas Over		4	9
by John Rudson		15	10
[r.h. col:]			
by William Daniell		10	0
by Alice Whiteley		19	0
by Thomas Williamson	1	16	0
by Samuell for oates	2	8	8
by Anthony Nicholson	3	10	0
by Thomas Fallowes		3	8
in linnen yarne 13ˡⁱ waight		[blank]	

[in excess of: 910   0   0]

Office endorsement: probate to deceased's relict Elizabeth.

63. JOHN ROBINSON OF STOCKPORT, YEOMAN.
S.Pr. 6 October 1619.
Will, sick.   W.T. 12 September 1619.

First I comend my soule into the hands of allmightie god my maker and continuall preserver, hopinge by the meritts of Jesus Christe to be one of the number of those that shalbe saved and my bodie to be buried in the church of Stockport at the discrecon of my executors hereunder named, Firste concerninge my Burgage wherein I dwell my mynd and will is and I do give and bequeath yt in manner and forme followinge That is to saie unto Olliver Robinson my eldest sonne all the said Burgage Buildinges Backsides as are now erected and builded with a fitt waie to the said Backside to him the said Olliver Robinson and to his heires for ever (Excepte the gardeinsteede) Soe that Alice Robinson my said wief shall have and enjoye to her sole and proper use all the new buildinge and Comon easemente on the Backside for and duringe her lief, or for and duringe soe longe tyme as she shall keepe herselfe chaste and unmarried, and that Olliver my sonne shall finde and allowe to her meate and drinke at or in the same house Item I give and bequeath to Frances Robinson my second sonne the said gardein plott formerlie Reserved conteyninge nyne yardes or thereaboutes to him the said Frances and his heires for ever to use and imploye the same to his beste benefitte and advantage by buildinge thereon at his pleasure and like libertie in all the said waies to him the said Frances Robinson his heires and assignes for ever Paienge therefore yearelie everie yeare unto the said Olliver Robinson and his heires the some of foure pence of lawfull money of England Item I give and bequeath unto Olliver Robinson my sonne the cupboard in the house Item I give and bequeath unto Alice my wief the Bedsteed in the parlour and all the beddinge now thereon and furniture thereto belonginge the seeled Cheste and the truncke in the said parlour Item I give and bequeath unto Anna Robinson one of my daughters the some of fortie shillinges Item I give and bequeath unto Richard hunt of Manchester my grandchilde the some of Tenn shillinges. Item I give and bequeath unto William hunt and James hunt his brethren to either of them Five shillinges. And for the reste of my said goodes my debtes beinge paid and funerall expenses discharged Then the said goodes to be devyded into three equall partes one third parte whereof I give unto Alice my said wief Item I give and bequeath unto France Robinson my said second sonne Jane Margerie Katheren Ellen Marie and Anna my daughters the other two third partes of all my goodes being unbequeathed to be equallie devided amongst them.

Executor: testator's wife Alice Robinson.
Witnesses: Thomas Elcocke and John Barrett.

Inventory: John Robinson of Stockport.   Taken: 27 September 1619.
Of: goods cattells and chattles.
Prisers: Henry Collier, George Whitticers, William Fletcher and Abraham Fieldinge.

	£	s	d
in new Sawne Timber		28	0
for odd Shelves and Breads		4	0
a sadle a bridle and a white nagge		26	8
in haye and the latter end of the winter pasture where the haye grew		50	0
for [*interlined*: fyre] woode		18	0
for [*interlined*: a] Swine		16	0
for a Cubboard in the house		20	0
three score and six pound of Pewter		40	0
three score and fyve pound of Leade		5	0
for Brasse		31	0
on featherbed, one bedstead, on Kadowe three blanketts twoe payer of sheetts, twoe bolsters on pillowe and twoe pillowbiers, a peece of a whitte Cadowe, one truncke and on Chest	5	6	8
in beddinge		32	0
Eight Chests and towe trunks		24	0
an Apple plate, a water plate and a sauce plate			18
towe Earthen Dishes			6
for fower litle painted glasse Dishes			12
for a blew Jugge			6
in glasses and a potte			4
Eight glasse bottells			8

140 *Stockport Probate Records*

for five pounde and a halfe of woollen yearne		5	6
one payer of flaxen sheets		10	0
on diaper table Clothe and three Dyaper napkins		10	0
on dozen of Napkins and Eleven		6	0
twoe payre of Course Sheetts		10	0
twoe pillowbeers, one Sife clothe, and on table Clothe		4	4
one table in the house, and one forme belonginge to it and twoe tresseboards in the house, fower buffett stooles, and on Chaire		11	4
in trine ware about the house		17	0
for one pack saddle, a tree, a wonntey and overlaye		4	0
a payre of Hampers and locks		5	0
in Iron ware		8	0
twoe blanketts and a little Cloathe		5	0
three poaks			12
a glasse casse			12
a Smothinge Iron			6
a Lanthorne			6
for twoe bills			18
twoe Iron wedges			6
a broken barrell of starche		6	8
in Turves and Coales, an olde payer of bedstocks and an olde sitting wheele		2	0
a grater with cassertrenchers			12
in spoones, dishes, a dishcather and trenchers			20
fower Cushens		2	0
a payre of Swifts and brasse Scales			6
a blacke Satten sute		20	0
a silver spoone		4	0
in Stone			12
twoe scales		4	0
His apparell Lynine and woollen	3	6	8
in readye money	4	12	1
in odd Implements		2	0
victualls		6	8
Sum	34	17	3
[*recte*	35	17	2]

Warres in the Shoppe praized ut supra viz

Ninetien payer of wosted stockings	3	13	2
wollen stockings thirtye fower payer		57	8
thirteen payer of Stockings for Children		7	7
twelve payer of wosted stockings more		30	0
a dozen and a halfe and one payre of gloves		41	10

three dozen and ten payer		30	4
a dozen and ten payer more		15	10
Nine dozen and a halfe		37	6
Ten doz and twoe payer more		25	8
ane other parcell of gloves		46	0
a dozen of purses		2	6
Fringe and Ribbininge		11	0
Chissells and punches		3	0
	Sum	19 2	1

Debts oweinge unto the testator

by Mr. Edmond Hayes		16	6
more in debts		18	0
	Sum	34	6
	Sum	55 13	10
	[*recte*	56 13	9]

Office endorsement: probate to the executors.

64. WILLIAM HULME OF STOCKPORT.   S.Pr. 16 November 1619.
Will, sick.   W.T. 6 November 1619.

First I gieve and bequeath my soule to Almighty God, and my bodie to Earthe. And for my worldlye goods I geive and bequeathe them as here after followethe, First my will is that Margrett my wyfe shall have all my whole goods, my detts beinge payed and my funarall expences discharged, Item my will is that my said wyfe shall keepe my Mother honestly and fitting for her callinge with meates drinke and apparall and lodginge durynge her lyfe; And further my will is that yf my Mother shall att anie tyme here after have Juste cause of dislyke of her findinge and keepinge that then my wyfe shall paye to her the some of £10 of lawfull Englishe money and then shee to be noe further charged with her; Item my will is that Margrett my wyf shall have and injoye my whole lands and howsinge durynge her lyfe; And after her decease my will is that John Hulme my brother shall have it to him and his heares for ever, and I doe freely geive it him.

Executrix: testator's wife Margrett.
Witnesses: John Redtche, Robert Hardman and Alexander Rodes.

Inventory: William Hulme of Stockport.   Taken: 13 November 1619.
Of: goods.
Prisers: George Chorlton, Robert Barlowe, John Rediche and John Robinson.

		£	s	d
one cowe			53	4
three hogges		4	0	0
foure shoates			13	4
in heye			40	0
in fewell			40	0
in mucke			3	0
the Coboard in the house withall uppon it		3	0	0
more in pewter			10	0
in brasse		3	0	0
one greate leade and one little one			16	0
in Iron ware			40	0
in tables			30	0
in Cheares and stooles			13	4
in wooden ware			50	0
one pair of tables				12
one gune			8	0
in quishenes			13	4
in chests			50	0
in beddstockes			40	0
three fether bedes		3	10	0
three chafbeddes			4	6
in boulsteres and pillowes			20	0
Curtaines and Rodes			6	8
three Cadowes		3	6	8
More in beddinge			33	4
in yearne			48	0
two swords and on dagger			20	0
in lynenes		5	0	0
three silver sponnes			20	0
in Money		5	10	0
in detts by bills		3	8	0
in Apparill		5	0	0
in Rides and lathes			10	0
in Corne			13	4
in byffe			3	4
in butter and cheise			13	4
in pullen			2	0
in sackes and poakes			6	8
two paire of boules			4	0
in weights and measures			4	0
in other Implements			10	0
	Sum	67	5	0

Office endorsement: probate to executors.

INDEX OF NAMES

This is not an index of persons, that is, we have made no attempt to gather together entries relating to single individuals. We are aware of the complex judgements involved in such an operation from our own researches, and feel therefore that readers should make their own identifications.

As a consequence, titles and other indications of status have been omitted, unless no forename is given. Variant spellings of names are given in round brackets. Missing forenames are indicated by a dash. Where we have had to assume a surname, e.g. for references such as 'my son James', the page reference is enclosed in [ ]. *indicates more than one entry on a page.

Abraham, —, 62.
Adshed (Adshedd), George, 45; Thomas, 20; —, 19.
Alcocke, Elnor, 107; Jeffrey, 114.
Allen (Allyn), Ann, 26; Margerye, 25; Mary, 19; Raph, 26*, 51, 67; Sibell, 108.
Allicocke, Alice, 136.
Amsden, Walter, 10.
Anderson, Thomas, 65.
Andrew (Andrewe, Anndrewe), Alex, 9; Alice, 4*; John, 4; Nicholas, 4; Phillippe, 10; Thomas, 4*, 32, 45, 47, 54, 56, 97, 130.
Ardern (Arderne, Ardernne), Alice, 121; Henry (Henrie, Henrye), 70, 121, 122*, 123; John, 70*, 121*, 122*, 123; Margarett, 122; Mary (Marie), 121, 122*; Raphe, [121*], 122*; Robert, 121*, 122, 129; William, 130*; Mr., 10.
Arstall, Robert, 113.
Ashton *alias* Wylde, Edward, 99.
Ashton (Asheton), Hugh, 107; Margaret, 60; Peter, 136; Raph, 88; William, 112, 137.
Asmall, Gyles, 105.
Aspinall, Alexander, 48.

Baguley (Bagaley), James, 136; Richard, 32 [*].
Bancroft (Bancrofte), Allexander, 69, Edward, 69; Godfrey, 85; Robert, 54; Roger, 69; Thomas, 105, 114; William, 69, 77.
Bardell, George, 10.
Barlow (Barlowe, Barrlow), Henry, 65; John, 106*, 112; Robert, 47, 105, 141.
Barnes, —, 48.
Barrett, George, 54, 136; John, 59, 63, 77, 80, 84, 137, 139.
Bate, Hugh, 43; Robert, 60; William, 43.
Baylie, Raphe, 136.
Baylis, Randall, 113.
Beckerstaffe, Ales, 16.
Benetson (Benesone, Benesson, Benessone, Benison), Edward, 116; Grace, 105; John, 24*, 65*, 66, 113; Thomas, 63, 88; William, 24.
Bennet, William, 104, 111.
Benton, Charles, 10.
Bexweeke, Robte., 27.

Bibbie, (Bibbye), Alexander, 113; Edward, 85*; Nicholas, 85.
Bickerton, Jo., 121, 123.
Birch (Birche, Byrche), Ales, 62; Alexander, 40, 62; Elizabeth, 60; George, 62; John, 40, 55, 62*, 63.
Blackborne, Richard, 85.
Black Prince, the xi.
Blackshawe, Thomas, 112.
Blane, Richard, xi.
Blomiley (Blomeyley,) George, 65; Nicholas, 33, 91, 137; Thomas, 113.
Boardman, (Bordman), Alex., 37; Otes, 112; Robert, 63, 91, 98; Thomas, 20, 37, 107, 136.
Boland (Bolande), John, 41, 42*, 43, 49, 63, 77, 96, 99.
Booth, Henrie, 1; Nicholas, 54; Wm., 123.
Bossevylle (Bossoyell, Boswell, Boswill), Alexander, 42, 65, 66, 73; Mr., 104.
Bowden, George, 32; Mr., 9.
Bowerhouse, Edward, 136; Raphe, 137.
Bowker, —, 107.
Bradley (Bradleye, Bradlie), Charles, 40; Elliz., 62; George, 43, 62*, 90; Izabell, 40; John, 62*, 105; Katherin, 107; Laurence (Lawrence), 54, 104, 114; Otes, 62*; Raph, 107; William, 99.
Bradshawe, Henry, 90.
Bramma, John, 99.
Brearley, James, 65.
Brentnall, William, 112.
Brentnough, William, 106.
Bretchgirdle, William, 106, 111.
Bretland (Breatland), Francis, 112; John, 63.
Bridge, Homfray (Humfrey), 5, 7, 16, 55; Robert, 1, 19; William, 106, 112.
Brodhurst (Brodhurste), Edward, 84; John 137.
Brooke (Brook, Broocke, Bruck, Bruke), Edward, 93, 114, 137; John, 108; Raph (Raphe), 44, 96, 102; Richard, 108, 122; Robt., 9; Thomas, 36, 48, 55.
Brooks, Edward, 73.
Brookshall (Bruckshall), George, 43; Thomas, 38.

144   Index

Browne, Edward, 114*; George, 136, 137; John, 2, 96, 106, 111; Rychard, 90.
Brundreth, Roger, 112.
Buckley *alias* Taylier, Ellen, 27.
Buckley, Ric (Richard), 3, 55.
Burdsell, (Beurdsell, Buerdsell, Buerdstell, Burdsill, Buredsell), Hughe, 16; James, 67*, 72, 73*, 88, 96, 98*, 108*, 118, 119, 130; John, 72*, 73, 118; Margerye, 73; Thomas, 2, 19, 26*, 34, 35, 73*, 118.
Burgess (Burges, Burgesse), Ellen, 105, 107; Hugh, 107; Jane, 5; John, 5, 18*, 54, 65[*], 105; Richard, 105, 114*; Robert, 105; Thomas, 106, 111, 113; William, 105.
Burghe, Robert, 83.
Byam, William, 90.

Callier, William, 122.
Camden, William xi.
Carrington, William, 38.
Cartwright, John, 29, 45*, 47, 48; Justynyan, 54.
Cash, (Cashe), John, 114; William 111, 112.
Chadwicke, George, 113.
Charlton, George, 113.
Cheadle, (Chedle), Willm, 9, 87, 111, 113*.
Cheet, John, 32.
Cheetam, (Cheetham, Chetam), Ambrose, 9; Raph, 107; Robert, 65; Thomas, 66, 137.
Chetman, John, 85.
Chewe, Roger, 43.
Chomley, Lady, 108.
Chorlton (Chorleton), Agnes, 48*, 50; Ales, 48*; Edward, 137; Elizabethe, 48*; George, 43*, 55, 141; James, 39*, 48*; Jane, 137; John, 9, 10; Margrett, 48*.
Chowcliffe, John, 9.
Chowlerton, George, 51.
Clarke, Hugh, 14.
Clayton, (Cleyton), Brian, 113; Rauffe, 19, 113.
Clough, John, 100.
Cockson, Richard, 112.
Collier (Collyer, Colyer), Alexander, 112, 113*; George, 55; Henry, 139; John, 32, 95; Raphe, 43; Robert, 112*.
Combes, Thomas, 20.
Cooke, John, 65; Thomas, 136.
Coppocke, Henrie, 114; James, 112; Richard, 107.
Cotterell (Cotrell), Allis, 102*, Ellin, 102; John, 61, 117; Robert, 92, 93, 117, 119, 136.
Coughen, Edward, 107; John, 108.
Cowley, Ann, 92; William, 92, 100.
Cowps, —, 85.
Crooke, Edward, 92.

Crosely, Charles, 100; Joane, 19; John, 100; Katheryn, 100*; Tho., 27, 100.
Cruft, Ellice, 55.
Cumberbach, John, 122.
Cusworth, John, 69.

Dale, Margarett, 118.
Dand (Dande), John, 137; Thomas, 73.
Damport (*see* also Davenport), Peter, 47; William, 44, 46.
Daniel (Daniell), Alexander, 6*, 15*, 68*, 69*; Ellen, 15*; Francis (Frances), 15*, 16, 69; George, xvii, 4, 6, 14, 15, 16; Henry, 137; Hugh, 138; James, 6*, 68, 69; Joane, [15], 68, 69*; John, 69, 85, 137; Raffe (Raph), 15, 68; Richard, 6*; Robert, 6, 105; William (Willm), 15*, 16, 68*, 98, 138.
Darbye, Laurence, 37.
Davenport (Davenporth; *see* also Damport), Ann 92; Humfrey, 54; John, 136; Katheryn, 92; William, 60*, 102, 103, 112, 130, 135*, 136; Mr., 55*, 92, 122.
Dawars, Robert,, 3.
Deane *alias* Williamson, Edward, 108.
Defoe, Daniel, xi.
Dickenson (Dickensonn, Dickinson, Dickinsonn, Diconson), Elizabeth, [130*], 138; Ellyn, 130; Henry, 117*; Joane, 7, 8*, 14; John, 8*, 26, 62, 108, 112, 136; Margaret, 130; Marie, 130; Radi, 14; Raphe (Rauffe), 7, 8*, 42, 62*, 130; Robert, [10], 62, 130, [136]; Thomas, 7, 8, 9*; William, 7, 8, 14, 41, 42, 43*, 44, 48, 61*, 62*, 80*, 92; Mr., 87.
Didsburye, Raph, 75; Thomas, 32.
Dixson, Ales, 105; James, 36.
Dixson, *alias* Lamkin, James, 105.
Dodge, Olliver, (Olyver), 4, 30, 54, 95, 96*, 106; Otiwell (Otywell), 5, 33, 45*, 47; Robert, 15, 43, 73; old good wife, 16.
Dokenfeld, *see* Duckinfield.
Downes, Phillip, 108; Raph (Rauffe), 20, 114; Robert, 106, 111, 136.
Duckenfield, (Dokenfeld, Duckenfeld, Dockfyld, Duckenfield), Robert, 87, 93, 99; William, 9.
Duncalfe, Thomas, 55.

Earwaker, J.P., xvi.
Elcock (Elcocke, Elcok, Elcoke), Alice, 61; Allexander, 9, 19*, 65, 80*, 108; Anne, 80; Dorothy, 80*; Frannces (Frannces, Francis: male and female entries together), 4*, 54, 80, 92, 95; George, 9, 19, 47*, 54, 60, 61, 65,

92, 101, 104, 117, 136, 137; Marie, 80; Nicholas (Nichollas), 9, 102*, 116, 119; Richard, 80; Sara, 118; Thomas, 32*, 65, 77*, 80*, 108, 139; William, 80; Mr., 15.
Elicord, Gorge, 65.

Fallowes, Alice, 66*; John, 115, 137; Margerie, 66; Robert, 66*, 67; Thomas, 138.
Faulkener *alias* Johnson, Thomas, 122.
Fawkner, Richard, 112.
Fearne, (Ferne) James, 39*, 49, 53*, 56.
Fell, James, 18, 19, 29, 91.
Fieldinge, Abraham, 139.
Flechar (Fletcher), Richard, 84, 85; William, 92, 94, 139.
Foden, Reynold, 107.
Fogge, Henerie, 16; Richard, 93; —, 94.
Fowler, Christopher, 108.
Fynney, Thomas, 107.
Fynsonn, James, 100*.

Gardner, Elizabeth, 83, 84; Hughe, 83; Phillippe, 10; Robert, 39, 83, 84.
Garlicke, Anthonie, 54.
Garnet (Garnett, Garnette), Edward, 66; Thomas, 19*, 20, 39, 76, 94.
Gee, Robert, 66.
Gemings, George, 45.
Gerard (Gerrard), Felix, 89; Ri. (Richard), 42, 43*, 44, 59, 60*, 89*; Thos. 89; Ursula, 89*, 90; Wm., 89, 137; Mr., 41, 43, 66.
Gibbon, John, 73, 107, 112.
Gibbons, John, 122.
Gibson, John, 9; Lawrence, 54.
Gilliver, Robert, 112.
Gloover *alias* Johnson, Richard, 25.
Glover, Richard, 27, 93.
Goddard, Tho., 67; Willm, 54.
Goodyeare, Henrie, 114.
Goole, Lawrence, 73.
Gortan, George, 137.
Grantham, Ales, 117; George, 117; Isabell, 117*; James, 117; John, 44, 45*, 65, 117*, 136; Margerie, 136; Raphe, 117; Willm, 117.
Greene, Edward, [50]; Elizabeth, 51*; Hugh, 114; John, 108; Thomas, 50.
Greens, Thomas, 9*, 10, 137.
Griffyn, Roland, 87.

Hatfield, John, 137.
Hall (Halle), Elizabeth, 4; Frances, 102; John, 3, 55; Lawrence, 107; Matilda, 95; William, 113.
Hampson, George, 10; John, 106, 111.

Hankenson, Richard, 113.
Hankesson, Richard, 37.
Hankinson, Francis, 48, 85; Randle, 137.
Hardey, William, 106.
Hardman, Margerye, 47*, 117, 118; Margreat (Margrite), 76, 80; Robert, 26, 47, 103, 141.
Harison, (Harrison, Haryson), Ales, 36*, 85; Ellen, 36*; Jane, [36]; John, 36; Reynold, 37; Robert, 55; William, 36, 37, 85, 114.
Harison *alias* Hughes, Robert, 48.
Harison *alias* Rawlinson, George, 43.
Harper, Roger, 59, 66, 84, 96.
Harrop, Thomas, 108, 137.
Hartley, William, 47, 108, 121.
Hay (Haye), Hugh, 114*.
Hayes, Edmond, 141.
Heald, James, 112.
Hearan, *see* Heran.
Heginbotham (Heyginbotham, Higgenbotham, Higinbothome), H., xvii; Nicholas, 107; Oliver, 20; Ottiwell, 16; Robert, 55; William, 55, 73.
Heigham (Higham), Edward, 113; John, 25, 71*, 72; William, 114.
Henshall, John, 43, 113.
Henshawe, Homfrey, 54; John, 16; William, 106; —, 68.
Henyson, Blanche, 16.
Heron (Hearon, Heyron, Herode, Heyrod, Heyron), Godfrey (Godferat), 15, 42, 69*, 88, 102; Hugh, 69; Margaret, 69; Myles, 30.
Hexam, Thomas, 55; William, 55.
Hey, Peter, 10, 41, 42*, 43, 63, 98.
Heyes, Peter, 9, 67, 91.
Heylde, Robert, 137.
Heywarthe, Henrye, 54.
Hibbart (Hibbearte, Hibbert), Robte, 99*, 123.
Higginson, William, 104, 111.
Higham, *see* Heigham.
Higinbotham, *see* Heginbotham.
Hill, Thomas, 122.
Hillane, John, 3.
Holland, Edward, 121, 122; Henry, 34; Mary, 121.
Hollinworth (Hollingworth), Alexander, 105; George, 114, 136; John, 113; Raphe, 107; Reginalde, 43; Reynold, 63.
Home (Houlme, and *see* Hulme), Alex., 9; Anthony, 65; Emma, 65; Henrye, 49, 63, 65*; Rauffe, 9; Rondulfe, 16; William, 54.
Honford, George, 108.
Hooley, George, 108 [and? *see* Howley].
Hopwood (Hopwoode), George, 137; John 75, 115.
Hordron, Robert, 83.

Holt, *see* Houlte.
Hough, Anne, 137; John, 9; Robert, 95, 105, 138.
Houlden, Katheren, 63.
Houlme, *see* Holme and Hulme.
Houlte, Thomas, 43; William, 55.
Howley, Kathleen, 50 [and? *see* Hooley].
Hudson (Hudsonne), Edward, 105; Jenkin, 105; John, 87, 106; Ric. (Richard), 90, 91, 123; Robt., 6; William, 9*, 27.
Hughes *alias* Haryson, Robert, 48.
Huland, Mistress, 122.
Hulme (and *see* Holme), Edmund, 107*, John, 141; Margrett, 141, Raph, 105; Thomas, 32, 105; Mistresse, 84.
Hunt (Huntt, Huntte), Elizabeth, 25*, 26; Ellyn, 26; James, 47, 105, 139; Raphe, 25; Richard, 139; Sampson, 20, 24, 45, 47, 51, 80; William, 139; Mr., 136.
Hurst, Katheren (Katherine), 79, 99*; Margarett, 79; Richard, 106*.
Hutchinson, Francis, 54*.
Hyde, Hamnet, 89, 90; John, 90; Ric., 55; Mr., 65.
Hyde *alias* Patricke, William, 111.

Jackson, Edward, 51; Hercules, 85; James, 85; John, 5, 66, 85, 86, 112; Margarett, 50; Raph, 107; Rauff, 37.
James, Richard, 10.
Janney (Jannye, Jynnie), Robert, 16; Robte, 105; William, 107.
Jennines, George, 87.
Jodrell, Edmund, 98.
Johnes, Alexander, 122.
Johnson, Raph (Raphe), 20, 24, 107; Ric., 55; Thomo., 1.
Johnson *alias* Faulkener, Thomas, 122.
Johnson *alias* Gloover, Richard, 25.

Karre, John, 53.
Kelley, Thomas, 137.
Kelsall (Kelsal), Ales, 32; Edward, 32*; Frances, 32, 34; James, 92, 105, 108; John, 31, 32*, 114; Richard, 32; Robert, 32; Wm., 31.
Kemp (Kempe), Alexander, 114; Edward, 92, 136; James, 73.
Kenyon (Cenyan, Kanyan, Kenion), Elizabeth, 117; Hughe, 9*, 71, 136; Jane, 130; John, 117; Margerie, 116, 118*; Raphe (Rafe), 116, 118, 120, 121; Richard, 93; Robert, 121.
Kirke, Humfrey, 106; John 54.
Knight, George, 51.
Knott (Knote), Alexander (Alex), 9*, 30, 113*.

Knowles, Robert, 9.

Lache, Robert, 55.
Lamkin *alias* Dixson, James, 105.
Lane, Robert, 89.
Latham (Lathome), Ellinae, 38; John 38; Laurence, 113.
Leckonbie, —, 121.
Lee, Richard, 108; Robert, 106, 112; Roger, 106, 111.
Lees, Nicholas, 90*, 91; Robert, 9; Roger, 112.
Leigh (Leighe), Anne, 1*; John, 1; Peter, 89, 108; Robert (Rabert), 111, 112; Roger, 71.
Lightbowne, —, 53.
Lingard, Thomas, 105.
Lowe (Low), Elizabeth, 58, 59; James, 19*; Jane, 3; John, 19, 61*, 85; Mr., 20*, 24.
Lumbston, Catteren, 102; John, 102*, 103.
Lynnen, Ellen, 62.
Lynney, Ellen, 41; Thomas, 112.

Makyn, Reynold, 20.
Manninge, Dorithie, 80.
Marburie, —, 121.
Marshowe, Robert, 3*.
Marsland, George, 102; Margaret, 67; Willm., 73; —, 3.
Massie, Henrie, 107; Thomas, 2.
Matley (Matlaye, Matly), Elizabeth, 107; John, 45, 47; Thurstan, 5.
Matley *alias* Rowson (Rowsson), Thurstan, 48, 75.
Mellor, —, 55.
Meykin, Reynold, 108.
Millington, John, 101*; Marie, 121.
Mills, Anne, 117, 118; Jane, 116, 118*; Marie, 117; Robert, 117.
Milnes, George, 112*; Robert, 3.
Molyneux, Richard, 89.
Monnson, Robert, 89.
Moores (Mores), Elline, 35; Laurence, 9, 10; widow, 73.
Morris, Willm., 85.
Mosley, Oswald, 59*, 60; Rowland, 59, 60.
Mosse (Moss), Alexander, 9, 19, 41, 77, 79, 90, 95, 105; Raphe, 87; Thomas, 29.
Mottershed (Mottershedd, Mottershede), Adam, 62, 130*; Anthonye, 71; Edward, 114*; Richard, 137; Thomas, 85*.
Mottram, Hugh (Hughe), xvii, 25, 74*; Margaret, 75*; Peter, 75; Raph, 75; William, 75*, 76, 115.

Nabbs, Matilda, 4; Richard, 2, 4.
Newcome, Francis, 92.

Newton, Alexander, 16; George (Georg), 51, 61, 75, 84, 99, 115; Raph (Rauffe), 55*, 113; Thomas (Tho), 34, 67, 84, 96, 98, 119; widow, 16.
Nicholson (Nicolson, Nicolsonne, Nyklesson), Alice (Ales), 40*, 118; Ambrose, 123; Anne, 118; Anthony (Anthonie), 63, 108, 118, 138; Dorothye, 40*; Ellen, 40; Frannces, 40; John, 101; Paul (Paule), 106, 112, 113; Raphe (Raffe, Rauffe), 10, 20, 24, 40, 43, 63; Theophilus, 118; Thomas, 20, 114; William (Willm, Wm), xviii, 6, 32, 40*, 41, 43, 45, 46, 47*, 48, 62, 85, 93, 114, 118.
Normansell, Richard, 50, 51; Thomas (Thos), 50, 66, 73, 90, 98*, 130; Urian, 50; Mr., 137.
Norres, William, 9*, 32.
Norton, Jane, 95.

Odcroft, Ellis, 47.
Ogden, Margerye, 41.
Oldham, (Ouldham), John, 37, 38, 41, 136; Raphe (Raph) 65, 71, 98, 99, 108*, 112, 114, 115; Thomas, 62, 90.
Olyver, John, 54.
Orme, Roger, 44, 46.
Orred, William, 107.
Osbaston, Thomas, 105.
Ouldfield, Hugh, 105.
Over, Thomas, 138.

Parker, George, 108, 112, 136.
Partington, Thurston, 55.
Partridge, Miles, 98.
Patricke, William, 106.
Patricke alias Hyde, William, 111.
Peares, Edmund, 111.
Peeres, Edmund, 106.
Peerson (Peereson), Edmund, 113; William, 60.
Percevall (Persyvall), Anthony, 87; Nicholas, 9.
Pickering, Edward, [50]; Margaret, 50, 51; Thomas, 51*.
Piggott (Piggatt, Piggot), Christopher, 61, 86, 87; Kateren, 136; Margerie, 51; Margret, 86, 87*; —, 3.
Pott, Elizabeth, 50; John, 32.
Potter, George, 73, 138; John, 73.
Pownall, Henry, 32; Robert, 107.
Pristnall, John, 105.
Pycroft (Picrofte), John, 106, 111; Raphe, 26.

Quynye, Mr., 10.

Radcliffe, Robert, 105, 114; William, 66.
Ratcliffe, Ed., 89.
Rawlinson alias Harrison, George, 43.

Reddish (Raddick, Reddich, Reddiche, Redich, Rediche, Redtche, Redyche), Ann, 66; Ellen, 62; George, 6*, 8, 16, 27, 32, 36, 53, 87; John, 27, 49, 63, 65, 84, 87, 108, 141*; Rauffe, 18*, 19*; Robert, 29; Robery, 55.
Renshaw, James, 113.
Rhodes (Roades, Rode, Rodes, Roodes), Alexander (Allexander, Alex), 26, 72, 94, 98, 141; Andrewe, 55; Edward (Ed), 26, 29, 72; John, 62, 72, 137; Thomas, 106, 136.
Richardson, John, 113; William, 20.
Ridgway (Ridgwaye, Ridgewaye, Rydgeye), George, 85; Hughe (Hew), 1, 30*; John, 30; Jone [30*]; Randull, 113; Robert (Roberte), 30*, 102; Thomas, 9; William, 29.
Rigbie, Elizabethe, 102.
Robinson (Robynson, Robynsonn), Alexander, 104, 116, 117*, 118, 120*; Alice, 138, 139*; Ambrose, 44, 46, 48; Anna, 139*; Anne, 117, 118; Ellen, [139]; Frances (France, Franncess), 117*, 138*, 139; Francis (Francs, Franncis, Francys), 44, 73, 87, 94, 103, 104*, 116, 118, 120*; Jane, 44, 103, 136, [139]; John, xvi, 33, 41, 44*, 45, 47*, 91, 104, 117, 119, 141; Katheren [139]; Margarett, 117; Margerie (Margery), 44, 117, 118, 139; Marie, 117*, 118, [139]; Martha, 117; Olliver, 138*; Richard, 9, 104, 116*, 117, 118*, 120, 121; Robert, 59; Thomas, 55, 107.
Robothom (Rowbothome), John xxiii, 60, 61; Katherin, 61*; Robert, 107.
Rocroft (Rocrofte), Alexander; 107, William, 55, 71.
Rowe, Henrye, 10.
Rowson (Rawson, Roleston, Rowsson, Rowsen, Rowston), James, 112; Thomas, 136; Thurston, 44, 45, 46, 51; alias Matley, 16, 48, 75.
Rudson, John, 137, 138.
Rydings (Rydinges), Henry, 65*, 87; Robert, 105, 137.
Ryle, Ales, 1*, Arnold, 114; Dorothie, 1; Edward, 1*, 43, 63; Elizabeth, 1*; Ellen, 1*; Henry, 32; John 1*, 114; Laurence, 105; Raphe, 32; Reginald, 112; Robert, 1*, 2.
Rysinge, John, 18; Thomas, 18; William, 18.

Sadler, Thomas, 138.
Samuell [?Surname or forename], 138.
Sandes (Sanndes), 137*.
Sclater, Anne, 90; George, 90, 91; Henrie, 90, 91.
Seddon, Elizabeth, 61; Raphe, 122.
Seele (Seylle), Laurence (Lawrence), 106, 107,

111; Raphe, 16, 20, 24, 26, 27; Robert, 16; widow, 65.
Sharman, George, 87.
Sharshall, Myles, 20.
Shaw (Shawe), Ellinne, 24*, 25; Ellinor, 98; Eme, 24; John, 105; Robert, 5, 24*, 25, 137.
Shawcross (Shalcrosse), John, 92, 93.
Shelmerden (Shelmerdyne), Edmund (Edmond, Edmonde), 1, 39*, 42; Edward, 36; Thomas, 10.
Shrigley, Frances (Frannces), 102, 137; Francis (Franncis), 65, 104.
Shuttleworth, Issabell, 62.
Siddall (Siddell, Sydall), Adam, 66*, 67; George (Georg), 65, 119; Robert, 66, 67, 106, 111; Samuell, 119, 130.
Sidebotham (Sydbothom, Sydebotham, Sydebothom), Charles, 99; John, 30, 48, 71*, 90, 91, 102, 137; Peter, 99; William, 116.
Simkin (Symkyn), Thomas, 39, 40, 41, 42, 43, 44, 60, 67, 69, 71*, 77, 90, 98.
Sinderland, John, 114.
Smale, Ric., 55.
Smallwood, Edward, 107.
Smith (Smithe, Smyth, Smythe), Allexander, 136; Edmonnde, 17, 18; Edward, 18; Ellen, 29*, 41, 107; Francis, 10*, 126; Hugh (Huge), 29*, 85*; James, 24, 25; John, 17*, 18, 44, 46, 55; Margaret, 98; Margerie, 17*; Nicholas, 137; Randolph (Randulphe), 17, 18 [19]; Richard, 48, 85, 107*; Robert, 17*, 18*, 19, 24; Thomas, 41, 54; William, xi, 90, 91, 122.
Spouner, John, 108.
Spragg, John 10.
Squyre, William, 105.
Stanfeild, Elizabeth, 113.
Stanley, Hugh (Hughe), 105, 137; Thomas, 137.
Storer, Arthur, 41, 62, 97; Mr., 122.
Summister, Allexander, 99.
Sutte, John, 37.
Swindells (Swindels, Swindles, Swyndels, Swyndells), Alice, 70; Edward, 71*; Hugh, 55; John, 65, 71*, 102*, 103, 105, 122*; Katheren, 51; Robert, 70; William, 1, 2, 70*, 71*, 96, 102.
Swinston, Roger, 69.
Sympson, young, 18.

Tatton, Robert, 112; William, 1.
Taylier *alias* Buckley, Ellyn, 27*.
Taylor, (Tayler, Taylier, Taylior, Tellier, Tailor), Allice, 77*; Anthony, 76*, 77; Edward, 27; Elizabeth, 76, 77*; Ellen, 76, 77; Frances, 27; James, xvi, 44*, 45, 47*, 103; Jeffrey, 75; John [78], 79; Margery, 44, 47; Raphe (Rauffe), 24*, 25, 62; William, 76*.
Thomston, John, 96; Kathreyn, 96; Margaret, 96; Raff, 96.
Thornecroft, William, 108.
Thorniley (Thorneley, Thornelye, Thorneyley), Edward, 43, 63, 108; Randle, 88; William, 71.
Toft, Raphe, 107,
Tollie, William, 10.
Tomlynson, Dorothie, 38*.
Torkington (Torkenton, Torkinton, Torkynton), Alexander (Alex, Allex) xvi, 5, 10, 40, 42, 43*, 62; Isabell or Ellizabeth, 62*; Izabell, 40, 42; John, 1, 2, 41, 113; Robert, 20; William (Wm), 41, 43, 59*, 108.
Tounge, Marie, 83.
Townsend, John, 10.
Twyffoard, John, 51.
Tym, Ellice, 54.
Typpinge, Thos, 79.

Urmeston, Mr., 137.

Vaudrey (Vadrey, Vaudraie), Ane, 76 [78*], [79]; Elizabeth, 108; Ellen, 76, [78*, 79]; George, 76*; Margery, 76; Richard, 76; Robert, 44, 104.

Wakefield (Wakefeild), Elizabeth, 51; John, 105; William, 4.
Walker, Raphe, 114; Richard (Ric), 38, 54; Thomas, 32.
Wall, Edward, 10.
Walley, Edward, 3.
Walmsley (Wallmsley, Walmersley, Walmeslie), Agneta, 38; Anne, 37; James, 44, 47, 48, 53.
Warburton, William (Willm), 119, 121.
Ward, Rob, 55.
Warren, Edward, 54, 55, 61, 62*, 136[*]; Gregorie, 92; Jerome, 92*, 93*; John, 19, 47, 113, 136*, 137; Margerie, 104, 136; Richard, 116; William, 113; family, xiv; old Mrs., 54; Mr., 20.
Wharmby, (Wharmbey, Wharmbie, Wharmeby, Wharmbye), Ales, 66; Bartholomewe, 107; John 35, 101, 106; Margarett, 51; William (Willm), 51, 63.
Whewhall, Robt, 100.
Whiteley, Alice, 138.
Whittakers (Whitachers, Whiticers, Whitticers, Whittikers), Anne, 72; George, 72*, 73*, 87*, 119, 139; John, 34, 72, 73*; Margerye,

Index 149

72*, 73; Marie, 72; Tho, 87.
Whittington, William, 98, 122.
Whyte, Jane, 92*.
Wilkinson, William, 113.
Williamson (Willyamson, Wyllyamson), James, 27*, 32, 44, 47, 52, 53*, 54*, 55, 56*; John, (Jo), 48, 53*, [55], 87, 113, 136; Margerye, 53; Nicholas, 47; Robert, 71; Rondulphe (Randolphe), 53*, [54]; Thomas (Tho), 44, 47, 53*, 54, 58, 93, 107, 136, 138.
Williamson *alias* Deane, Edward, 108.
Willms, Stephen, 98.
Wilson, John, 91*; Richard, 137.
Winington (Wynnington), Robert, 66; Mr., 136.
Wishall, Hugh, 3.
Wither, John, 108.
Withington (Withinton), Francis, 26; Robte, 26.
Wolsencrofte, James, 108, 113*.
Wood (Woodd, Woode,) Alexander, 33; Anne, 8; Elizabeth, 107; George, 3*, 38, 136; Henrie (Henrye), 54, 105; John, 107; Laurence, 105, 114; Marie, 108; Martin, 65, 66; Robert (Robt, Robte), 26, 29, 34, 43, 98; Roger, 20, 29*.
Woodward, Mr., 137.
Woolfendyne (Wooffendyne), Raphe (Rauffe), 20, 136.
Worth, Robt, 63.
Worthington, James, 43; Thomas, 106, 111; —, 20.
Wright, Laurence (Lawrence), 65, 106, 137.
Wylde *alias* Ashton, Edward, 99.
Wynne (Winne, Wynn), John, 27*, 39*, 48, 77, 84; Nicholas, 38*, 39; Robert, 83.
Wynnynton, Mr., 9*.

Yale, David, 43, 93, 97.
Yonge, John, 107.

INDEX OF PLACES

We have ventured to indentify a few places as lying within Stockport, primarily with the aid of the relevant volume of *The Place Names of Cheshire*, ed. J. McN. Dodgson (English Place Name Society, vol. XLIV, 1970); similarly we have used the common spelling of places identified from this volume in our index. References to *The Place Names of Cheshire*, are indicated by [1]. We locate a few places in Stockport which are not given in *The Place Names of Cheshire*, and have indicated this by italic type, and by a heading ? Stockport.

Variant spellings are indicated by round brackets; an * indicates more than one entry on a page.

Adlington, 19, 20, 75, 105.
Adswood (Adswodd, Addeswoodd), 20, 69*, 111, 112.
Ashton upon Mersey Bancke, 112.

Baguley, 18, [32], 108.
Blacklach, 69.
Bolton, 53,
The Bothams, Stockport, 1.
Bramhall[1] (Bromhall), xvii, xviii, 14, 16, 55, 60, 62, 69, 107, 136*, 137.
Bredbury[1] (Bradburie, Breadburie, Bredburie), xvii, 1, 19, 66, 75, 102, 126, 127, 129; Bredburie Hall, 121.
The Bridgend, 136.
Brinnington[1] (Brinington, Brynnington), xvii, xviii, 27*, 66, 90, 91, 117, 122.
Buckinghamshire, 89*.

Canterbury, xv.
Castleton, 54.
Cheadle[1] (Chedle), 54*, 108.
Cheadle Hulme, 137.
Chester, xiii, 97, 99, 108, 136.
Chorlton, 75.
Cloudwood, 107.
Compstall[1] (Combstall), 105.
Congleton, xi, 135.
Cross Acres, 55.
Crosse Lache, 111.
Cruckiley, Cheshire, 122.

Daniells, 135.
Dean Rowe, 105, 111.
Derbyshire (Derbieshire), 54, 55, 137.
Didisburie, 51.
Disley, xvii, 107.
Dukinfield, xvii.

The Edge, 32.
Edgley, 73, 111.
Etchells[1] (Ecchills, Etchalls, Etchulles), xvii, xviii, 24, 55, 73, 111.

Fallowfield, 111.
Fulshaw, (Fulshawe), 107, 111.

Gamesworth, 107.
Godley, 70.
Goytt, 55.

The Hake, 107.
Hale, 107.
Hanford, (Handford), 20, 111.
Hanslope, Bucks., 89*.
Harrow-on-the-Hill, Middlesex, 89.
Hathorne, 32.
Hawarden, county of Chester, 70, 121, 123.
The Heald, 70.
Heaton, Lancs., 10, 44, 55, 87, 122.
Heaton Norris, xvii, 14, 46, 90.
Heaviley, xvii.
Hempshawgate, *see* Impeshawgate.
Henbury[1] (Henburie), 55, 122.
Henfabancke, 54.
Heweston, 26.
Hillgate[1] (Hilgate), Stockport, 105, 111*, 135, 136; Hilgate Barn, 135; Hilgate Feild, 118.
The Hill top, Stockport, 16, 90, 91.
Holt, 32.
Hope, 54.
Horderne, 118; *Horderne Barn, Stockport*, 104; *Horderon Barne*, 111.
Horton, Northants., 89.
The Houghe, 105.
Hyde, xvii, 71, 72.

Impeshaweyate [probably Hempshawgate[1]], 16.

Kettleshulme, 107.
Knott Crofte, 4.

Ladibridge, 106.
Lancaster, county of, 40.
Levenshulme (Levensham, Levensulme), 29, 40, 62, 85.
Lincoln, 89.
Liverpool, xiii.
London, xi, 65, 108.

Longlee, 65.
Longrakes, 14.
Longshut Head[1], Stockport, 6.
Lyme, 105.
Lyndall, 104.

Macclesfield (Maclesfield), xi, 62, 98, 105, 137.
Manchester, 14*, 46*, 59*, 60, 135, 139.
Marple (Merple) xvii, 19, 54, 55, 72, 73*.
Middlesex, 89.
Mile End[1] (The Myles End), Stockport, 92, 112.
The Milnegate, Stockport, 136.
The Mooresyde, 24.
The Mooresyde House, 59.
The More, 135.
More Syde, 111, 116.
Morley Steyre, 111.
The Myles End, Stockport, 112.
Nangreave[1] Stockport, xvii, 48, 106.
Newton, 116.
Norbury[1] (Northbury), xvii, 3, 76.
Northamptonshire, 89.
Northenden, 1*.

Offerton, xvii, xviii, 9, 14*, 16, 67.
Openshaw, 85.

Paddocke Carr[1] (Padockarre), Stockport, 111.
The Park[1], Stockport, 118.
Poynton, 20, 104, 107, 136*.
Prestburie, 75.
Priestfields, 55.

Reddish (Redich, Rediche, Reddich, Riddiche), xviii, 20, 40, 112, 118; Woodhall in Rediche, 40*.
Rhodes, 108.
Right Bank, 111.
Romily (Romeley), xvii, 70, 122.
Rungey [?Ringway], 105.

Sale, 104, 106.
Shaw Heath[1] (Shawe Heathe), Stockport, 48.
Staffordshire, 48.
Stockport, The Bothams[1], 1; factory in, xi; Hempshawgate[1] (Impeshaweyate), 16; Hillgate[1], 14, 15, 16, 59; Hillgate Barn, 135; Hilgate Feild, 118; Hilltopp[1], 16, 90, 91; Longshut Head[1], 6; market, xi; Mile End[1] (The Myles End), 92, 112; Milnegate[1], 136; Nangreave[1], xvii, 48, 106; New Bridge[1], 71; Paddocke Carre[1], 111; The Park[1], 118; school, 41, 58; Shawe Heathe[1], 48; Parish, townships of xvii; Towne Endes[1], 40.
[?]Stockport, The Hake[1], 107; *Horderne*, 118; *Horderne Barn*, 104; *Horderon Barne*, 111; *Mooresyde House*, 59; *The More*, 135. *More Syde*, 111, 116; *Streete House Lane*, 32.

Stone (Stoone), 48.
Street House Lane, 32.
Styal (Styall), 107, 111.

Tarvin, xi.
Thurston, 1.
Torkington, xvii, xviii.
Towne Endes, Stockport, 40.

Wabanckhill, 136.
Walle butts, 24.
Watersyde, 106.
Werneth, xvii, 71, 73, 106.
Whitcroft, 3.
Wilmslow (Wilmeslowe, Wylmeslowe), 54, 105.
Withington, 32, 137.
Woobutes, 135.
Woodes House, 135.
Woodford (Widford), 105, 107.
Woodhall in Reddiche, 40*.
Woodley, 107.

York, xv.